GUIDANCE AND COUNSELING AROUND THE WORLD

Victor J. Drapela, Editor
University of South Florida

University Press of America™

Library of Congress Catalog Card Number: 79-64966

THIS BOOK IS DEDICATED

TO THE SCORES OF STUDENTS IN

COMPARATIVE GUIDANCE WHO HAVE

DISCOVERED THAT THE MORE WE

UNDERSTAND THE LIFE OF PEOPLE

IN OTHER COUNTRIES, THE BETTER

WE UNDERSTAND OURSELVES

FOREWORD

Edwin L. Herr

The publication of <u>Guidance</u> <u>and</u> <u>Counseling</u> <u>throughout</u> <u>the</u> <u>World</u> brings to the reader a comprehensive and contemporary view of the national conditions from which guidance and counseling emerge. It acknowledges that neither the factors which cause guidance and counseling to flourish nor the behavioral interventions which guidance and counseling represent are restricted in national origin. While certain scholars have had influence on guidance and counseling theory and practice beyond their own countries, many nations could claim contributions to the international shape and practice of guidance and counseling if their professional story became better known.

The study of guidance and counseling throughout the world provides the professional practitioner within any country a reassurance of the importance of guidance and counseling to human reclamation, to the personalizing of mass education, to individual purposefulness. Such study puts the practitioner in the company of other like-minded individuals, without the barriers of language, who are applying their skills to the needs of their countrymen. It reinforces the fact that human needs know no political boundaries.

For the scholar, the study of guidance and counseling in international terms permits the analysis of the effects of various experimental conditions -- policies, organizational structures, staff preparation, practices -- upon outcomes. As such, understanding of the comparative effects of guidance and counseling techniques or models can be significantly advanced.

To any interested individual, practitioner or scholar, the study of guidance and counseling in international perspective enhances a sensitivity to the needs of persons of different cultural or ethnic background. Whether living in the United States or elsewhere, awareness of the pluralism of backgrounds, experiences, and beliefs of persons seeking guidance and counseling assistance reinforces the professional goal to individualize that assistance as fully as possible.

Many other advantages can accrue to the counselor or scholar versed in the approaches to guidance and counseling used in other nations. Rather than recite those, it is useful to consider some of the factors which provide the context to which guidance and counseling responds. Since each of the following essays deal with the specifics of these within a nation or geographical region, the intent here is to consider a broader perspective.

Conditions Fostering Guidance and Counseling

Societies throughout the world are in transition. In some cases, the changes they are undergoing are revolutionary and in others evolutionary. It is a rare nation, if it exists, which is not influenced by turmoil surrounding its economic climate, belief systems, value structure, employment or unemployment rate, educational provisions, male/female relationships or other emphases.

The impetus to social change in many parts of the world manifests itself in striving for economic growth as the means to provide for rising mass aspirations for a better quality of life, for occupational mobility, for greater personal options. In order to achieve economic growth, most nations have moved to widen their industrial base and to adapt diverse technological processes.

Economic growth requires job opportunities, occupational specialization and both basic education for literacy and higher education capable of supplying persons capable of designing, maintaining, and operating the required technological processes. Such shifts in occupational structure and educational provision redistribute people among occupations, breaking down hereditary associations with certain occupations and relating wealth to knowledge and skills rather than family lineage. Such phenomena are particularly apparent in the shifts of nation after nation from agrarian dominance to industrial dominance as well as from population dispersion in rural areas to urban population concentration.

With particular pertinence for guidance and counseling, both international organizations and governments have become increasingly aware that the major questions regarding technology and economic growth are not technical but human questions. It has become widely acknowledged among nations of diverse political persuasion that investment in human capital, the development of a work force func-

iv

tionally adequate to a specific nation's level of and goals for industrialism, is a necessity. To develop human capital is to acknowledge that underemployment and unemployment are not just individual problems but a collective tragedy for a nation committed to social and economic progress. What has become obvious is that the availability of skilled and productive workers can even out many of the comparative advantages which nations enjoy because of climate and natural resources.

A key factor in the growing recognition that human capital is a nation's greatest treasure is the complementary recognition of children and youth as the "people of the future." Singer (1972) in a study for the United Nations of the processes of economic and social development has argued that "expenditures for children is the most important part of human investment." Among the ten principles found in UNICEF's Declaration of the Rights of the Child (1974) is "equal opportunity to develop his abilities, his individual judgment, and his sense of moral and social responsibility, and to become a useful member of society." Such a principle clearly argues for providing mechanisms by which children and youth can become aware of their own characteristics, and the opportunities to use them in selecting among occupational and social options. In political terms, the result may be the development of human capital, or personal development, or both.

The changes in national geography, political systems and economic circumstances which are occurring throughout the world ultimately affect every individual in a particular society and, indeed, frequently those in other societies as well. Sometimes these effects are direct; sometimes they are indirect. Nevertheless, these changes affect the feelings of security people have about themselves and their environment; how they relate to other people; the achievement motives which they are likely to pursue; their knowledge about and feelings of ability to master the opportunities available.

Enter Guidance and Counseling

As the emotional aspects of life in various societies intensify under the influence of rapid change and as the educational and occupational structures diversify, nations throughout the world are turning to the implementation of guidance systems and counseling services to assist their populations deal with the personal questions which ensue in such circumstances.

The formalization of guidance and counseling services which is occurring throughout the world is not to suggest that guidance and counseling does not continue in the family, among peers, and through other informal mechanisms. It obviously does. All societies, including the most primitive, have mechanisms to distribute certain forms of information to its members regarding behavior or occupational roles. Rather, the point at issue here is that the complexity

of life is requiring forms and quantities of information and analysis
of it which is increasingly beyond the power of many, if not most,
families and other informal mechanisms to provide. Increasingly,
too, societies are penalizing persons for not knowing about and using
accurate and current information. In a period of extremely rapid
national change, neither families nor peer groups nor other informal
processes can provide information or considerations of personal
direction which meets such requirements.

This does not mean that the family or the peer group has no
influence on the decisions that their members make. This is obviously
untrue. It is to say rather that in complex, information rich
societies, principally those which are heavily industrialized, families
and peer groups need to be augmented by mechanisms external to them
if the challenges of choosing, planning, and preparing for educational, occupational, and personal life styles are to be dealt with
purposefully and effectively. In less complex or information rich
societies, the requirements for such processes may be less
sophisticated but they exist nevertheless and in increasingly
insistent terms.

Although the fact is not widely discussed in the professional
literature, guidance and counseling processes are sociopolitical in
their manifestation. The characteristics of the society in which
guidance and counseling systems or services are implemented have a
great deal to do with the types of problems which are considered
appropriate for counselors to deal with and they have much to do with
the techniques which are considered ethical or professionally
responsible.

In large measure, the questions and presenting problems which
youth and adults bring to counselors are socially defined. Problems
of personal choice, achievement, social interaction, self-initiative,
marriage, dating, prestige, do not occur independent of the societal
time and place which a given individual occupies. The social
"permission" to consider such questions and to behave in accordance
with the available answers differs among Socialist and Capitalist
nations, East and West, or on other factors. The anxieties, behavioral deficits or indecisiveness which persons experience as they
compare themselves with what their society -- in the person of
parents, teachers, and employers -- expects of them may arise from
similar psychological processes across cultures but are stimulated
by different environmental circumstances.

Just as the questions which societies "permit" their citizens
to ask vary cross-culturally so do the resources which these
societies place at the disposal of their citizens to deal with such
questions. Thus, both the content with which guidance and counseling
systems deal and the organizational shape or the range of services
they provide depend upon a complex set of political, economic and
social factors in any given society.

vi

Super (1974) has suggested that there are four conflicting
trends in the provision of guidance and counseling among various
nations. These are (1) guidance for manpower utilization versus
individual human development; (2) occupational choice versus
vocational or career development; (3) information dissemination versus
counseling; and, (4) professional versus lay guidance. These conflicting trends continue to be evident in surveys of national
approaches to the provisions of guidance and counseling. The reader
will find them useful reference points to apply to each of the
essays which follow.

In addition to the conflicting trends identified by Super, it is
useful to consider other perspectives. From a cross-cultural vantage
point, a major question arises about whether the guidance and counseling that societies provide their citizens is intended for those few
who experience maladjustment and rejection by the social system and
need to be rehabilitated or, instead, the many who can profit from
assistance to enhance their personal development and growth. Put
more simply, nations differ on whether guidance and counseling are
for a few persons, specially labeled as problems of some sort, or for
all. A second question which many nations are now confronting is
whether guidance and counseling should occur only after a personal
problem is clearly present and limiting the person's capacity to cope
with life or before such problems exist as a way of educating persons
to those attitudes, knowledge, and skills which will reduce the
likelihood that the stresses and challenges of life will become problems. There are enormous sociopolitical issues involved however you
answer such questions.

Clearly, as the world becomes smaller, at least in figurative
terms, the stresses and strains associated with the struggle for
personal dignity, literacy, and economic self-sufficiency are shared
by larger portions of the world's population. On balance, the
implicit recognition of the right of each individual to participate
in that struggle is a positive matter. It brings with it, however,
the obligation for nations to provide their citizens the guidance
and counseling assistance required for them to confront the struggle
in a free and informed fashion.

References

Singer, P. Study of children and economic and social development. _ESI Features_. May 22, 1972

Super, D. E. The broader context of career development and vocational guidance: American trends in world perspective. In E. L. Herr (Ed.) _Vocational guidance and human development_. Boston: Houghton Mifflin, 1974 (Chapter 3).

UNICEF and the rights of the child. New York: UNESCO, 1974.

Additional sources

Drucker, P. _Technology, management, and society_. New York: Harper and Row, 1970.

Herr, L. L. Career development concepts and practices: Some international perspectives. _Counseling and Human Development_. September 1978, 11 (1), 1-12.

Wolfbein, S. Planning for work in a world community. In E. L. Herr (Ed.) _Vocational guidance and human development_. Boston: Houghton Mifflin, 1974 (Chapter 21).

PREFACE

Although the American guidance profession has generated a vast repertoire of literature that covers virtually all aspects of counselor involvement, no textbook for international and comparative guidance studies was available for years. To fill this vacuum, a group of counselor educators published a small experimental textbook two years ago under the title <u>Guidance in other countries</u> (Tampa: University of South Florida Bookstore, 1977). The book was used at several universities for instructional purposes and was read by scores of counselors who ordered it individually. By now, the book is out of print.

The feedback by readers that was received stimulated the publication of the present book which is a revised and substantially expanded version of the experimental text. Some of the revisions and additions are the result of that feedback. However, the format of the book primarily reflects the desire of the editor and the authors to stimulate intercultural, comparative studies in counselor education curricula and to provide a basic, reliable instructional resource for such academic courses. The book is equally suitable for in-service training of counseling practitioners and for individual study by counselors, particularly those who plan to use foreign travel for professional enrichment.

The book offers a theoretical and a methodological basis for international, comparative guidance studies. However, its main focus is informational. Representative samples of guidance work in more than twenty countries throughout the world are described by qualified authors who are familiar with the social and cultural factors that

influence the various guidance models. In many cases, additional
readings are recommended.

The book is a cooperative work of a consortium of authors who
come from different backgrounds, both professionally and culturally.
Some are counselor educators, others are administrators, or counseling practitioners. Some are Americans, others are from a score of
other nations. As editor of this volume, I sent out a chapter outline to all authors who agreed to become involved. This was done to
provide a degree of evenness in treatment and comparability among the
various cultures and guidance models that are discussed.

Nevertheless, the great differences in the authors' backgrounds
is reflected in individual chapters of the book. In my view, this
variability is inevitable in a volume that taps so many professional
resources which so differ from each other. If I had to err, I preferred to do so by overly protecting the cultural integrity and professional convictions of individual authors rather than by enforcing
uniformity of content at the expense of unique personal and cultural
attributes. Some authors use the American spelling, while others
find the British spelling preferable. Since some of the terms spelled
in the British manner involve formal titles of institutions or periodicals, I decided to accept the duality of spelling throughout the
entire book.

I am indebted to many persons who assisted me during the implementation of this project; to the holders of copyright who made it
possible for us to quote other sources; to the professional colleagues who offered their time and talents to write parts of this book;
and to my wife, Gwen, for her encouragement and caring.

Victor J. Drapela

AUTHORS

V I O L E T   N.   A R E N E
Federal Ministry of Education, 1-3 Moloney Street, Lagos
NIGERIA

C A T H E R I N E   A V E N T
Inner London Education Authority, County Hall, London SE1 7PB
GREAT BRITAIN

H E A T H E R   C.   B A I N
Faculty of Education, University of Alberta, Edmonton, Alberta T6G 2E1
CANADA

S E A N   B E A U S A N G
Richmond Estate, Blackrock Road, Assisi, County Cork
REPUBLIC OF IRELAND

L A W R E N C E   M.   B R A M M E R
Educational Psychology, University of Washington, Seattle, WA 98195
U. S. A.

D O R O T H Y   C L A R K
Colomane West, Bantry, County Cork
REPUBLIC OF IRELAND

N A T H A N   D E E N
Guidance and Counseling, University of Utrecht, Tiberdreef 4, Utrecht
THE NETHERLANDS

THOMAS J. DONAHUE
Taipei American School, 731 Wen Lin Road, Sec. 1, Shih Lin, Taipei
TAIWAN

VICTOR J. DRAPELA
Counselor Education, University of South Florida, Tampa, FL 33620
U. S. A.

M. O. A. DUROJAIYE
Faculty of Education, University of Lagos,   Lagos
NIGERIA

OLIVA M. ESPIN
Counselor Education, Boston University, Boston, MA 02215
U. S. A.

EDWIN L. HERR
Pennsylvania State University, University Park, PA 16802
U. S. A.

THEODORE LANDSMAN
Psychology, University of Florida, Gainesville, FL 32611
U. S. A.

RUTH MALKINSON
2 Mahilever Street, Rehovoth
ISRAEL

JOHN MORACCO
School of Education, Auburn University, Auburn, AL 36830
U. S. A.

AUDREY NEWSOME
University of Keele, Ispringpool, Keele, Staffordshire ST5 5BN
GREAT BRITAIN

JOHN G. PATERSON
Faculty of Education, University of Alberta, Edmonton, Alberta T6G 2E1
CANADA

DONALD PEMBERTON
Westgate Elementary School, 3560 58th. St. N., St. Petersburg, FL 33710
U. S. A.

WALTER L. POWERS
Applied Psychology, Eastern Washington University, Cheney, WA 99004
U. S. A.

SHARON E. ROBERTSON
Faculty of Education, University of Calgary, Calgary, Alberta T2N 2E1
CANADA

J O H N   J.   S M A L L
University of Canterbury, Christchurch 1
                                  NEW ZEALAND

E.   L.   T O L B E R T
Counselor Education, University of Florida, Gainesville, FL 32611
                                  U. S. A.

J O H N   M.   U R B A N O
Dept. of Employment and Youth Affairs, PO Box 2817-AA, Melbourne
                                  AUSTRALIA

A.   G.   W A T T S
Nat'l Institute for Careers Education, Bateman St., Cambridge CB2 1LZ
                                  GREAT BRITAIN

A V N E R   Z I V
Psychology Department, Tel Aviv University, Tel Aviv
                                  ISRAEL

CONTENTS

xix

THE CASE
FOR COMPARATIVE STUDIES

In the September, 1974 issue of the Personnel and Guidance
Journal, Leo Goldman has made a strong case for comparative studies
in guidance and counseling. In a special feature entitled "Guidance
USA: Views from abroad" he published invited reactions of eleven foreign colleagues to what they had seen in the United States. Some
of them studied at American universities, others toured the country
to observe its guidance system. Goldman (1974) explains the purpose
of his project:

> Itoccurred to me that it would be valuable for us here to see
> ourselves as these others see us...

> What I asked the visitors to emphasize, and what I have
> emphasized in selecting the excerpts for use here, are the
> points of difference and similarity between what they see
> in their own countries and what they saw here. I asked
> them especially to try to relate those differences and
> similarities to the values and customs and backgrounds of
> the two countries. This, it seems to me, is one of the
> most valuable outcomes of international study and visitation--
> greater perspective and insight, on both sides, as to who we
> are and why we do as we do. (p. 40)

It is this comparative perspective that we need to keep while
surveying guidance and counseling activities around the world. It
is the fundamental approach that has been adopted for the purpose
of this book. Section One sets the stage for optimal exploration,

1

by the reader, of individual countries and geographical areas, of cultures, and guidance models. It offers a conceptual clarification of comparative studies and spells out concrete applications of this approach in the learning process.

Chapter 1 presents the rationale of comparative guidance and counseling and points out what benefits counselors may gain by becoming involved. Chapter 2 proposes a comparative methodology in counselor training curricula and in-service workshops. The recommended methodology has been tested in both settings with positive results.

Reference

Goldman, L. (Ed.) Guidance USA: Views from abroad. Personnel and Guidance Journal, 1974, 53, 40-56.

1

RATIONALE OF COMPARATIVE
GUIDANCE AND COUNSELING

Victor J. Drapela

In our daily life, we use comparative approaches more than we
realize. For instance, before buying a car, we compare the relative merits of various models; and after we have decided on the model, we compare prices in several dealerships to get the best deal.
The same applies to shopping for food, clothing, and various services. If it were not for our ability to make effective comparative
judgments, we would be at the mercy of others. Coping with circumstances of modern life would become difficult. It is fair to say
that one's skill in applying comparative thought processes is commonly associated with maturity and experience. Conversely, the inability of making comparative judgments is seen as a sign of naive-
ty and of ineffective living patterns.

The crude example of shopping for a car can be applied to other
areas, e.g., personal life philosophy, goals, and values, which do
touch the very core of our personality. A dramatic shift from traditional ethical standards to criteria based on the individual's
conscience has occurred in the past several years. Conventional
life styles have been challenged and new ones have emerged. In
this fluid situation, only individuals sensitive to the relative
merits of current trends can select a framework that would give
meaning to their lives and ensure their self-fulfillment.

A new frame of reference

Most of us will agree that there is a great difference between shopping for a car and forming one's philosophy of life. For

3

one thing, when we buy a car, we have to take it the way it comes
from the factory. We can order additional features, a CB radio or
radial tires, but unless we are mechanics by profession or avoca-
tion, we cannot buy the engine of one model and the body of another.
We have to decide on the overall quality of the one product and
make the best use of it.

When it comes to values and living patterns, the choices are
obviously much wider, and the number of possible combinations is
virtually unlimited. If we wish to lead an "examined life" in a
pluralistic society, we need to develop a keen sense for assessing
values and the intrinsic worth of various life styles. We cannot
do this effectively by mere objective observation. Values and ensuing behaviors are adequately understood only by those who are
willing to adopt what Combs and Snygg (1959) call a "perceptual
frame of reference." This approach makes observers into participants who look at other people's behaviors, and the underlying
values, from the vantage point of those who are being observed.
This does not imply that the·observer-participant has to accept
the values or the behaviors which he or she observed perceptually.
Nevertheless, it is the only way of understanding others as they
understand themselves.

Experienced counselors and members of other helping professions
are aware of the uniqueness of each of their clients. They realize
that unless they perceive the concerns of clients from the point of
view held by clients rather than from their own point of view, they
may touch the surface, but will fail to grasp the meaning of the
problem. Unless helping professionals have the ability to vicari-
ously "walk in the moccasins" of their clients, they will offer
little help, and frequently will add to the degree of maladjustment.

Comparative studies

The preceding discussion pointed out that professional guidance
counselors, and graduate students in guidance curricula, should have
acquired the two basic prerequisites for a successful pursuit of
comparative studies. The first one is the ability of examining the
relative merits and weaknesses of current phenomena. The second is
the ability of perceiving values and behaviors from the vantage
point of their originator (behaver)--through the perceptual frame
of reference. The next step is to conceptually describe the meaning and the scope of comparative studies.

Any inquiry which uses the comparative method falls into this
broad category. Linguistics use the comparative method to identify relationships between various languages and to explore their
origins and development. Comparative anatomy clarifies similarities and contrasts between humans and lower animals. However, in
most cases the comparative method is applied to cross-cultural or

4

international investigations. How is a particular profession practiced in various nations, what are the goals, the methods employed,
etc? Such studies are meant to uncover parallels and contrasts,
and to provide new insights for professionals in their respective
fields.

In this context, guidance is perceived as a worldwide effort
to help individuals overcome obstacles in various life situations
and attain optimal developmental levels. Many features of the
guidance effort are common to all societies, but operational patterns and the scope of guidance services differ from one country
to another. Generally, counseling is the core service and the
principal helping process of guidance both for dealing with individuals and with groups. But the level of counseling may range from
therapeutic interventions by highly trained professionals to mere
information giving by people with minimal training. The terminology is equally uneven: guidance, counseling, orientation, career
planning, pastoral care, ideological training, or character formation.

In addition to formal guidance services, there are culturally
rooted customs in family, religious groups, and social institutions
of any given country that contain basic elements of guidance:

> Young people are aided to develop socially, to form their
> value structure, to plan their education, and to prepare
> for a career. The process of socialization is the result
> of many informal guidance efforts that operate in every
> society, from the most primitive to the most advanced.
> Many languages recognize the difference between instruc-
> tion and counseling or guidance, such as the German terms
> Unterricht (teaching), Beratung (advising, counseling),
> and Erziehung (value-related upbringing). (Drapela 1975,
> p.442)

Comparative studies cover the entire spectrum of guidance and
counseling efforts as they have developed around the world; in some
countries, both the organized and the unstructured processes, in
others, where no organized guidance exists, the spontaneous societal influences only.

A brief historical sketch

Although guidance and counseling in the United States have
grown into a major profession since the days of Frank Parsons, international studies in the field failed to keep pace with that
growth. Parsons placed great emphasis on contacts with guidance
pioneers abroad, but that part of his legacy was overlooked, and as
a result, a sustained, continuous effort in comparative guidance
has not materialized for decades. In May, 1966, the American Per-

sonnel and Guidance Association (APGA) approved a policy statement which stated its "international responsibility" in these terms:

1. To help its members develop a broader understanding of the international dimensions of their profession. To this end each of the constituent Associations of APGA is encouraged to develop the international aspects of its own specialized field, and to make appropriate recommendations...

2. To urge those responsible in colleges and universities to emphasize appropriate international perspectives in professional preparation programs in counseling, guidance, and related fields.

3. To encourage world-wide professional communication, including exchange of professional information and literature.

4. To promote the international exchange of persons preparing for or professionally engaged in personnel work and guidance.

5. To develop continuing liaison with professional organizations in other countries and with international organizations in personnel and guidance and related fields.

6. To maintain liaison with governmental and private agencies and professional organizations concerned with international education and the international exchange of persons.

7. To encourage emphasis in regional and national conference programs on the international aspects of the personnel and guidance profession. (American Personnel and Guidance Association, 1966)

In the fall of 1966, President Johnson signed the International Education Act which was approved by Congress and became law. The Act provided for the strengthening of American educational resources toward international studies and research. However, in the turbulent years that followed, especially with the escalation of the U.S. involvement in Vietnam, the counseling profession was absorbed in the mounting crisis situation on the domestic scene. Most counselors were looking for answers to imminent problems, and they felt that comparative studies would merely complicate their outlook, and offer them no help. It is accurate to state that the rank and file of the counseling profession considered international concerns a commendable but impractical endeavor. They relegated it to the level of a narrow subspeciality of marginal value to be pursued by experts which had no impact on the day-to-day operation of an average guidance worker.

This attitude is gradually changing. In 1976 APGA sponsored a survey among its members to determine the degree of interest in international studies and relations. Close to 1,000 APGA members indicated that they wanted to become actively involved in an on-going international program, they requested regular news releases in APGA Press organs, exchange of information, study trips abroad, structured courses in comparative guidance, and a greater emphasis on international programs at APGA Conventions. A committee has been appointed to promote the cause of international relations in the Association.

Present international contacts

Most people realize today that, no matter how large a country is, or how wealthy it is, it cannot live in isolation from the rest of the world. The American isolationist movement of the era prior to World War II was counterproductive then, and would be self-defeating today. Global interdependence is developing among countries of various sizes, cultures, and political systems. Even a small, under-developed country with untapped mineral or oil resources is now treated as a valuable partner by technological giants who depend on the import of raw materials for their industrial output.

Global interdependence is a fact of life in social developments and value-related changes as well. Events in one part of the world influence the life of people in other countries. A "local" war in a remote area may trigger a world-wide holocaust involving the super-powers, if it is not checked in time. Social unrest in one country frequently stimulates similar developments in other countries due to the instant reporting capability of world-wide communications net-works which penetrate even the airways of totalitarian countries. For instance, in the late 1960's, significant parallels emerged in the youth culture of the United States, of Western Europe, of Soviet bloc countries, and Japan. The global interdependence continues to develop, and its momentum is increasing with every new transistor radio brought to the highlands of Peru, to the shores of the Zambezi River, or to the jungle of Sumatra. Within the next few years, a satellite television network will reach all parts of the globe and bring people still closer together.

Levels of international studies

Since the end of World War II, UNESCO tried to serve as a clearinghouse for international exchanges in the field of education and culture. In 1951 the world organization helped establish the International Association for Educational and Vocational Guidance (IAEVG) to serve a parallel purpose in the field of guidance. Fifteen years later, another organization emerged, the Round Table for the Advancement of Counseling (IRTAC). Both these organizations have scheduled regular conferences and seminars for counselors from all parts of the world.

Exchange of information, materials, and professional contacts among various countries stimulated the initial, basic level of international studies. Its chief aims involve opening and maintaining channels of communication, forwarding guidance data from one country to another, storing them, and reporting them to researchers for use in theoretical investigations. The raw data are translated into hypotheses, and the validity of such hypotheses is tested. As Kerlinger (1965) points out, behavioral research involves systematic and controlled processes that can be duplicated, and thus the obtained results are accepted with a degree of critical confidence. However, even at this level of comparative studies, there is some ambiguity, since behavioral variables are defined only in part by "hard" data in quantified form. Behavior cannot be adequately understood if "soft" data reflecting values, cultural traditions, and the like are neglected.(Wrenn 1978)

The second level of comparative studies aims at presenting the assembled, classified, and interpreted information on foreign guidance trends to members of the internationally oriented group within the profession. The results of research conducted at level one are then further analyzed by interested professionals. However, the main emphasis is on the international scene rather than on the use of foreign information for "domestic" purposes.

The third level of comparative studies goes one step further and uses the foreign data for the improvement of skills and for personal enrichment of counselors whose professional interest in the international scene may be but marginal. They simply wish to broaden their perspective and they welcome a fresh, interesting approach to gain new insights and to clarify their professional commitments and personal values.

The stucture of this book is geared to concerns prevalent at the second and the third level of comparative guidance studies.

Benefits for counselors

It has been repeated over and over again that the effectiveness of counselors lies in what they are rather than what they say or do in the course of the therapeutic process. Counselors should be genuine persons, they should have an interesting outlook on life, and their interests should be multidimensional. Hibernating in a cocoon of cultural isolation and provincialism leads to attitudinal rigidity which Tyler (1969) identifies as a debilitating handicap in counseling.

8

Obviously, a counselor who is willing to understand how people thousands of miles away live and think will be much more sensitive to the ethnic subcultures in the school or agency where he/she works. A counselor exposed to greatly differing life **styles** will be much less shocked by unconventional life styles which are found in contemporary society. By the same token, such a counselor will not be overly impressed by the mere fact that a social phenomenon is new or unusual. Comparative guidance experiences enhance the counselor's critical acumen to the point of taking social developments in stride, and avoiding unprofessional, faddish attitudes.

The perceptual frame of reference which needs to be applied for understanding other cultures and prevalent behavior patterns in foreign countries has been discussed earlier in this chapter. It runs parallel to Rogers' (1957) construct of "unconditional positive regard" for the client and to the attitude of "accurate empathic understanding" formulated by Truax and Carkhuff (1967). Both are seen as necessary conditions to cause therapeutic changes in individuals. Since comparative studies foster an increase of perceptual understanding, positive regard, and empathy for culturally different behavior, they reinforce basic therapeutic attitudes and skills in the counselor.

Another useful outcome of comparative guidance studies is the clarification of personal values and professional commitments. Many of us become so absorbed in our daily routine that we lose sight of the ultimate meaning of our work. We come close to being technicians rather than professionals. It is significant that clarification of values has become one of the foremost guidance concerns in recent years. Simon et al. (1972) systemized a new set of techniques to help young people (and educators) clarify their values. While their approach has been very successful, it may gain even greater depth by adding an international, or inter-cultural, dimension to the process, i.e., clarifying values against the backdrop of a foreign philosophy of life.

Parenthetically, we should mention here an overriding concern of our time--the preservation of world peace. Rokeach (1973) found the desire for "a world at peace" to be the highest value priority among both men and women in the U.S. On the other hand, attitudinal prequisites conducive to world peace, e.g., cooperative nurturance, have not been sufficiently developed. Counselors clearly share in the responsibility to promote such attitudes in a world which stresses competition. Besides greater cooperation and social relatedness among people in their own country, counselors can also emphasize the global perspective of cooperation among nations. Adequate exposure to comparative studies will help them in this task.

A very tangible outcome of comparative inquiries is the critical assessment of guidance practices and methods used in the country where we work. Our professional activities appear in a slightly

9

different light, when exposed to comparison with parallel work abroad. At times, they look brighter, at other times, they seem to lose some of their luster. As Noah and Eckstein (1969) point out, comparative studies may lead to "borrowing" from others. Even a system which seems at first quite foreign to our culture may provide clues to modifying our existing guidance practices, or introducing new ones on an experimental basis.

Summary

As we have seen, comparative attitudes are prevalent in daily life. In our present learning endeavor we intend to make them more explicit, and combine them with assessing behavior of others through the perceptual frame of reference. In the process, both similarities and contrasts between one's own guidance and foreign models will be discovered.

The studies can be carried out at three levels, of which the first is comparative research with strong theoretical orientation. The second level involves the application of research findings to more tangible international programs. The third level makes use of international data for the personal and professional enrichment of guidance practitioners.

As counselors participate in comparative studies, their outlook widens, and their sensitivity increases. A process of values clarification is stimulated, and professional commitments are reexamined. The proposed format offers comparative studies for the benefit of rank and file practitioners in the guidance profession rather than limiting them to highly specialized and rather small interest groups.

References

American Personnel and Guidance Association. Policy Statement, May, 1966. Mimeo.

Combs, A.W. & Snygg, D. Individual behavior. A perceptual approach to behavior. New York: Harper & Row, 1959.

Drapela, V.J. Comparative guidance through international study. Personnel and Guidance Journal, 1975, 53, 438-445.

Kerlinger, F.N. Foundations of behavioral research. New York: Holt, Rinehart & Winston, 1965.

Noah, H.J. & Eckstein, M.A. Toward a science of comparative education. New York: Macmillan, 1969.

Rogers, C.R. The necessary and sufficient conditions of therapeutic personality change. Journal of Consulting Psychology, 1957, 21, 95-103.

Rokeach, M. The nature of human values. New York: Free Press, 1973.

Simon, S.B. et al. Values clarification: A handbook of practical strategies for teachers and students. New York: Hart, 1972.

Truax, C.B. & Carkhuff, R.R. Toward effective counseling and psychotherapy: Training and practice. Chicago: Aldine, 1967.

Tyler, L.E. The work of the counselor. (3rd Ed.) New York: Appleton-Century-Crofts, 1969.

Wrenn, C.G. Values and counseling in different societies and cultures. International Journal for the Advancement of Counselling, 1978, 1, 45-62.

Suggested readings

(Because of the scarcity of published works that deal specifically with comparative guidance and counseling, the titles listed below cover a wider area of international studies. However, the concerns discussed in these publications are closely related to the interests of students in comparative guidance and counseling.)

Beck, C.E. (Ed.) Perspectives on world education. Dubuque: Brown, 1970.

Bedal, C.L. (Ed.) Special issue: Guidance in other countries. The School Guidance Worker, 1973, 29, 1-56.

Brickman, W.W. (Ed.) Comparative education: Concept, research and application. Norwood, Pennsylvania: Norwood Editions, 1973.

Catterall, C. Psychology in the schools in international perspective. Volumes I and II. Columbus: International School Psychology Steering Committee, 1976 (1st Vol.), 1977 (2nd Vol.).

Deutsch, S.E. International education and exchange: A sociological analysis. Cleveland: Case Western Reserve University Press, 1970.

Donahue, T.J. Guidance resources for counselors and administrators in international schools. East Lansing: Institute for International Studies in Education, Michigan State University, 1978.

Education on the move. Toronto: The Ontario Institute for Studies in Education; Paris: UNESCO, 1975.

Goldman, L. (Ed.) Guidance U.S.A.: Views from abroad. Personnel and Guidance Journal, 1974, 53, 40-56.

Kenworthy, L.S. The international dimension of education. Washington: NEA, 1970.

King, E.J. Comparative studies and educational decisions. Indianapolis: Bobbs-Merrill, 1968.

King, E.J. Other schools and ours. Comparative studies for today. London: Holt, Rinehart & Winston, 1973.

Lawson, T. (Ed.) Education for international understanding. Hamburg: UNESCO Institute for Education, 1969.

Sanders, I.T. & Ward, J.C. Bridges to understanding. New York: McGraw-Hill, 1970.

Seelye, H.N. & Tyler, V.L. Intercultural communicator resources. Provo, Utah: Brigham Young University, Language & Intercultural Research Center, 1977.

Super, D.E. The broader context of career development and vocational guidance: American trends in world perspective. In Herr, E.L. (Ed.), Vocational guidance and human development. Boston: Houghton Mifflin, 1974, pp. 63-79.

The study of environment in school. International Bureau of Education. Geneva: UNESCO, 1968.

Tolbert, E.L. (Ed.) Special issue: Career guidance in other countries. Vocational Guidance Quarterly, 1976, 24, 294-365.

Wrenn, C.G. Values and counselling in different societies and cultures. International Journal for the Advancement of Counselling, 1978, 1, 45-62.

2

COMPARATIVE METHODOLOGY

Victor J. Drapela

Before choosing the appropriate methodology for our learning experiences, we should briefly review the spectrum of potential approaches to international studies. They can be placed on a continuum between two extreme positions. On one end are loosely structured learning experiences by which students are exposed to various aspects of life in a foreign country--a substitute for a study trip abroad plus some academic credits. On the other end is the pure research model that is concerned with relationships of specific variables but is oblivious of potential cultural experiences by the researchers.

An example of the former are the so called area studies in interdisciplinary social sciences (e.g., Slavic or Scandinavian studies). Their purpose is to get to know a particular country, its people, and its culture. This involves exploring the geography and climate of the region, its history, geopolitical position, and its prevalent religious, political, and social structures. A cultural landscape of major impact unfolds for the students when they listen to the country's music, read its literature, or watch film presentations of national dances, folklore artifacts, and typical street scenes from rural and urban regions. While statistical data offer useful information on the overall status of a country, the meaning of developing social trends within that country can be assessed only to the degree that one has experienced the rhythm of daily life-- work and leisure activities of people living there. By stimulating such concerns, interdisciplinary area studies frequently lead to foreign language courses, and eventually, to a visit of the foreign country.

15

In contrast, the research model emphasizes objective, "hard" data that are descriptive of a particular phenomenon (e.g., the degree of directiveness in guidance) to be compared in two or more societies. A research strategy has to be devised with built-in controls to assure that the findings of the study are not affected by extraneous variables and that appropriate critical standards are maintained. Noah and Eckstein (1969) explain the role of a comparative researcher versus a comparative amateur through the analogy of what interests a zoologist and a big-game hunter. While the hunter shoots as many animals as are available, the zoologist collects only certain specimens and ignores the rest. For the researcher, a great volume of information (particularly, subjective experiences) is of little value. The emphasis is on appropriate criteria to separate "hard" data from subjective observation, and relevant information from irrelevant material.

Selecting a method

As had been mentioned in the first Chapter, the information presented in this book is for the benefit of guidance practitioners and graduate students who had little previous experience in comparative studies. Our method does chart a middle course between the two extremes described above. It aims at promoting growth and professional enhancement of counselors by helping them experience the impact of a foreign culture. It includes comparative approaches in a wider context, not restricting their focus to specific variables, but analyzing guidance practices abroad and relating them to our own professional scene.

Every guidance model reflects cultural values, national traditions and social structures prevalent in a given country. This linkage is frankly admitted, even emphasized, in countries where counseling services were initiated on a professional basis. Priorities were spelled out, goals set, e.g., vocational and career planning, ideological orientation, or personal development. However, even in geographical areas where no formal guidance services exist, we find established processes that assist people to come to terms with their society. Yet "coming to terms with society" is a concept which means different things in different countries. Thus, we can formulate a twofold theorem: (1) All guidance efforts have a common denominator; they share like concerns no matter whether they are formally organized and professionally administered, or unstructured and barely defined. (2) Conversely, as a result of the different value systems and social structures which undergird them, guidance efforts in various countries differ from each other to a high degree.

Applying the method

Although rigorous research methodology is not suitable for our present purpose, there is need for a well defined structure. It helps clarify the learning process, facilitate class involvement, and spell out concrete objectives. The fact that comparative guidance is a relatively unexplored field makes the need for clear structural guidelines even more explicit. The sequence of learning components proposed here will be of particular help to instructors and students in the early stages. As a rule, each of the components should be sufficiently developed before the next one is introduced, allowing of course for overlaps whenever appropriate. An overview of the learning process is presented in Figure 1.1.

Component I: Gathering of information on life in general in the country under study.--A variety of dependable sources should be tapped to form a mosaic-like picture of the current cultural and social situation in the country. To minimize distortions, Bereday (1964) cautions students to watch for preconceived ideas and biases. Ideally, he suggests, one should learn the language spoken in the country--certainly an advantage but not a prerequisite. Whenever possible, the information about the foreign country should be acquired from current primary sources that originated there, or were written by natives or long-term residents of that country. Since this is not always possible (because of language barriers), secondary sources have to suffice. When using them, we need to have adequate assurances of accuracy and objectivity. This does not imply that primary sources are always unbiased. However, biases held by people from a foreign country are more apparent, and offer in themselves significant insights into that cultural orientation. In addition to written materials, there are other important clues available for the assessment of the cultural climate, e.g., samples of folk art, native music, typical dress patterns, preferred foods, and modes of habitation. A review of the region's history clarifies national traditions (and hangups), such as the role of women and the importance of family life. The social structure of the country is closely linked with its political system, with its economic situation, its labor market, and the overall standard of living.

Component II: Gathering of information on education and guidance in the foreign country.--It is well to begin with a survey of the educational system and the level of literacy in the country. Is guidance linked with the school system or with vocational agencies? How is guidance defined, what are its rationale, and predominant patterns? Is it formally organized or are its functions exercised informally by various social institutions? What is the top priority of guidance efforts: promoting the uniqueness and growth of individuals, or normative adjustment of behavior to fit explicit standards of society? Are the prevalent guidance activities related to educational, vocational, personal-social, or ideological needs? Which methodology seems to be preferred: counseling individuals or group work, a high or low degree of directiveness? How frequent are contacts with clients? What personnel is involved in carrying out guidance functions (teachers, counselors, psychologists), and what

17

COMPONENT	I	II	III	IV	V	VI
ACTIVITY	gathering of information on foreign country under study			non-evaluative juxtaposition of the foreign guidance model and our own guidance model; identifying similarities and contrasts	evaluation of the foreign guidance model according to our standards; learning from successes and errors of others	clarification of our personal values and professional commitments; realistic assessment of guidance and counseling in our own country
	life in general	schools, guidance & counseling work	self-assessment of guidance model			
FRAME OF REFERENCE	p e r c e p t u a l (internal): observing structures and behavior from the vantage point of the foreign culture				o b j e c t i v e (external): observing structures and behavior from our own vantage point, as outsiders, admitting our biases	
SHORT TERM BENEFITS	gaining new insights through cognitive and experiential learning processes				improving critical analysis skills	acquiring new self-insights, more independence
LONG TERM BENEFITS	broadening of our professional perspective; openness to new ideas; increase in cross-cultural sensitivity; enhancement of therapeutic attitudes and skills (unconditional positive regard, accurate empathy, flexibility)					

Figure 1.1. Overview of the comparative learning process as applied to intercultural studies in guidance and counseling.

18

type of training do counselors receive? What is the social status
of guidance workers in the country? Are statistical data available
on the number of professional personnel or guidance centers? Does
any guidance association exist in the country?

Component III: Self-assessment of the foreign guidance model
by its own standards.--What is the assessment of the foreign guidance effectiveness by administrators and practitioners? Is the
guidance model consistent in adhering to its stated principles?
Do its services promote the envisioned goals? What are the admitted strengths and weaknesses of the system? What proposals have
been offered by theorists or by rank and file workers to upgrade
guidance effectiveness, e.g., change in emphasis, upgrading of
training for personnel, etc.?

Component IV: Non-evaluative juxtaposition of the foreign
model and our own.--What parallels and contrasts seem apparent at
first glance? Are the differences real when we analyze the two
models in depth? Which parallels are most significant? Do they
reflect similar trends in the foreign youth culture and in our own?
Based on the present developments of guidance on either side, can
we expect convergence or divergence of the two guidance models in
the future?

Component V: Evaluation of the foreign guidance model according to our own standards.--Assuming the external frame of reference
(the role of objective observers) and admitting our cultural biases,
how do we evaluate the effectiveness of the foreign guidance model?
Does the foreign model offer strategies that could be incorporated
in modified form in our own guidance work? Are there any theoretical assumptions, practices, or methods in the foreign model that
have proven to be counterproductive and should be avoided?

Component VI: Clarification of our own personal and professional commitments.--The insights provided in the previous five
components help us form a new perspective on the "why" of our professional work, and on the role we are to assume as counselors in
our educational and social settings. How do our personal values
differ from those prevalent in the foreign culture we have studied?
Although we may theoretically reject certain approaches found in
the foreign guidance model, e.g., tendencies toward conformism, or
the lack of appreciation for different life styles, are we not using
parallel approaches in our work? Do we consistently apply the
principles that we profess? Or do we see a conflict between our
personal values and the role society expects of us as counselors?
How should we resolve such a conflict? How can we guard against
radical negativism that considers existing social structures beyond
reform and also against excessive conformism that would make us
into mere agents of the current establishment?

Concrete learning patterns

In the next paragraphs we will consider concrete steps that are useful when making comparative guidance studies available to counselor trainees and practitioners, especially those who wish to become leaders within the profession. We will operationally apply the comparative method described in the previous section to pre-service and in-service training experiences, and suggest ways of using travel to foreign countries for personal and professional growth.

Pre-service study pattern.--Ideally, the comparative dimension should permeate all academic courses in counselor training curricula. However, this assumption is at present unrealistic, since relatively few counselor educators have been adequately exposed to comparative studies themselves. On the other hand, most counselor education departments have at least one member with adequate foreign travel experience and with some knowledge about professional work done in other countries. Such a faculty member can initiate a course of comparative guidance, or at least make comparative studies the central issue of a guidance seminar. Additional resource persons can be found outside the counselor education program among instructors of other departments and foreign students; also off campus among knowledgeable people in professional and business circles. As a rule, it is far more suitable to concentrate on exploring one or two foreign guidance models in depth rather than cover a lot of territory in a superficial way which usually leads to over-simplifications and misconceptions. The following suggestions apply to the learning process of comparative guidance in an academic setting:

(a) The course format should be structured as a cooperative effort of instructor, resource persons (if needed), and class members. Components One and Two should be introduced by the instructor and a resource person to provide basic information on the foreign country, to identify available resources, and to stimulate involvement of class members right from the start. Individual students should be given responsibility for researching various areas of life in the foreign country, e.g., its history, cultural traditions, social patterns, political structure, educational system, and guidance activities. Specific projects should be assigned to individual students, e.g., provide samples of foreign art work, clothing, or food. Well defined, individual assignments are more apt to produce tangible information to be shared in class.

(b) During the first two Components the students, with the help of the instructor, are to experience the foreign cultural environment through role playing. For instance, they can portray the role of a parent, a teacher, a vocational counselor dealing with

20

a young person; they can act out group dynamics of a socialist collective, of an Israeli kibbutz, or of a Latin American extended family.

(c) Components Three through Six are to be developed primarily in group discussions. Students should prepare for class interaction (and for the earlier mentioned role playing) by readings suggested for each section of this book, and by drafting brief position papers on various subjects to organize their thoughts. The quality of written materials along with the degree of participation in class discussions are appropriate criteria for evaluation of individual performances.

In-service study pattern.--Workshops for practicing counselors have to be structured with a great deal of flexibility to meet the specific needs of the participants. The format of such workshops can range from a half-day mini-seminar to a series of several classes arranged almost like a pre-service study. Here we will concentrate on in-service training experiences that have to be kept brief. First, to avoid superficiality, the scope of the study has to be appropriately narrowed, in come cases to a single, salient characteristic of a foreign culture reflected in the guidance priorities of the country. Yet in spite of the limited range of the study, the impact factor of the foreign culture must not be lost or even reduced. Obviously, audio-visual and other resource materials have to be carefully selected to support the main theme of the workshop. It helps if the workshop leader has one or two assistants who have become familiar with the subject matter and can facilitate the smooth flow of the program. An example of a four hour workshop structure follows:

(a) Introduction of the overall topic by the workshop leader or resource person; explanation of workshop process and objectives (30 minutes).
(b) Audio-visual follow-up; displays of materials from the foreign country as suggested in Component One and Two (45 Minutes).
(c) Role playing of various life situations typical of the foreign culture under study as discussed in the section on pre-service study patterns (30 minutes).
(d) Break with refreshments typical of the foreign cuisine (30 minutes).
(e) Discussions of topics outlined in Components Three through Six (about 20 minutes each), preferably in small groups, with summary reports at the end of the workshop. The main conclusions of the group should be retrieved and mailed out to workshop participants along with a letter confirming their attendance.
(f) Evaluation of the workshop by participants.

Foreign travel.--Comparative studies at pre-service and in-service training levels logically lead to visits of foreign countries. Bereday (1964) confirms this to be the usual pattern among serious students of comparative education.

Meeting foreign counselors in their home settings provides deeper insights into their work, their attitudes, and their lives. One should acquire at least a rudimentary knowledge of the language spoken in the host country. Even a few halting phrases communicate one's willingness to perceive things from the local perspective.

Valuable experiences can be gained at international meetings and workshops which are available for counselors every year. Informal exchange of ideas in small groups is as important as the plenary sessions. There is no substitute for direct contacts of people from various countries who react to each other's opinions at close range and clarify their mutual concerns in a climate of professional and social rapport.

Individual travel should be prepared well in advance by study of the country to be visited, and by making contacts with foreign guidance professionals who may be willing to act as informal guides for the traveler. Letters should be written at least six weeks prior to departure from home indicating the dates of arrival and departure in the addressee's area, primary interests in the guidance field (vocational, rehabilitation counseling, etc.), and any other information that may help the foreign host prepare a meaningful program. Parenthetically, it should be added that "travel as education" is a legitimate income tax deduction item in some countries, when properly documented.

Group travel abroad is sponsored by various institutions such as universities or professional organizations which assume responsibility for both the physical and professional arrangements to be made abroad. Such trips can be taken as academic courses for credit. The major advantage is the professional leadership of a competent instructor who coordinates a group of like-minded people. Students have an excellent opportunity to share ideas and discuss personal impressions. The format of such trips varies according to emphases intended by the organizers. It is well to become thoroughly familiar with the proposed structure of the project (e.g., size of group, program of professional and recreational activities, housing arrangements, degree of regimentation, etc.) before joining.

Summary

The methodology suggested here for comparative studies in guidance and counseling follows a middle course between rigorous research and mere amassing of information about a foreign country. While Bereday (1964) suggests four basic steps, i.e., description (gathering of data), interpretation (evaluation of data), juxtaposition (establishing differences and similarities), and comparison (simultaneous evaluation and conclusion), the method proposed here structures the learning sequence in greater detail—an approach that is more suited for this pioneering stage. The six steps or components are applicable to learning patterns of academic courses and in-service workshops organized for counseling practitioners. Although researchers may find this method less sophisticated, it facilitates growth and affirmative reform. It is both dynamic in character and utilitarian in purpose—criteria envisioned by scholars of the stature of Nicholas Hans and Vernon Malinson. (King 1968)

References

Bereday, G.Z.F. Comparative method in education. New York: Holt, Rinehart & Winston, 1964.

King, E.J. Comparative studies and educational decision. New York: Bobbs-Merrill, 1968.

Noah, H.J. & Eckstein, M.A. Toward a science of comparative education. New York: Macmillan, 1969.

Section Two

NORTH AMERICA

The title of this volume requires the inclusion of a separate section covering the North-American scene of guidance and counseling, although the information may not be new to many readers. This applies particularly to the professional scene in the United States whose comprehensive repertoire of guidance literature is known to people in the helping professions throughout the world.

To avoid the futile effort of "carting coal to Newcastle," the essay on the United States has been kept intentionally brief, has avoided repeating generally known data, and has instead concentrated on currently developing trends and on the image of U.S. guidance in other countries. To be of assistance to readers less familiar with American guidance literature, a list of suggested readings has been included that contains basic resource material for additional study of guidance and counseling in the United States.

There was another reason for the inclusion of this section-- the desire of juxtaposing guidance and counseling in the United States and Canada. In many quarters, little distinction has been made between the two professional communities. The Canadian guidance movement has been often, incorrectly, perceived as a mere geographical extension of professional efforts south of the national boundary. True, Canadian guidance has been greatly influenced by its neighbor, as the authors of Chapter three readily admit. However, they also repeatedly emphasize the desire of Canadian counselors "to stand apart from the United States and its past influences" and document this determination by current efforts inspired by the unique cultural configuration of the country. Of particular inter-

est to readers of this book is the stated emphasis on international involvement by the Canadian guidance community.

The co-authors of Chapter 3, John Paterson, Sharon Robertson, and Heather Bain, are associated with Canadian universities. The author of Chapter 4, covering the United States, is an American counselor educator.

3

CANADA

John G. Paterson, Sharon E. Robertson, Heather C. Bain

Canada is one of the three countries which comprise North America. Guidance and counseling, like all facets of life in this country, has been heavily influenced by developments in the United States. In the past fifty years, most of the Canadian "giants" in this field received their training in the U.S., as graduate programs of counselor education were unknown in Canada until very recently. In spite of the traditionally close adherence to the American model, since the early 1960's some uniquely Canadian trends have started to surface. These new dimensions in counseling are closely related to the social and political structures in Canada, as they have existed, and do exist, in the 1960's and 1970's.

The country

Canada is a country made up of ten provinces joined in a Confederation. Politically, Canada is a democratic country with a Parliament based upon British tradition. This country has historic ties with Britain and the Queen of England is also the Queen of Canada, although she is represented by a Governor General in this country. France also has historic ties with Canada and was the other European power involved in the colonization and settlement of this vast nation. Canada is now a bilingual country, with close to one-third of Canadians speaking French as their first language. The Province of Quebec is predominantly French speaking, while in all other provinces English is the primary language spoken.

An important factor in Canadian life is the division of power between the National Government and the Provincial Legislatures. In Canada, control of education rests with the provinces, and each profession within education is under provincial jurisdiction. For this reason, it is almost impossible to discuss counseling in Canada as a whole. There are vast differences in the philosophy and implementation of guidance programs among provinces and among regions. Up until 1965, there was no national association to foster developments, or even exchange information among practicing counselors in this country. The last two decades have seen many changes in Canada and these changes have included both the threat of separation by Quebec and the demand for more autonomy, particularly by the Western provinces. These developments have been countered by a national unity movement which has resulted in a strong demand for more Canadian content in education throughout the land. Perhaps Canada is maturing as a nation; at least now Canadians are looking to their own past as a source of strength for the future. (Paterson and Masciuch 1972)

Canada, then, is a vast and enormously wealthy country with great regional disparities in life style and income level. Education, including guidance and counseling, is a provincial matter, and each province has developed in a different and unique fashion. Since 1965, there has been a Canadian identity in guidance and counseling, promoted by the success of the Canadian Guidance and Counselling Association and its journal, The Canadian Counsellor.

The present Canadian scene

A common stereotype of the Canadian tourist abroad presents a person more polite, more conservative, more unsure of self, and more confused than the American counterpart. Like all stereotypes, this one is unfair, but does have some base in reality. Now, as Canadians change, so will the stereotype.

In 1967 Canadians celebrated the 100th birthday of their country with Expo '67 in Montreal. Here it was shown that Canadians could host major international events successfully, and citizens throughout Canada began to take pride in their country hitherto unknown. Expo '67 was followed in Montreal by the Olympics, while in the West, the successful staging of Pan-American and Commonwealth Games helped to change the international "inferiority complex" of many Canadians.

As a group, Canadians are probably still conservative. Because this country has not embraced the "melting pot" philosophy, there is still wide diversity in cultural traditions and backgrounds among Canadians. The English--French language dichotomy is not really a representative look at the ethnic structure of this country, as almost one-third of Canadians trace cultural and language roots to other parts of the world.

Canadians now seem to be rediscovering pride; pride in their heritage and cultures, regional pride and, of course, national pride. This has resulted in an expanded political vote for Canada in the 1970's and 1980's. Similarly, Canadians in guidance and counseling are becoming more active internationally. Canada has recently hosted a world conference of the International Association of Educational and Vocational Guidance (IAEVG). Canadians sit on the Executive Council of this Association, as well as the International Round Table for the Advancement of Counselling (IRTAC). In the last decade, Canadian leaders in this field have been invited to teach and speak in all parts of the world. Perhaps in counseling, as in other areas, Canadians stand ready now to make their contribution. (Paterson 1975)

Educational processes

Since primary responsibility for education in Canada lies with each province, educational programs, facilities, and personnel vary from province to province according to past history, current affluence, and present societal trends. Maintenance of such diversity has one advantage in that the rights of the people of each province are more likely to be ensured and their wishes met. On the other hand, such diversity leads to confusion regarding a student's status in moving from one province to another, and requires that students and teachers make adjustments as the situation demands. In a highly mobile society, such confusion is not infrequent and counselors can often help students cope with the change.

In spite of these differences, there are similarities in the organization of education across provinces. By law, children must attend school until the age of fifteen or sixteen years (depending on the province), although this might be modified in special cases. The usual pattern is that children enter school at about the age of five, beginning with Kindergarten and then continuing on for twelve or thirteen years within the public school system. Schools are divided into three levels: elementary (Grades 1 - 6), junior high (Grades 7 - 9) and high school (Grades 10 - 12). Within the various levels, alternatives are available according to the needs of the child. For example, there are special classes for the gifted, and for children with physical handicaps, mental handicaps, learning disabilities and emotional distrubances. At the high school level, students may choose between an academic or a vocational route. This choice is usually made after consultation with teachers, guidance counselors, parents, and principals regarding the students' past and present performances, aptitudes, abilities, interests, and future goals.

At the post-secondary level, students can choose from a number of options depending upon their past achievement level. They may enter a university where degrees are offered at the undergraduate and possibly graduate levels, or they may choose a technical school.

29

We have also seen the emergence of what is referred to as "community college" in recent years. These colleges usually offer two year non-university programs, although students may receive university credit for certain courses if they wish to transfer.

In some provinces, a number of vocational centres have been established for those who have for some reason "dropped out" of the school system, but as adults wish to be involved in academic upgrading. Such programs offer possibilities for the disadvantaged adult which previously did not exist.

Within Canada, there is an accelerating tendency for more people to obtain more education. In a review of the data on higher education and student unemployment needs, Beech (1977) noted that from 1966 to 1975, the proportion of people entering the labour market in Ontario with some post-secondary education has increased from 24.9% to 43% and was estimated to be 50.5% in 1986. Not only did university graduates have the highest participation in the labour force (82% as opposed to 46% for elementary and 62.6% for high school graduates), but they also had the lowest unemployment rate.

In recent years there has been a greater emphasis on offering alternative courses and programs for adults. With increased numbers of women and youth, since World War II, looking for work, competition in the job market has increased considerably. For those without experience, particularly youth, one alternative has been to seek further educational qualifications. (Beech 1977) But besides this, as we move into the era of post-industrial society, education is being viewed as a life-long process and the demand for alternatives in adult education has increased. (St. John MacDonald 1978; Woodsworth 1973)

Concept of guidance and counseling

In the Canadian context, guidance and counseling are usually viewed as complementary disciplines with guidance having the broader scope, and counseling being one of the services or activities in the guidance program.

"Guidance" in the Canadian context might be defined, in the words of Banmen,

> ... as an ongoing process, developmental in nature, and consisting of specialized services planned to enable the individual to understand and accept himself in the light of his abilities, aptitudes, and interests so that he may become increasingly self-directed and competent to make appropriate adjustments in a dynamic society.

A closer look at the term guidance suggests that a number

30

of different services are included: appraisal services,
counseling services, information services consulting
services, placement and follow-up services, and orientation services. (Adkins, Banmen, Jackson, Moher and
Nevison 1971, pp. 29-30)

As the definition implies, the objectives of guidance and
counseling are considered to be identical. In counseling, whether
in a one-to-one relationship or in a small group, the focus is
usually on helping the individual to develop greater awareness and
acceptance of self and others as well as greater decision-making
and problem-solving skills.

Guidance rationale and goals

The rationale for guidance and counseling lies in a basic concern for the individual as a unique human being with a right to
realize his or her own worth, dignity and potential. It assumes
that an individual's behavior is a purposeful attempt to satisfy
personal needs within a society, as they are perceived by the person, and that self-direction and responsibility in making one's
own decisions are basic rights of all human being. (Herman 1972)
The objectives and goals of guidance and counseling are, therefore,
consistent with the goals of education in the Canadian democratic
society. Here, the primary purpose of education is seen as helping
students develop to the maximum of their potential as individuals
and as members of society. The facilitation of a student's intellectual, social, physical and emotional growth is essential in
achieving this purpose. (Turgeon 1973) Counselors are considered
to be specialists in the area of socio-emotional and cognitive
development, and thus play an integral role in the educational
process. (Christie and Williamson 1973)

While traditionally counselors have been primarily concerned
with clients who had more serious problems, a gradual change in
thinking has been evident over the last decade or so. It is argued
that, because counselors' skills are particularly suited to promoting positive human development, developmentally normal children as
well as those with particular difficulties may benefit from the
specialized services which guidance and counseling can offer. It
is further argued that this approach may prevent problems or alleviate them in their early stages. Thus, the emphasis in Canadian
counseling is shifting from an essentially remedial, therapeutic
approach to one which is primarily developmental and preventive in
nature. (Brosseau 1973; Grant 1977; Van Hesteren 1971) This does
not imply that counselors no longer see children, on an individual
basis, for remedial purposes. It does mean that fewer children
are seen in this manner and that the counselor has been encouraged
to work with teachers in classrooms, with groups of children in
classroom, with parent groups and with teachers in staff development. (Blowers and Paterson 1976)

31

Models for guidance services, particularly at the elementary school level, usually focus on the counseling, consulting, coordinating, and evaluative functions of the counselor. (Herman 1974; Jeffares and Peters 1974) It is argued that in a time of budget restrictions, this model has two major advantages: (1) a maximum number of students can be helped by a specialist; (2) the expertise developed by the counselor is passed on to others who are also close to students.

Organizational patterns of guidance and counseling

Guidance and counseling in Canadian school systems are usually found under pupil personnel services within the organizational hierarchy. Definitions of pupil personnel services are of two types--descriptions of functions of specialists and descriptions of goals of services. Pupil personnel services are supportive of classroom functions and their aims are complementary to the aims of education. Such services are usually performed by school counselors, remedial specialists, speech and hearing clinicians, school psychologists, school social workers, health specialists, and research personnel. Special education for exceptional children often falls within their scope. (Paterson 1970) As noted by Herman (1972), "a major objective of pupil personnel services is to provide for the student the best psychological climate for learning so that he may develop self-assurance, self-understanding, and decision-making competency."(p. 5) Such services are for students of all levels of ability, achievement, and adjustment. The goals of the pupil personnel workers are consistent with those of guidance, and counselors must cooperate with other members of the pupil personnel services as well as teachers and administrators to help students achieve to their full capacity in all aspects of their lives. (Paterson 1972)

Representation of pupil personnel services varies greatly from city to city. Each province has developed services in slightly different ways and services range in terms of adequacy according to budget constraints and the availability of qualified personnel and necessary facilities. Almost universally, though, there is a real shortage of specialized help in rural areas. Almost all pupil personnel workers, except health specialists, are qualified first as teachers and secondly as specialists within their discipline. This does not apply to post-secondary counselors.

Priorities of guidance and counseling

Professional literature in Canada suggests that the most frequently reported counselor activities are the traditionally accepted areas of educational-vocational counseling. (e.g., Brown 1974) Personal problem counseling is not as frequent an activity as educational or vocational counseling, but it is regarded as one of the most important functions of a counselor, as indicated, for example, in Mott's (1973) study, by counselors, principals, and teachers.

According to Herman (1974), school counseling has been subjected to the artificial trichotomy of educational, vocational, and personal-social foci. This division implies that the three areas should be dealt with as discrete problems. In actuality, they are inter-related and should be seen as integral components of the total experience of each student. This is consistent with the current thinking in Canada that primary emphasis be placed on the total development of the individual. Thus, there is an attempt to give equal attention to all three areas of responsibility in counseling services (Grant 1977), varying in emphasis according to the needs of students at any particular time.

Prevalent methodology

Canadian counseling theory and literature indicate an increasing shift in emphasis to a developmental and preventive approach to counseling. Correspondingly, it seems that there might be, in the practical situation, an increasing emphasis on group work, as counselors cannot hope to meet the needs of all students on an individual basis. Thus, they are encouraged to refer those students who are seriously dysfunctional to other specialized services within the school system or to agencies outside the school system.

Christensen (1976) has noted a gradual shift towards a more directive approach in counseling where the counselor attempts to help the client re-examine values, learn interpersonal skills, and develop understanding. Efforts are also being directed towards identifying interpersonal coping skills and knowledges as well as to developing effective ways of teaching those skills and knowledges. Certainly, if we look at the increasing use being made of programs for affective development, career awareness, life skills, decision-making, communication skills, values clarification, and parent education, Christensen's claim would appear to be accurate. Counselors in collaboration with teachers are increasingly using behavior modification techniques, Adlerian psychology, reality therapy, and transactional analysis to develop classroom atmospheres which are more conducive to the enhancement of the child's total development and the development of a positive learning climate.

In a study of elementary counselor role activities, Merchant and Zingle (1977) reported that "frequent" activities clustered into three categories: (a) counseling; (b) consulting; and (c) coordinating. Over 85% of the counselors reported that they provided individual counseling on a continuing basis for those children presenting learning or adjustment problems. Counselors reported that they were involved in parent and teacher consultation, the emphasis being on individual conferences with particular reference to children having specific difficulties. Consultation, then, appeared to be concerned with individuals and crisis-oriented rather than concerned with the normal, expected development of all children. The latter type of consultation was an "infrequent" activity of these counselors.

Such activities as the identification of seriously dysfunctional students and their referral to various agencies and professionals were considered as coordinating functions. Over two-thirds of
the counselors reported to be involved in such functions. Other
frequent activities included child study or child assessment. This
covered testing, analyzing cumulative record information to better
understand the child, and recommending children to be screened for
special classes of gifted students or slow learners. Infrequent
counselor activities included staff development and group work.

A study by Merchant and Zingle (1977) indicated that most elementary school counselors were still primarily involved in the traditional counseling activities. Similar results were obtained by
Brown (1974) whose responding counselors reported infrequent involvement in group work, testing, inservice for other professionals,
public relations activities, and research and evaluation. However,
most of the counselors expressed a desire for greater involvement
in all of these areas except testing. Psychological testing was
neither a frequent nor a popular counselor involvement, although
many Canadian experts see it as an important diagnostic tool in
helping students, teachers, and counselors make better decisions.
(Adkins, Banmen, Jackson, Moher and Nevison 1971)

Thus, it appears that despite the emphasis in current theoretical models of guidance and counseling on a developmental and preventive approach, there is, in practice, little implementation as
yet of this approach. The trend towards group work is just beginning in the practical setting--there is a lag from theory to practice. This is probably still true in 1979, although the data presented by Brown (1974) and by Merchant and Zingle (1977) are a few years
old.

Guidance personnel

In the last decade a number of surveys have been conducted to
gain information regarding the status of guidance personnel at all
levels of education in Canada. At the elementary level, three provincial surveys (Altmann and Herman 1971; McCulloch 1971; Interim
Report on the Survey of Elementary Counselling in B.C. 1971) and
two national studies (Oksanen and Van Hoose 1972; Merchant and Zingle
1977) have been conducted. Several provincial surveys at the high
school level have been reported. (Massey 1973; Mott 1973) In addition, Johnston and Miles (1975) reported a study of community college counseling personnel, while Brown (1974) sampled members of the
Canadian Guidance and Counselling Association (CGCA). Such studies
have been hampered by problems arising from inaccurate information
sources, misunderstandings in the definition of basic terms such as
"counselor" and by low response returns. Consequently, a comparison
of the results of the Canadian surveys are not particularly meaningful. However, some of the more recent studies are considered here.

Oksanen and Van Hoose (1972) found that of the 267 Canadian

34

elementary school counselors covered by their study, 50% were employed on a full-time basis. About 18% held a graduate degree in guidance; 75% had an undergraduate degree with guidance qualifications; and 7% had no degree but some guidance training. Somewhat similar results were reported by Merchant and Zingle (1977) who found that 77% of the 162 elementary counselors in their study had an undergraduate degree. About 22% held a guidance certificate without an academic degree and about 10% had no formal guidance training. About half of the counselors (57%) were employed full-time. However, 15% served as elementary-secondary school counselors, 12% as elementary teacher-counselors, and 4% as elementary school administrator-counselors. About two-thirds of the full-time counselors were responsible for over 750 pupils.

In a more limited study by Brown (1974) various levels of training were again evident among the 49 counselors surveyed, 56% of whom worked in secondary school settings. In this sample, 65% held a Master's degree, graduate level diploma, or better. Furthermore, 88% had completed a counseling practicum and 25% had done an internship.

Johnston and Miles (1975) reported on the staffing of counseling services at 83 post-secondary, non-university educational institutions across Canada. Of the 200 full-time counselors in the study, 37% held Bachelor's degrees, 62% Master's degrees, and only 2% more than Master's degrees. Of those reporting an area of specialization in their studies, 60% specialized in areas relevant to counseling. The counselors were predominantly male (68%) and primarily in the 26-35 age range. Experience was usually limited to six or fewer years (53%). Only 10% of the colleges indicated that they employed paraprofessionals on the counseling staff which in this study meant anyone with less than a Master's degree in counseling or equivalent.

As Guttman (1973) noted, there are no formally recognized requirements for certification as a counselor in Canada. Most provinces do recognize course work leading to a Master's degree or diploma in counseling. While these credentials are not formally required for a person to function as a school counselor, a teaching certificate and teaching experience are. This applies in all provinces of Canada except Quebec where a teaching certificate has never been required except in some Anglophone school districts. Instead, the Province formally recognizes the Corporation of Guidance Counselors as the representative professional body in counseling. According to provincial law, one must have a Master's degree in counseling, or its equivalent in a diploma, for admission to the Corporation. Issues relating to standards for counselors at the various educational levels are still being debated and counselors are encouraged to upgrade their professional qualifications.

Professional training for counselors

A survey of selected training programs for school counselors offered by Canadian universities was conducted in 1971 by Guttman (1973). Fourteen counselor education programs were identified. It should be noted that the data would not cover all programs in operation today and that only Anglophone universities were represented in the survey. Guttman concluded that there appeared to be three distinct models of counselor education in Canada: (1) a two-year program which is integrative in its approach to counseling theory and practice; (2) a one-year program (part- or full-time) which follows a course requirement outline; and (3) a diploma or certificate program which is very similar to guidance programs offered through provincial departments of education. For the most part, the one-year Master's degree program seemed to be the dominant model.

On surveying the one-year programs, Guttman found that most of them were similar in the number of course requirements, the content of the courses, and the counseling activities offered through practicum experience. The course work frequently included: Principles of Guidance and Counseling; Techniques of Guidance; Theories of Counseling; Group Work in Guidance; Theories of Vocational Development; Organization and Administration of Guidance Services; and optional courses such as Theories of Personality; Individual Testing; Adolescent Development; etc. While Guttman was critical of the programs for not including courses on group counseling skills, communication skills, and behavior modification skills, it would appear that many of these courses have been incorporated into the programs of today. Furthermore, courses on family counseling, on counseling girls and women, and on human sexuality are increasingly finding their way into the more advanced programs. Among the Master's programs, there is still some variation with regard to a thesis requirement; in some programs there is no such requirement while in others a thesis is required.

Guttman (1973) reported that the counseling practicum or internship was the main feature of the training programs. She also noted the vast differences in practicum courses "on such variables as the scope and depth of the experiential activities in counseling, the expectations of the role performance skills of the counselor trainee, and the nature of the counseling supervision in the practicum experience." (p. 255) Such differences probably still exist today.

An area which was not covered in the Guttman (1973) survey was the state of doctoral programs in this country. Currently there are at least five such programs in operation with the level of development varying considerably.

The professional association

One of the outstanding aspects of guidance and counseling in Canada has been the spectacular success of the Canadian Guidance and Counselling Association (CGCA). Perhaps CGCA has been the most prevalent force in promoting a Canadian identity and approach to counseling problems at all levels of society.

Many Canadian counselors are, and have been, members of the American Personnel and Guidance Association (APGA). CGCA is now a very different type of organization, but it was from APGA that the Canadian Association drew early strength. Gilbert Wrenn, Henry Borow, Maurice Freehill, George Gazda, and Donald Super were a few of the prominent APGA members who spoke to early conferences and assisted Canadian executive members in early planning.

The CGCA was founded at a fledgling conference in Niagara Falls, Ontario in 1965. The first President of the Association was John Andoff, a vocational counselor with Canada Manpower. In its early stages, CGCA was heavily dominated by counselors from the Provinces of Quebec and Ontario in central Canada. The cornerstones of the Association were laid at the first truly national conference in Quebec City, in 1967. The first issue of <u>Canadian Counsellor</u> was published at that time by Myrne Nevison of the University of British Columbia. The second President of CGCA, Aurèle Gagnon, promoted the Association's constitution, ensuring truly national representation as well as bilingualism.

Since 1967, CGCA has had regional or national conferences in all provinces of Canada and has achieved international prominence through the excellence of its publication. Canadian biennial conferences have become well known and consistently attract a worldwide representation. As an association, CGCA has also encouraged and supported the two major international groups--IAEVG and IRTAC-- and at present has its members on the executive councils of both organizations and as editors or consulting editors of major international journals.

To date, much of the success of CGCA has occurred because the Association has resisted temptations to formalize its operations and break into divisions or interest groups. Conferences have been held throughout Canada, not only in major convention centres. Some areas have regional councils, others do not, as membership remains on an individual basis, with much flexibility within the Association. Counseling in Canada is a provincial responsibility; so this Association wields little power, but has now immense influence in counseling circles of Canada and throughout the world.

Summary and conclusions

Canada is a country of great variety geographically, historically, culturally, linguistically, socially, and economically. Education is under provincial jurisdiction, and as such reflects this national variety through regional differences in philosophy and implementation. For this reason, it is difficult to generalize about guidance and counseling in Canada as a whole.

However, there are some basic similarities and national trends emerging across the provincial boundaries. The common rationale that lies behind guidance and counseling is a concern for the individual as a unique human being with a right to realize his or her own dignity, worth, and potential. One assumption lying behind this proposition is that of education as a life-encompassing and life-long process. As such it is seen to continue beyond the classroom walls and often beyond the years of formal schooling. It includes not only intellectual achievement, but encompasses also the realization of social, emotional, and physical potential. Counselors in Canada are seen as having an integral role in the educational process, through fostering the development and integration of an individual's many potentials.

Traditionally, a counselor's activities have been primarily concerned with the educational and vocational spheres. Although there is always a lag between psychological theorizing and practical application, there is evidence within the Canadian counseling reality of a move to integrate the educational, vocational, and personal-social spheres. In the future, it seems, we will see counselors adopting a truly integrative approach in the realization of a student's educational potential.

The last decade has witnessed, in Canadian guidance literature, a change in emphasis to a developmental and preventive approach. In reality, there has as yet been little application of these ideas in the practical situation. Most counselors still see students with special difficulties on an individual basis, their contacts being remedial or crisis-oriented. The next two decades should give rise to the implementation of the developmental and preventive emphasis by counseling practitioners. It is likely that counselors will-- more and more--identify and refer seriously dysfunctional students to specialized services outside the school system, and thus spend more time in working with groups of children, with teachers in class-rooms and in staff development, with parents, and in communication and cooperation with other pupil personnel workers who have contact with the students.

Canada is maturing as a nation. She is showing evidence of a strong Canadian identity and national pride. Canada wants to be Canadian; to stand up apart from the United States and its past influences. Thus, the world is likely to witness in the country's guidance and counseling future: firstly, many trends and ideas that are uniquely Canadian; and secondly, an expanding and very active role internationally.

References

Adkins, A.A., Banmen, J., Jackson, D.W., Moher, J. & Nevison, M.B. Objectives and functions: Answers to a series of questions on guidance and counselling from Canadian authorities. School Guidance Worker, 1971, 26 (5), 29-39.

Altmann, H. & Herman, A. Status of elementary counselling in the province of Alberta. Canadian Counsellor, 1971, 5, 41-45.

Beech, H.D. Higher education and student employment needs. Canadian Journal for Higher Education, 1977, 7 (3), 1-22.

Blowers, E.A. & Paterson, J.G. The teacher, the counsellor and other children. The School Guidance Worker, 1976, 32 (1), 13-16.

Brosseau, J. Consulting--a potpourri? Canadian Counsellor, 1973, 7 (4), 259-267.

Brown, T. Present and preferred functions of CGCA members. Canadian Counsellor, 1974, 8 (3), 175-184.

Christensen, C.M. Editorial--Changing role of the counsellor? Canadian Counsellor, 1976, 10 (2), 45-48.

Christie, T.G. & Williamson, J.A. The counsellor--an affective educator. Canadian Counsellor, 1973, 7 (4), 241-247.

Grant, M.L. Career emphasis with a difference: Counselling secondary school students in Vancouver. School Guidance Worker, 1977, 33 (1), 29-34.

Guttman, M.A.J. A survey of selected school counsellor training programs in Canadian universities. Canadian Counsellor, 1973, 7, 250-257.

Herman, A. Student personnel services: A rationale. In Herman, A. (Ed.) Introduction to guidance. Toronto: Holt, Rinehart & Winston, 1972, 3-6.

Herman, A. The school counsellor as educator. The School Guidance Worker, 1974, 29 (6), 19-21.

Interim report on the survey of elementary counselling in B.C. Pulse, 1972, 1, 1-6.

Jeffares, D. & Peters, L. The elementary school counsellor: A role description. School Guidance Worker, 1974, 29 (6), 9-13.

Johnston, E.F. & Miles, F.A. Canadian community college counselling services--how are they staffed? Canadian Counsellor, 1975, 9, 169-181.

Massey, B.J. A survey of counsellor, student, teacher, administrator, parent, and school trustee attitudes and factors influencing attitudes toward present high school counselling services. Unpublished doctoral dissertation. University of Alberta, 1973.

McCulloch, B.   Elementary guidance in Ontario--a survey. <u>Ontario School Counsellors' Association Review</u>, 1971, <u>4</u>, 15-25.

Merchant, D. & Zingle, H.   Elementary school guidance in Canadian urban areas: A study of present counsellor functions. <u>Canadian Counsellor</u>, 1977, <u>11</u>, 201-209.

Mott, T.R.   Perceptions of the high school counsellor role in Alberta. <u>Canadian Counsellor</u>, 1973, <u>7</u>, 49-57.

Oksanen, I. & Van Hoose, W.H.   Status of elementary school counselling in six Canadian provinces. <u>Canadian Counsellor</u>, 1972, <u>6</u>, 271-274.

Paterson, J.G.   A case for teacher training and experience for pupil personnel workers. <u>Canadian Counsellor</u>, 1970, <u>4</u>, 161-164.

Paterson, J.G.   Administration of elementary school counselling services in urban settings. In Zingle, H.W. & Fox, E.E. (Eds.) <u>The elementary school counsellor in the decade ahead</u>. Toronto: Holt, Rinehart & Winston, 1972, 149-153.

Paterson, J.G.   Where now? <u>The Alberta Counsellor</u>, 1975, <u>6</u> (1), 7-11.

Paterson, J.G. & Masciuch, H.   Accountability and the future role of the counsellor. <u>The Alberta Counsellor</u>, 1972, <u>3</u>, 11-15.

St. John Macdonald, M.   Here to stay? Women, counselling, post-secondary education. <u>School Guidance Worker</u>, 1978, <u>33</u> (6), 10-14.

Turgeon, P.   The school counsellor: Where are we heading as a profession? <u>School Guidance Worker</u>, 1973, <u>29</u> (2), 15-22.

Van Hesteren, F.N.   Foundations of the guidance movement in Canada. Unpublished doctoral dissertation. University of Alberta, 1971.

Woodsworth, J.G.   Changing concerns in educational and vocational counseling. <u>Canadian Counsellor</u>, 1973, <u>7</u>, 149-153.

4

UNITED STATES OF AMERICA

Victor J. Drapela

The United States of America is a land of immigrants. Since
the days of the Pilgrims, people from many nations came to its
shores and gave of themselves and of their native cultures to weave
a social pattern that has become present-day America. Few ethnic
groups were able to preserve their cultural identity in this melting
pot of nations. Most newcomers became "Americanized" in the first
or second generation.

By the same token, the many genetic and cultural influences have
created a pluralistic society with a broad perspective in interpret-
ing events, setting goals, and chosing life styles. If there ever
was an "American way of life," it was not a systematized, clearly defined living pattern as we find it, for instance, among the Nordic
peoples of Europe. Rather it has emerged as a mixture of hard drive
for survival, materialism, pragmatism, and competitive entrepreneur-
ship on one hand; and individualism, self-directiveness, flexibility,
and tolerance of religious or philosophical diversity, on the other.

Foreigners who visit the United States for the first time are
amazed by the cultural-social climate of a country that seems to
function reasonably well in a situation of apparent chaos. This
feeling is intensified by the eagerness of most Americans to explore
their nation's weaknesses rather than strengths: in government, economy, ethics, law enforcement, education, and health care. Yet in
spite of the publicly voiced criticism of national affairs--or, perhaps, because of it--most Americans share a gut feeling that "things
will work out all right," and they plan their future lives based on

41

that assumption. Although American society has been for generations materially satiated and thus appears to be spoiled, it has acquired a high tolerance of·trauma and an ability to recover quickly from setbacks. Some consider these qualities to be marks of national vigor, while others view them as symptoms of superficiality or insensitivity. Be it as it may, the events from Kennedy's death in 1963 through the period of racial confrontations and the Vietnam nightmare to the bizarre mass murder-suicide in the Guyana jungle have shaken the present generation, but have failed to unnerve it.

While the high degree of ethical permissiveness that blossomed in the late 1960's has largely survived, the political extremism of that period has not. New trends are emerging among young people toward a more realistic posture in general. The philosophy of "doing your own thing" under all circumstances is tempered by concerns for other people's needs and rights, especially those of racial and ethnic minorities, of women, the handicapped, and the old. Self-awareness, personal and group values, health habits, and stages in the individual's life cycle have become important issues, along with efforts at conserving energy and the natural resources of the country.

The guidance movement

Guidance as a helping professional activity grew out of the vocational assistance provided for new immigrants by Frank Parsons and a group of idealistic people around him in the first decade of the century. While the vocational aspect of guidance remained strong, organizationally, guidance has been integrated within the educational system of the country. The current thrust of guidance work has outgrown the four year high school, where many vocational decisions are made, and is increasingly branching out to elementary school as it did earlier to institutions of higher education.

The concept of guidance has been defined in many ways. Shertzer and Stone (1976) report that over one hundred definitions have been identified in professional literature. For readers who may be less familiar with American professional literature I am presenting a composite definition that reflects the general consensus of counselors in the United States. Guidance is perceived as a helping process by which clients get to know themselves, i.e., their strengths and limitations, accept themselves and clarify their values, get to know the world they live in, and develop effective ways of interacting with people. The outcomes are increased self-directiveness, maturity, contentment, and social identification.

Guidance services

The guidance process is carried out by means of various services that overlap and complement each other, such as counseling with individuals and groups; appraisal by psychological testing and by non-test methods; educational, vocational, and personal-social information; placement; etc. The core service of American guidance is counseling which focuses upon the needs of clients as individuals and helps clients understand the meaning and the optimal use of other guidance services. Many counseling approaches are being employed side by side, ranging from the client-centered to the behavioral model. However, they all share the basic principle of the counselor's commitment to the client rather than to the employing institution. Society in general, and the school or other institutions in particular, are helped indirectly through the enhancement and social maturity attained by individual clients. Whether this theoretical orientation is always put into practice is, of course, another question.

During the past two decades an emphasis on group counseling has gained ground within the guidance profession. The thrust culminated around 1970 when some counselors felt that group work may replace individual counseling almost completely. Since then, a more balanced view has prevailed. While it is admitted that group work is not a panacea, it is considered to be a very useful counseling tool and is favored by many counselors and clients.

Guidance personnel

In the early days, guidance in American schools was predominantly in the hands of teachers and was closely linked with the curriculum. However, along with its expansion it assumed a separate identity and organizational structure within the educational system. By now, guidance is entrusted to professionally trained counselors who are members of the school personnel team. They are in close liaison with teachers, administrators, and other helping professionals, many of whom divide their time among several schools. There is an emphasis on cooperation between counselors and parents, particularly at the elementary school level. Some counselors have been involved in organizing groups for parents in the schools they serve and offering courses in parent effectiveness training.

The typical training program for American guidance counselors is a one or two year Master's curriculum which includes course work in psychological, social, and research foundations along with theory and practical experiences in individual and group counseling, as well as other guidance services. The professional education typically includes a supervised counseling practicum. Some counselors have received additional training in an Education Specialist curriculum which leads to a degree midway between M.A. and Ph.D., while others have earned a doctorate.

Professional groups are carefully monitoring existing counselor training programs (about 420 in the U.S.) to assure maintenance of appropriate standards. This involves selection and retention of students, content of courses offered, degree of practical training experiences, and attitudinal characteristics as well as human relationship skills attained by trainees. The Association for Counselor Education and Supervision, a Division of the American Personnel and Guidance Association, adopted in 1978 a Manual for accreditation procedures of counselor training programs. It spells out in detail required minimal standards to be met by institutions that desire to receive full accreditation. This step has far reaching implications for fostering quality education of American counselors. (ACES 1978)

These basic standards apply to counselors working in non-school settings as well. However, while some agencies or mental health centers maintain very high standards, other institutions employ as counselors people who are not adequately trained. This inequality of professional qualification has stimulated a movement promoting mandatory counselor licensure by the State where a counselor works.

Current trends

The American guidance profession is currently in a state of soul searching. After a decade of dramatic value shifts, it has arrived at a crossroad and is forced to assess the validity of its traditional programs. The effectiveness and relevance of basic guidance functions are questioned. New roles are envisioned for counselors in terms of client advocacy and social proactivity. The issue of values and philosophy seem predominant in many professional discussions. Smith and Peterson (1977) observe:

> The counseling process can be a means by which individuals
> can examine cultural values and goals and modify for them-
> selves the destructive elements by bringing them in line
> with humanistic and democratic values. The process begins,
> of course, with counselors becoming aware of their own
> value orientations that will make subtle imposition of
> values less likely. (p. 316)

Some authors question even the guidance rationale itself. In Ivey's (1976) opinion, traditional counseling is no longer sufficient as a helping effort, since it frequently pacifies individuals and makes them adjust to a situation that is in itself unhealthy. Rather than accept the world as it is, he urges counselors to work toward change and to help humanize the social system. Cook (1972) believes that counselors are ideally suited to assume the role of change agents, particularly in schools where they serve as liaison persons between students and the professional staff.

Loud voices are heard in favor of extending guidance services, particularly through outreach programs, to population groups whose needs had been largely neglected in the past. These include women (Hansen 1972), racial minorities (Vontress 1976), persons caught in

44

mid-life career changes (Entine 1976), and homosexuals (Norton 1976). This theme of horizontal expansion has dominated the current discussion in the guidance community and has led to a reassessment of professional priorities and to tangible outcomes.

Also, career education and vocational planning have emerged as top priorities in the practice of developmental guidance from elementary school on through the final stages of education. Career development is considered a life-long process (Super 1957) not only within the initially chosen field of work, but also by means of radical changes of occupational involvement. Such mid-career readjustments are accepted by society as every person's prerogative. This implies the need for vocational guidance services far beyond high school or college levels. The American School Counselor Association and the National Vocational Guidance Association are particularly concerned with these issues.

The image of U.S. guidance abroad

Since guidance in the United States has for long occupied a prestigious status in the international community, many foreign counselors have chosen to receive their professional education at American universities. This, in turn, has provided the U.S. guidance profession with a valuable critique by qualified people who speak from different cultural perspectives. The paragraphs that follow are a summary of most frequently repeated observations by foreign colleagues. Some of them were abstracted from a special feature edited by Goldman (1974) and published in the Personnel and Guidance Journal under the title "Guidance USA: Views from abroad." (cf., the introduction to Section One) But the majority of them were obtained during "International Visitors Forum" discussions at APGA Conventions in the U.S. and at international gatherings abroad. They refer almost exclusively to guidance at the secondary school level:

(1) Most foreign observers are amazed by the vastness and variety of ongoing guidance programs in the U.S. and by the budgetary resources involved. Those who have been familiar with the American scene since World War II note a dramatic expansion during that period.

(2) U.S. counselors are seen as generally well trained and highly motivated. Additional training opportunities are considered abundant for those who wish to advance their training. However, American counselors are also criticized for being anti-intellectual, parochial in outlook, and overly enthusiastic about anything that is new, no matter what its worth.

(3) Counseling skills are seen as a major forte of the typical American counselor. The emphasis on psychological counseling, self-understanding and self-enhancement is seen by some as exaggerated, with little concern given to early career planning. This is explained by the tendency of counselors to channel high school students into college education although they are of marginal caliber, thus delaying

45

career choices that should have been made earlier. The American labor market is seen as overly complex, with few government regulations, particularly with regard to required apprenticeship experiences.

(4) In spite of their extensive professional training, U.S. counselors are seen as overinvolved in activities that could be adequately discharged by competent clerks, i.e., academic scheduling, and as having little time for their guidance tasks. At times, the guidance role perception is seen as blurred among the school personnel, and even among counselors themselves. In past years, the emphasis on accountability may have forced counselors to accept unprofessional roles to "look good" on work efficiency reports.

(5) Foreign observers are impressed by the volume of research that is being generated every year in various counseling settings. Much of the research has blazed new trails and foreign colleagues are monitoring the results with interest. On the negative side, it is said, a wide gap exists in U.S. guidance between sophisticated research projects and the actual implementation of guidance programs by practitioners.

(6) Perhaps one of the reasons, foreign observers feel, why American practitioners are unable to test current research data in their work is the need to respond to crisis situations rather than plan on a long-term basis. Drug abuse is seen as one of the most pressing current problems. American society, in general, is perceived as constantly changing. Young people are said to be exposed to an excessive number of stimuli. It is not an easy setting to live in, unless one is used to it from early youth, foreigners feel. In spite of the extensive counseling services available in the U.S., much maladjustment remains. Foreign observers ask: Is counseling ineffective? If it is effective, how much maladjustment does this society generate?

(7) It is admitted by most foreign observers that the prevalent emotional problems in the U.S. are typical of all "overdeveloped" countries, such as West Germany or Japan. The high degree of specialization fragments the human psyche. It also fragments the impact of therapeutic intervention. Counselors are urged to deal with the total person, to become enlightened generalists rather than retreat to an over-specialized level that does not treat the total person.

To view these critical remarks in perspective, it is well to remember that foreign observers have a generally high opinion of the guidance profession in the United States. Occasional negative comments are in line with the standard of excellence they expect and are not a sign of ill will.

Professional organizations for counselors

While counselors are free to belong to as many professional

organizations as they wish or to none at all, most of them do belong
to the American Personnel and Guidance Association. Since its foundation in 1952 it grew to become the single largest professional organization of counselors with a membership of over 40,000 persons.
It has thirteen national Divisions and fifty-two regional Branches,
including a European Branch.

APGA provides for its members an official newspaper, Guidepost,
that is published eighteen times a year, and a professional period-
ical, the Personnel and Guidance Journal, which has ten issues per
year. It also publishes books, monographs, and films, and organizes
workshops. Every spring, APGA holds a National Convention with key-
note addresses and smaller content sessions for which about 500 one-
hour slots are available. The association has its placement service
and offers professional insurance to its members.

APGA Divisions pursue, within the larger organizational framework,
their own specialized interests. They publish thirteen professional
journals of their own. I am presenting here the list of current APGA
Divisions to indicate the scope of professional interests in counselor
ranks:

American College Personnel Association; Association for Counselor
Education and Supervision; National Vocational Guidance Association;
Association for Humanistic Education and Development; American School
Counselor Association; American Rehabilitation Counseling Association;
Association for Measurement and Evaluation in Guidance; National
Employment Counselors Association ; Association for Non-White Concerns
in Personnel and Guidance; Association for Religious and Value Issues
in Counseling; Association for Specialists in Group Work; Public
Offender Counselors Association; and American Mental Health Counselor
Association.

References

ACES (Association for Counselor Education and Supervision). Accreditation procedures manual for counselor education. Washington: American Personnel and Guidance Association, 1978.

Cook, D. R. The change agent counselor: A conceptual context. The School Counselor, 1972, 20, 9-15.

Entine, A. D. Mid-life counseling: Prognosis and potential. Personnel and Guidance Journal, 1976, 55, 112-114.

Goldman, L. (Ed.) Guidance U.S.A.: Views from abroad. Personnel and Guidance Journal, 1974, 53, 40-56.

Hansen, L. S. We are furious (female) but we can shape our own development. Personnel and Guidance Journal, 1972, 51, 87-93.

Ivey, A. E. An invited response: The counselor as teacher. Personnel and Guidance Journal, 1976, 54, 431-434.

Norton, J. L. The homosexual and counseling. Personnel and Guidance Journal, 1976, 54, 374-377.

Shertzer, B. and Stone, S. C. Fundamentals of guidance. Boston: Houghton Mifflin, 1976 (3rd Ed.).

Smith, D. and Peterson, J. Counseling and values in a time perspective. Personnel and Guidance Journal, 1977, 55, 309-318.

Super, D. E. The psychology of careers. New York: Harper, 1957.

Vontress, C. E. Counseling middle-aged and aging cultural minorities. Personnel and Guidance Journal, 1976, 55, 132-135.

Suggested readings

Combs, A. W. et al. Helping relationships: Basic concepts for the helping professions. Boston: Allyn & Bacon, 1971.

Gazda, G. M. (Ed.) Basic approaches to group psychotherapy and group counseling. Springfield, IL: Thomas, 1975 (2nd Ed.).

Hansen, J. C. (Ed.) Counseling process and procedures. New York: Macmillan, 1978.

Herr, E. L. Vocational guidance and human development. Boston: Houghton Mifflin, 1974.

Holland, J. L. Making vocational choices: A theory of careers. Englewood Cliffs, NJ: Prentice-Hall, 1973.

Hoppock, R. Occupational information: Where to get it in career education. New York: McGraw-Hill, 1976.

Kemp, G. C. Foundations of group counseling. New York: McGraw-Hill, 1970.

Krumboltz, J. and Thoresen, C. Behavioral counseling. New York: Holt, Rinehart & Winston, 1969.

Pietrofesa, J. J. et al. The authentic counselor. Chicago: Rand McNally, 1971.

Rogers, C. R. On becoming a person: A therapist's view of psychotherapy. Boston: Houghton Mifflin, 1961.

Shertzer, B. and Stone, S. C. Fundamentals of counseling. Boston: Houghton Mifflin, 1974 (2nd Ed.).

Shertzer, B. and Stone, S.C. Fundamentals of guidance. Boston: Houghton Mifflin, 1976 (3rd Ed.).

Super, D. E. et al. Career development: Self-concept theory. New York: College Entrance Examination Board, 1963.

Tolbert, E. L. An introduction to guidance. Boston: Little, Brown, 1978.

Tyler, L. The work of the counselor. New York: Appleton, Century, Crofts, 1969 (3rd Ed.).

Van Hoose, W. H. and Pietrofesa, J. J. Counseling and guidance in the twentieth century. Boston: Houghton Mifflin, 1970.

Wrenn, C. G. The world of the contemporary counselor. Boston: Houghton Mifflin, 1973.

Periodicals

Personnel and Guidance Journal; Counselor Education and Supervision; Vocational Guidance Quarterly; The School Counselor; Elementary School Guidance and Counseling Journal; Journal of Specialists in Group Work; Humanist Educator; Counseling and Values; Journal for Non-White Concerns in Personnel and Guidance; Guidepost. Washington: American Personnel and Guidance Association Press.

Section Three

LATIN AMERICA

In spite of its size and wealth in cultural and material resources, Latin America has received undeservedly little attention
in the arena of international studies. This may have been caused
by the relative lack of involvement of most Latin-American nations
in international affairs. For many generations, people in other
parts of the world saw Latin America as a self-contained geographical,
cultural, and political sphere where things are being done with a
flair for the unpredictable. The novels by Graham Greene which have
a Latin-American scenario offer clues to the prevalent feelings on
life in Latin America held by Europeans and North-Americans alike.

The dramatic developments in the last twenty-five years have
shown Latin America as a changing continent. The first Chapter of
this Section elaborates on the theme of cultural and social changes
which are still under way and relates their significance to the
emerging field of guidance and counseling. Rapid modernization of
developing countries produces a loosening of traditional family patterns and leads to uncertainty and value conflicts among individuals,
particularly the young. While pointing out prevalent trends throughout the continent, the author of the Chapter is careful to dispel
the mistaken notion that Latin America is a cultural or social commonwealth comparable to the United States and Canada. Oliva Espin
is herself a native Latin-American with work experience in Cuba, Panama, and Costa Rica where she served both as counselor and college
professor.

The second Chapter of this Section deals with guidance developments in Brazil. There is no doubt that by its vastness and economic strength the country represents an appropriate sample of forthcoming trends on the continent. It also suffers from social problems typical of many other South- and Central-American countries. Donald Pemberton describes both the reality of guidance work in Brazil and the theoretical and legal bases on which it operates. He has first-hand knowledge of the country where he lived for many years and which he regularly visits.

It is unfortunate that we cannot include a report on Mexico, as we had intended, in the present edition of the book. Guidance work and counselor education in that country has expanded in recent years significantly. Initially, there were strong U.S. influences involved. By now, however, Mexican professionals are charting their own approaches quite independently of foreign models.

5

A CHANGING CONTINENT

Oliva M. Espin

Any study of Latin America must begin with the understanding that Latin America is not a single unit. What we refer to as Latin America is a unit in geographic terms only. There are differences in race, language, political organization, and cultural values among the Latin American countries.

Within each Latin American country, there are also important differences. Most nations in Latin America are populated by a variety of races, creating major cultural differences within a single country. There may also be a number of languages spoken in a single country, as is the case of those nations with a large and varied Indian population.

Racial heritage is often a key difference between the Latin American nations. Countries with a strong black influence, such as the Dominican Republic or Panama, differ in their character and cultural traditions from the Andean countries with their strong Indian heritage. European influence, on the other hand, is marked in countries such as Costa Rica, Chile and Argentina.

Latin American political systems are anything but homogeneous. Costa Rica has had a tradition of constitutional governments almost since her independence more than a century ago, while Haiti-- independent for a longer time--has had a series of dictatorships. Cuba's political situation, on the other hand, is unique among the countries of Latin America.

While most Latin American countries share the common heritage of the Spanish conquerors, there are other countries—such as Brazil, almost a continent in itself—where another language is spoken and which have quite a different historical tradition.

Obviously, then, to talk about guidance and counseling in Latin America as a whole is an almost impossible task. Differences among the Latin American countries manifest themselves through the guidance system, as well as through language, cultural heritage and politics. Chile, for instance, has had guidance programs at the secondary school level for years, and instituted an elementary guidance program in 1966. That same year, UNESCO assigned a consultant to Bolivia to begin planning a secondary school guidance programs for the first time. Latin American training programs for guidance personnel range from highly specialized graduate programs to limited paraprofessional training.

In spite of all these differences, however, there are certain values shared by most Latin Americans and pressing issues that are common to all countries of the continent. These values and issues are worth discussing, since they affect the field of guidance and its role in Latin America.

Change as the common denominator

Latin America is changing—no one can deny that. Change is taking place socially, politically, and educationally. But most of all, change is taking place at the ideological level. Cuba's political changes, her educational and socio-economic development, are influencing all Latin American countries. Politicians, businessmen, educators and students alike all see Cuba's situation either as an example to emulate, or as a danger and a threat. However it is experienced, this influence affects the ideological outlook of Latin Americans planning programs at all levels and in all fields.

A sense of urgency prevails in Latin America. Those who have had access to education are developing a sense of responsibility for their less privileged countrymen. They are searching for new ways to improve the human condition on their continent. The need for human liberation in its fullest sense has become the central theme of Catholic theology on this continent where the world's largest Catholic poulation lives. The most effective utilization of human resources is the concern of politicians and educators in all Latin American countries. The field of guidance is developing within this context.

The cultural context

The guidance movement originated in the United States as an expression of the early twentieth century social movement. Appropriate vocational choices and educational advancement were seen not only as individual needs, but as instruments for the betterment of society in general. In that same sense--though the cultural context and the historical moment are different--the profession of guidance and counseling can also exemplify "a new dimension in social responsibility in Latin America." (Lechter 1970)

In this critical historical moment, guidance programs could become central to the development of human potential in Latin America. However, they might also be seen as just another export from the United States, having no real meaning for the young people or the nations of Latin America.

Certain specific cultural differences between Latin America and North America are especially relevant to the field of guidance. Carter (1966), for instance, has noted the absence of a Puritan tradition in relationships, rigidity of the instructional program, importance of the extended family, and the political influence of student elections.

Work, education, and the extended family

The absence of a Puritan tradition in Latin America decreases the importance of work, and makes work a less important element in self-concept formation. Moreover, socio-economic mobility is less prevalent in Latin America than in the United States. Jobs are frequently obtained through relatives and friends, and there is a high correlation between job status and family status. Thus, social class and family status influence the range of jobs that are available, and may determine the jobs that are "respectable" for a person to undertake.

Geographical mobility is less prevalent in Latin America than in the United States. Consequently, most Latin Americans grow up and spend their adulthood in the same area where their extended family lives and where old friends or neighbors keep close ties. For this reason, parental influence on children may be supplemented by the influence of grandparents, aunts or uncles, and even neighbors and friends of the family. Conflicts between parents and adolescents are often ironed out through the effective intervention of a grandmother or aunt. Adult relatives, the parish priest, other elders in the community, or a sympathetic teacher are frequently helpful to adolescents dealing with vocational decisions and personal problems. Adolescents may choose not to seek counseling services not only because other adults are available as helpers, but also because "talking about one's family" with strangers is considered disloyal and inappropriate in Latin America.

Only when the vocational choices or personality problems in question are beyond the understanding or experience of the adults in

55

the young person's network, does the idea of consulting an expert seem relevant. In such cases, talking to a guidance counselor about "vocational doubts" carries less stigma than seeing a psychologist or psychiatrist. As in the United States, seeking psychotherapy may be seen as an indication that the person is "crazy". In spite of such stigma, however, more sophisticated Latin Americans will seek professional assistance with psychological problems. Usually the counselor at school is either not prepared to deal with those problems, or s/he is perceived as lacking adequate preparation.

As more youngsters gain access to education in Latin American countries, there is a growing need for outside helpers who have greater expertise than the adults in the family. Especially in the lower socio-economic classes, a youngster who goes beyond the sixth grade may already have more formal education than anyone else in the family. For many young people, teachers and counselors may be the only adult role models demonstrating what a person can do with an education.

Importance of politics in students' lives

An important aspect of the lives of Latin American students is their deep involvement in national political issues. When a fifteen year old class president expresses an opinion on a bill before the legislature, this is not just another social science class exercise. The opinion of this student may influence other students, adults with the same opinion will cite the student's opinion as support, and the student's argument may be used to exert pressure over the legislature. In some tragic moments of Latin American history, college leaders have been killed for expressing their political opinions. Some of the student demonstrations of the 1960's in the United States can give us an idea of what it can mean to be a college student in Latin America at such a time.

Even in peaceful times, students--especially those at the university level--show a much greater involvement in national politics than is characteristic of students in the United States. In a research study on college women in Latin America and the United States (Espin 1974), immediately following presidential elections in Costa Rica, Venezuela and the United States, Latin American subjects showed a significantly greater interest in politics and had a greater involvement in presidential campaigns than the U.S. subjects.

For many Latin American students, political leadership in college is a determinant of political leadership at the national level at a later date. Fidel Castro, Rómulo Betancourt, Raúl Haya de la Torre--to cite but a few--began their political careers as student leaders. Student parties carry the ideology and programs of national parties to the college level and sometimes even to the high school level in Latin America. In one instance, a student leader in a private girls' school was defeated because her older brother was a college leader and a member of the communist party. Both teachers and students at the high school feared the influence of the family's ideology on the prospective school president, who was barely fifteen years old.

In this context, then, the school counselor can be placed in the position of helping a student decide how to vote, how to determine the consequences of expressing a political opinion, or why and when to attend a demonstration. The counselor, too, is likely to have equally strong political opinions, especially if s/he is young and has just completed a college degree. It is indeed very difficult for a Latin American counselor to maintain objectivity, while helping a student make political decisions. These decisions may potentially affect the counselor's own future through political changes in the country which may result from students' actions.

The educational system

Most Latin American countries have an educational sequence consisting of six years of elementary school, followed by five or six years of secondary education for those planning to attend college. Each country has some form of vocational or commercial secondary education that may have two or three years in common with the college preparatory program. Usually, however, these non-academic programs start immediately after sixth grade.

A minimal number of children finish the sixth grade, especially in rural areas. Once they can read and write, children are taken out of school to work in the fields, sell lottery tickets, shine shoes, or engage in similar activities to supplement the family's income. In most countries this is illegal, but it happens nevertheless. Latin American governments are hard put to enforce this legislation, when in fact the oldest child's earnings may be the family's only income.

A small percentage of the population finishes high school and only about 1% of Latin Americans achieve a college degree. Family income correlates directly with educational level, although there are increasingly more exceptions to this rule. Literacy rates vary dramatically, both from country to country and between rural and urban environments within the same country. Some Latin American countries face an additional educational problem, created by the need to teach Spanish to a large population of Indian children whose own native language is not Spanish.

The typical Latin American curriculum has been characterized traditionally by its rigidity. Once a youngster embarks on a course of study, changes in the original decision imply the loss of two or three years of schooling. Certain vocational decisions must

57

be made after completing the sixth grade, when the student chooses
between commercial school and a college prep academic program
("bachillerato"). Guidance professionals may play a key role in a
youngster's decision at this time.

For those students who choose to attend a vocational school,
several unique programs have been developed in Latin America, such
as the Universidad del Trabajo in Uruguay, the work-study program
in Brazil, and the National Apprenticeship Program in Colombia.

On the other hand, only by starting high school again can a
commercial or vocational school student gain access to college.
Since several years have usually elapsed between the original decision and the change of vocational plans, the loss in time and
financial resources is obvious. This situation also applies to
any adult who, after graduating from a commercial or vocational
school or perhaps following some work experience, wishes to attend
college. This person must return to high school again in order to
gain admission to college. There are evening schools for this purpose, but the student must have a great deal of energy and persistence to undertake a full high school program and work full-time
simultaneously.

The rigidity of programs both at the high school and college
levels discourages many persons who would otherwise continue their
education. When a student finds s/he has begun a program of study
that seems inappropriate for his/her vocational interests or intellectual abilities, the prospect of attending high school or college
again and losing several years of formal education in order to
change vocational goals, is most discouraging. Many prefer to quit
school and join the work force instead, despite little or no preparation.

Thus, there is a great need for appropriate guidance services
in order to help children make the best choices at such an early
age. Even if guidance is provided, however, it is unrealistic to
expect a child to adhere to a life decision made in elementary
school.

The curriculum in each nation is for the most part determined
by the Ministry of Education of that country (or of the state, in
a federal system). Some countries permit electives at the high
school level, but once a school determines which electives should
be offered, all students within that school usually take the same
courses. Ministry of Education inspectors visit all schools,
private and public, to ensure that curriculum guidelines are being
followed properly; a school's certification by the Ministry depends
on the fulfillment of the Ministry's curriculum requirements. At
certain intervals, usually after the sixth grade and after the last
year of secondary education, students take comprehensive exams prepared by the Ministry. Graduation with a diploma or certificate

of studies is contingent upon passing these examinations.

Aware of the burdens imposed on students and their parents by rigid academic programs, and seeking to make education more relevant, most Latin American countries have embarked upon some type of educational reform during the past two decades. As a consequence, the curriculum is becoming more varied in most countries. However, there are still few electives, and programs remain basically rigid at the present time. Because of the limited number of available electives, the Latin American guidance counselor's work focuses primarily on decisions for the future, rather than on decisions about course selection in any given semester.

A large proportion of students in Latin America attend private schools, corresponding to their social class. Frequently, these schools are sex segregated. It is not unusual for a student to begin kindergarten and finish secondary education at the same institution, thus spending twelve or thirteen years at the same school. This practice gives teachers and counselors a developmental perspective on individual students that can be of value in helping the student.

Frequently, teachers in these schools are not fully certified, but rather are in the process of obtaining a degree. They often teach part-time at the secondary level to pay their way through college, and frequently they do not intend to continue teaching after graduation from college. A typical example might be an engineering major who teaches physics at the high school level. These teachers, like most college students in Latin America, attend the university on a part-time basis.

Teachers in Latin America may be college-educated or may be trained in Normal Schools. Students who decide to pursue a teaching career might choose to attend a Normal School after two or three years of secondary education, obtaining a teaching certificate in the same time they would otherwise have finished a college preparatory high school program. Both the part-time teacher who is not fully certified and the teacher certified through a Normal School are an answer to the shortage of teachers in Latin American countries.

The field of guidance

Latin American guidance counselors have to contend with a linguistic difficulty in defining their profession. The verb "aconsejar," the Spanish word for counseling, means "to tell a person what to do", generally in a moralistic way. The word "orientación" (Spanish) or "orientação" (Portuguese), translates better as "guidance", but unless followed by the word "professional" (i.e., "orientacion profesional"), the word means "to tell a person where to go," as when you tell someone how to get to Main Street.

While this may be a beautiful metaphor for the counseling profession, it also creates confusion as to what exactly a counselor
is supposed to do. In the Latin America cultural context, where
most people control familiarity with respect for authority, it is
easy for a client to expect the counselor--who may even have been
a schoolmate of the client's mother--to tell him/her exactly what
to do. The student may judge the counselor to be incompetent if
this does not happen. Still worse, the student may fear that the
counselor will act or think "just like my mother" and will consequently "tell me what to do" quite literally, without considering
the student's needs. In either case, Latin American counselors
are hard put to define their profession.

Guidance and counseling are viewed in Latin American countries
as part of the educational system. A few other programs, such as
the Centro de Orientación Familiar in Costa Rica (Center for Family
Guidance), may employ counselors to provide some services, such as
sex education. However, most guidance which is not strictly educational is considered the domain of psychologists and social workers, rather than that of counselors.

Most colleges and universities in Latin America provide their
own student personnel programs, counseling centers for vocational
and personal counseling and other activities and programs related
to student welfare and students' adjustment to the institution and
to their educational and professional goals. These services are
frequently staffed by professors who teach guidance and counseling
courses at the institution.

At the secondary level, guidance counseling services originated chiefly as a consequence of recent educational reforms. The
need for guidance services had been present all along, but as social mobility increased in Latin America, it became clear that students required professional assistance in making sound vocational
choices. At the present time, almost all Latin American countries
provide some sort of guidance in school settings.

The stated goals of the guidance programs are to help students
make informed vocational and educational choices, solve minor personal problems and adapt socially, and to foster student development
in general.

Even before guidance was an official aspect of educational
services, some Latin American countries, such as Costa Rica, had
a system through which a "guidance teacher" was assigned to each
group of 30 or so students at the same grade level. The guidance
teacher's responsibility was to teach a daily or weekly class focused on a topic related to student development. Subjects might
range from dating to choosing a career.

These guidance teachers served at the same time as homeroom
teachers and counselors, serving as a liaison between home and

school. For all practical purposes, they acted as individual and group counselors in many ways. These teachers did not have any special preparation for their work, other than their desire to help students, above and beyond the teaching of specific subject matter. In fact, they were in most cases chosen because of their desire and ability to work with students on a more personal level. Each guidance teacher was left to his/her own resources, however. For this reason, the level of effectiveness of guidance teachers varied considerably. After 1964, when educational reform began in Costa Rica at the secondary level, it was usually an effective guidance teacher who became the school counselor.

It was the responsibility of the new guidance counselor to serve as a resource for other guidance teachers and to coordinate guidance efforts. This system worked fairly well in some schools, but led to a duplication of efforts in many schools--or worse, to two completely unrelated or even contradictory sets of activities and recommendations. Sometimes the guidance teachers perceived the counselor as an intruder. Other times, the guidance counselor was too occupied with administering tests required by the Ministry of Education to have time to provide other needed services.

If properly organized, however, such a system involving coordination between the guidance counselor and guidance teachers can be extremely valuable. More students may be served effectively, once the counselor begins to serve primarily as a consultant to the guidance teachers. In fact, the elementary guidance movement in the United States is trying to use this model in which the school counselor serves as a consultant to classroom teachers.

Although a general concern for student welfare is at the root of any guidance program, there is not necessarily agreement as to what is best for the students concerned. The Ministries of Education, as mentioned, design certain tests to be given to students and guidelines to be followed by guidance counselors in all schools. However, priorities within each school are largely determined by the philosophy of the school--especially in the case of private schools--and by the individual counselor's areas of expertise.

Most counselors are required to do extensive testing to help students make vocational choices, or to decide the causes of some learning disability. In this sense, Latin American guidance programs tend to follow the Minnesota model, although there are variations from country to country as to what tests are used and how they are used. The Ministry of Education may require that certain general tests be given to the nation's whole student population, although the purpose of that particular test in the context of a specific school might never be clear to the counselor.

Most counseling that takes place in schools is certainly focused on vocational and educational issues, but as all counselors know, these issues can be related to personal problems that may sometimes be quite serious. Since the training of most guidance counselors in Latin America focuses on educational and vocational problems and testing procedures, counselors confronted with students' personal problems tend to refer students to psychologists or psychiatrists in the community, unless they themselves have a degree in psychology or otherwise feel competent to deal with the issues presented. Dealing with "normal" developmental problems of students is a part of the school counselor's work, however.

In this context, the guidance methodology prevailing in most Latin American countries is a combination of individual and group counseling. Use of the latter modality depends more on the expertise of the counselor than on any other consideration. Many guidance counselors--such as the Costa Rican "guidance teachers"-- like to "teach" guidance in the classroom, but this method resembles a classroom discussion on some extracurricular topic more than group counseling.

Guidance as a profession

During recent educational reforms, many Latin American countries determined that there was a need for counselors in the schools, and therefore mandated the establishment of guidance programs at the secondary level, even before any university in the country was training counselors. The sudden demand for guidance personnel has created its own problems, in terms of the professionalization of counselors. In some instances, sensitive and interested teachers were enrolled in "crash courses" over the summer and were declared to be guidance counselors. As a consequence, these new counselors did not know quite what they were supposed to be doing, unless they had previously received training outside of the country. This extreme situation did not occur in all Latin American countries, but in general, there are still not enough trained counselors to meet the demand. Many of those who are fully certified to work as counselors have studied in foreign countries.

While most Latin American countries now recognize the professional status of psychologists and have established licensure requirements for persons practicing as psychologists, this is not the case for counselors. The demand for guidance services is so great and the supply so limited that standards are overlooked in most countries, in order to provide students with some type of services. Although these services might not be optimal, some services are provided that might otherwise be unavailable if only well-trained and certified counselors were employed. A positive aspect of this situation is that counselors are perceived by most teachers as equals, not as outsiders trying to impress them with superior knowledge. Consequently, counselors' suggestions are more likely to be accepted without suspicion. This may, of course, have the opposite effect, in that teachers may reject the opinions

62

of someone who, after all, does not have that much more training
or expertise than the teachers themselves.

As in the United States, the counseling profession remains
vaguely defined for those who are not involved in it or do not
have direct contact with it. In many schools, guidance counselors
are used as disciplinarians, substitute teachers and administrators.
These problems are familiar to school counselors in the United
States as well, but Latin American counselors usually face other
additional problems. Latin American counselors experience a lack
of legal recognition and a minimum of status and support to a
greater extent than counselors in the United States.

The most serious hindrance encountered by counselors in Latin
America is their limited opportunity for professional communication, especially in terms of professional publications or associations. The guidance literature in Latin America tends to
cover one of three or four specific areas. First, there are a
number of descriptions of what guidance is and how it can be helpful to students, combined with organizational charts and other
kinds of descriptions of counseling positions in both the administrative structure of the Ministry and the school. Second, there
is literature dealing with translations and validations of foreign
tests or with the development of some national testing materials.
(Adis 1966) Third, there are a number of articles describing
specific techniques or approaches such as peer counseling programs
for adolescents. Several books have been published which address
themselves directly to the students making vocational decisions;
these books can be used effectively by the guidance counselor.
(Salas 1969) Finally, there are some materials concerning counselor
education. In this respect, Latin Americans have made a unique
effort aimed at educating counselors in distant places, through
the development of booklets and radio conferences on topics in
counselor education. (Ministerio da Educação e Cultura 1961)

Most of this literature is published by the Ministries of
Education (Varela 1969), for internal use and, consequently, is
fairly unoriginal and repetitious. International organizations,
such as the Panamerican Union (Dintrans et al. 1967) and the
International Association for Vocational and Educational Guidance,
have published some materials describing programs in different
countries. The journals of national or regional psychological
associations also publish articles of interest to guidance counselors. However, since these publications are basically for psychologists, it is difficult for counselors to develop a sense of
professional identity, since Latin American counselors do not
have their own professional organizations.

Counselor education courses are taught at the graduate level in
several Latin American countries--in Costa Rica, for instance,
where a two-year program leads to an M.Ed. in Guidance. Other

countries, such as Colombia, offer undergraduate programs in
counseling and guidance which seem to be quite successful.
(Wittmer 1972) This is not surprising, since most undergraduate
preparation in Latin America is very specialized and a high degree
of professionalism is fostered at that level.

Whatever their level of preparation, Latin American guidance
personnel feel a need to develop programs and models of guidance
that are specifically Latin American. Adaptations of programs
imported from the outside are looked upon with suspicion by counselors in training and by students in general. Since many Latin
American counselor educators have been trained in the United
States, and since most consultants hired are also originally from
this country, there is a tendency to attempt to translate and re-
produce what has been developed in the United States for United
States needs. This trend is not confined to the field of guidance.
However, imports related to human relations and the social sciences
are looked upon with more suspicion than imported knowledge in
technical fields. It is important to note that in the United States
as well, applications of traditional models of counseling are being
questioned in programs which respond to the needs of people whose
cultural background is not white middle class.

The need to develop models of guidance that are more fully
relevant to the Latin American milieu goes hand in hand with the
present search for Latin American identity and liberation. Obviously, Latin American students cannot be helped to lead effective
lives in the future through the indiscriminate application of
models which, even in the United States, have proved ineffective
with Third World students.

Conclusions

Many guidance functions are carried on within the limits of
the extended family in Latin America. Other adults in the student's
social network, both outside and inside the school, also participate
in this process. The need for specialized counseling services has
begun to develop, however, as more Latin American students pursue
secondary and post-secondary education, taking their educational
and vocational decisions beyond the understanding and experience of
those adults who would usually have given advice in the past.

While some cultural and historical characteristics of present-
day Latin America create a need for guidance services, others tend
to interfere with the acceptance and best use of those services.
Models of guidance that will incorporate the specific characteristics, values and needs of the social and personal situation of
Latin American students are urgently needed.

If properly understood and used, guidance and counseling can

64

play an invaluable role in developing and maximizing human resources in Latin America. The richness of cultural tradition and the advances of modernization can be combined by individual students in their own personal development. However, if only North American models of guidance are considered, and if professionalization remains at a low level, guidance can play a stultifying role, at best, and a culturally devastating role, at worst, by helping to destroy what is best in Latin America in the name of development and education.

There is a slow but sure trend towards increased professionalization of counselors in Latin America. There is also a deep sense of the need for self-determination and development. We can hope that a combination of these trends will create an effective guidance movement unique to the Latin American continent. Only the future can tell us what will happen, not only to the guidance movement, but to the quality of human life in Latin America.

References

Adis, C.G. Instrumentos de medición psicológica en Centroamérica: encuesta sobre necesidades y recursos. Instituto de Investigaciones y Mejoramiento Educativo, U. de S. Carlos, Guatemala y Centro de Investigaciones Psicológicas, U. de Costa Rica, 1963. In Investigaciones Educativas en America Reseña Analítica, No. 1. Washington: Union Panamericana, 1966, 3-5.

Carter, R. E. Problems of communication in Inter-American programs. Personnel and Guidance Journal, 1966, 44, 1051-1055.

Dintrans, R., Lemus, L.A., Reyes, A., and Naranjo, G. La orientación educativa y profesional en Chile, Guatemala, Panamá y Venezuela. Washington: Union Panamericana, 1967.

Espin, O. M. Critical incidents in the lives of female college students: A comparison between women from Latin America and the United States. Doctoral dissertation, University of Florida, Gainesville, 1974.

Lechter, R. Counseling: A new dimension in social responsibility in Latin America. Unpublished paper presented at APGA National Convention, New Orleans, 1970.

Ministério da Educação e Cultura. Cadernos de orientação educacional. CADES, Radio Ministerio da Educação e Cultura, Brasil, 1961.

Salas, S. Orientación vocacional al encuentro de mí mismo. Santiago de Chile: Biblioteca Latinoamericana de Educación, Editorial Universitaria, 1969.

Varela, M. A. El programa nacional de orientación: Naturaleza, rendimiento y necesidad de mejoramiento. Guatemala: Ministerio de Educación, 1969.

Wittmer, J. Counseling and counselor education in Colombia, South America: A case for undergraduate preparation. Counselor Education and Supervision, 1972, 11, 279-283.

Suggested readings

Espin, O.M. and Renner, R.R. Counseling: a new priority in Latin America. Personnel and Guidance Journal, 1974, 52 (5), 297-301.

Jordan, J.E. Review of research on counseling and special services in Latin American education. Latin American Research Review, 1966.

Psychology in Latin America: A bibliography. Revista Interamericana de Psicologia, 1975, vol. 9, no. 3-4.

Wolf, E.R. and Hansen, E.C. The human condition in Latin America. NY: Oxford University Press, 1972.

6

BRAZIL

Donald Pemberton

Brazil differs from other Latin American countries due to both its vast area (it ranks fifth in size in the world) and the Portuguese as the predominant language. Brazilian society is composed of people with African and Eurasian heritage, in addition to a decreasing number of indigenous Brazilians. As a result of extensive internal migration much of the population is concentrated in the coastal areas.

Over 90% of the population is Roman Catholic, but for many the allegiance is merely family tradition. The extended family, particularly among the wealthy, exerts a strong influence on its members from child rearing on to providing good jobs for graduating sons, daughters, nephews, and second cousins. Although the role of women has improved over the last few decades, the traditional authority role of the male is not yet a thing of the past.

There is a marked contrast between the modern cities suffering from the problems of urban life common in industrialized countries everywhere, and the sleepy towns and villages in the countryside with primitive accomodations and services. However, even in the urban areas, the sizeable lower class continues its marginal existence away from the economic mainstream, at least partially due to the high rate of inflation.

Under military rule, the Brazilian economy has evolved and diversified. This has created a larger middle-class and rising expectations which are not being fully met. The military has governed since the overthrow of the democratic system in 1964. Certain elections are permitted but censorship is prevalent.

Life in Brazil is generally relaxed, no matter what the governmental system may be. Even in the large, bustling cities, people enjoy leisurely visits over a cup of "café-zinho," frequently in a sidewalk cafe, while watching the world go by. There are two important national pastimes that have grown into institutions of sorts. One is the soccer game which stimulates high passions among spectators. The other is dancing, particularly the national "Samba" dance. Music, dance and merriment culminate each year in the four day celebration of the "Carnival" just prior to Ash Wednesday.

Rationale for Brazilian guidance

Individuals active in Brazilian education agree on the need for guidance services in the school setting. The necessity for counseling is admitted not only by those in education, but also by laymen. However, some Brazilians still question the value of guidance. Oliveira Lima (1965) believes that counseling is a luxury since there are many teachers who are not fully qualified. This reflects the opinion that guidance is more appropriate in the developed educational systems of industrialized countries. Yet, the prevailing opinion is that guidance can help the young come to terms with their changing culture and help the educational system become more effective.

The changing socio-economic structure of Brazil is repeatedly cited as justification for guidance services. (Varebe 1973) Technological advances and the mass migrations from rural areas to urban centers have exerted a strong influence on society. A committee of counselors identified as reasons for guidance: the depersonalization of society; new and changing occupations; and the increased number of females entering the work force. (Elementos básicos... 1975) Most authors do stress the necessity to assist the individual in coping, adjusting, and in decision making.

Brazilian guidance is viewed as a catalyst for improving the educational system. Counselors, in conjunction with teachers and educational administrators, develop an integrative and cooperative team approach that helps enhance the students' learning experiences.

Development and objectives of guidance: Legislative enactments

Guidance was established nationally when the Brazilian Congress enacted the Organic Law of Industrial Education. (Brasil 1942) Guidance services previously were available only in select schools and agencies. Legislation has defined counseling as "Orientação Educacional," or "school guidance."

68

Initially, counseling was limited to industrial and technical schools. Subsequent legislative enactments extended guidance services to secondary, commercial, and agricultural institutions. (Brasil 1943 a; 1943 b; 1944) In the period of two years guidance and counseling became legally required within a variety of educational levels and settings. The noticeable exception was the lack of counseling services at the university level.

The two primary objectives of Brazilian guidance defined by law remained consistent: (a) to assist the student in career planning and vocational choice; and (b) to aid the individual's personal development. Despite major changes in government, a steady emphasis on career guidance is evidenced in legislation which affirms the counselor's role, i.e., assisting the student in professional and career decisions. (Brasil 1942)

This emphasis can be linked with efforts at maximizing human effectiveness within a developing technological society; also with particular needs of Brazilian youth who wish to enter university training. According to educational policies prevailing in the country, high school graduates must pass highly competitive entrance examinations before they are admitted to a university. A student who successfully completes the examination is admitted into a specific field of study, such as law, engineering, medicine, or education. It is difficult to transfer to a different field of study without repeating the complete entrance examination process.

Personal counseling is often defined in the context of vocational decision making. Recent legislation infers that an individual who is personally and socially adjusted will make the proper career decisions. (Brasil 1971) Another law further emphasizes the interdependence of personal and career counseling by its definition of guidance as assisting the student in personal development and career choice. (Brasil 1973)

The counselor's role of monitoring student health is a unique feature of the Brazilian guidance model. Federal guidance legislation specifies the counselor's function of establishing that the student is sufficiently healthy to maintain school attendance. (Brasil 1943 b) This counseling objective is relevant because of the lack of school nurses and the poor nutritional and health conditions in certain areas.

A different facet of Brazilian guidance is the counselor's role in working with the family and the community. (Brasil 1942) Due to the tremendous influence the Brazilian family exerts on its members, it is important that the counselor develop an active relationship with the client's family. The Law of Directives and Foundations of National Education (Brasil 1961) insists that counseling is to be in cooperation with the family. This illustrates the degree to which guidance in Brazil responds to the nation's cultural demands.

Guidance practitioners' perspective

The objectives of counseling, as defined by guidance practitioners, are similar to those cited by legislative enactments, including the emphasis upon vocational counseling. The guidance process is viewed as democratic, allowing the individual the responsibility for decisions. However, due to the rigidity of the socio-economic and political system, it can be argued that the decision-making process by clients is not totally free. Subtle coercion may originate from an awareness of the authoritarian political system, the influence of the family, and the lack of career alternatives.

During my personal contacts with counselors in the state of Sao Paulo as recently as early 1979, the practitioners emphasized that their work was quite similar to the theoretical model of Brazilian guidance. They felt it was important to assist the student in educational and career planning, personal concerns, and in decision making. Furthermore, they had an active role within the school setting, helping coordinate programs and provide the stimuli for action.

The practitioners' concept of personal and career counseling is characterized by its directiveness. Parents, teachers, and community resources are involved in the counseling process. There is evidence that Brazilian students prefer and respond more readily to directive counseling. (Goldberg et al. 1974) Due to the Latin-American characteristic of respecting authority figures, counselors would be viewed as vacillating and weak if they did not assume an active and directive role.

Elementary school counselors work with students individually and in groups. Group work is used both for developmental and career guidance, while individual counseling is mainly therapeutic in nature. Counselors also invite guest speakers, assist students with health and academic problems, and conduct field trips. Secondary school counselors concentrate on career guidance, even through individual contacts with students.

Assessment is most prevalent in the vocational and technical institutions. These industrial and commercial training schools (Senai-Senac), maintained by the federal government, have the most extensive and developed counseling services in the country. Aptitude and ability assessment and interest surveys are used in assisting individuals with their career decisions. Counselors also help students who have personal problems or academic difficulties and offer current information on educational and professional opportunities.

Although the expansion of guidance services have been mandated by law, in the view of counseling practitioners, the growth

70

has been slow and varied from region to region. Teachers and other elements in the educational setting, unfamiliar with guidance and counseling, often misperceive the practitioner as an administrator, a psychologist, or a disciplinarian. As a result, there are erroneous referrals, and a hesitancy by many of the teachers to implement guidance activities.

The poor health and nutritional conditions of students was a source of concern to the counselors interviewed during my recent visit to Brazil. The academic failure rate is as high as 40% due to improper diets and hygiene. The practitioners, through working with parents, teachers, and community resources, help improve the students' health and thus significantly lower the failure rate. Nevertheless, students continue to drop out of school at an early age and enter the job market without the necessary training or skills.

Training of counselors

Legislation in reference to the training of counselors has not remained constant. The early laws were general and all-inclusive, while recent legislative enactments have tended to be more specific. This can be explained by the lack of training facilities in the early, formative years of Brazilian guidance. In later years, as guidance training institutions and the numbers of counselors increased, legislation has been enacted which reflects these changes.

Recent legislation stipulates that counselors must be graduates of: (a) a college of education with a major in guidance; (b) a graduate level counselor program; or (c) a counselor training program in a foreign country. (Brasil 1973) The majority of practitioners have completed the four-year undergraduate program. The content of the counselor training curriculum is left to the University's discretion. However, there are certain required instructional hours and a supervised practicum. Prior to entering the profession, practitioners must register with the appropriate state authorities and show proof of training, practicum, and teaching experience.

Future trends

Brazilian guidance·is reaching a critical stage in its development. Whereas in the past there were not sufficient numbers of practitioners, that situation has been partially remedied by the many counselor training programs in major universities and in smaller colleges. The expansion of guidance is now dependent on greater financial support at the federal level.

There are indications that the federal government will soon make a significant financial commitment towards education. Since salaries of guidance practitioners are usually paid by municipal or state governments, there is a small number of counselors in the public schools under local or regional control. However, in the national industrial and commercial training schools guidance services are extensive, as the practitioners are paid by the national government. Since the federal government has demonstrated its commitment to guidance by enacting legislation and ensuring the implementation of counselor training programs, it is expected that funds will be made available to hire more practitioners.

The earlier discussed objectives and methodologies of Brazilian guidance will likely remain constant. Counselors will continue to be defined as educational specialists who formulate guidance programs which intergrate the various elements in the school and community. It will be necessary for practitioners to remain flexible, due to their diverse roles as consultants, coordinators, and mediators.

Brazilian guidance will become a model for other developing countries, if it receives the financial support to ensure its expansion. A primary concern of third world nations is to maximize their human resourses. Brazilian guidance legislation, government authorities, and practitioners, have identified occupational and career counseling as the foremost guidance objective. As a result of this emphasis, realistic occupational choices and adjustment to the world of work have increased within the Brazilian labor force and are helping the country's socio-economic structure to become more viable.

References

Brasil (The Government of Brazil). Legislative publications:

    Decreto Lei 4073. 1942.
    Decreto Lei 4244. 1943 a.
    Decreto Lei 6141. 1943 b.
    Decreto Lei 9613. 1944.
    Decreto Lei 4024. 1961.
    Decreto Lei 5642. 1971.
    Decreto Lei 72846. 1973.

Elementos básicos para implantação da orientação educacional.
São Paulo: Divisão de orientação tecnica, 1975.

Goldberg, M. et al. Avaliação de competencia no desempenho do
papel de orientador educacional. Cadernos de pesquisa, 1974,
Dezembro.

Oliveira Lima, L. Tecnologia, educação e democracia. Rio de Janeiro:
Civilização brasileiro, 1965.

Varebe, M. Orientação vocacional. São Paulo: Faculdade de filosofia,
ciencias e letras, castro alves, 1973.

Section Four

WESTERN EUROPE

The separate treatment of guidance in Europe in two sections is an anomaly, particularly with regard to the East-Central European areas that have many traditional ties with Western culture. However, the current social-political realities have to be taken into account and the philosophical differences reflected in the Western and in the Marxist-socialist guidance orientations cannot be denied or glossed over. Yet in spite of the political division of Europe, we need to recognize the many cultural parallels and similarities of educational systems that exist on both sides of the artificial boundary line.

Since an extensive introduction to the West-European area is provided in Chapter seven, only a few remarks on the organization of the material and brief biographical data introducing the authors are in order. The sequential listing of countries which have been selected to represent typical guidance models of Western Europe is in alphabetical order. This principle, used throughout the book, reflects the conviction of the Editor that attempts at ranking various guidance models according to selected criteria is highly subjective and inappropriate. In fact, all guidance models presented in Section four, while having much in common, also offer unique contributions to the total repertoire of the professional community.

The authors of the chapters are guidance professionals of varied cultural backgrounds and job-related titles. All of them have an accurate understanding of the social, cultural, and professional scene which they describe. They are listed here in the order of

75

the essays they have contributed.

Thomas Donahue, author of Chapter 7, spent several years in Europe, as guidance director in an American school in West Berlin and as counselor in the Netherlands.

Victor Drapela who authored Chapters 8 and 12 (Federal Republic of Germany and Sweden) is a European by birth and maintains ongoing communication with European guidance professionals from his home in the United States.

E. L. Tolbert, author of Chapter 9 (France), is an American counselor educator who travels to Europe, especially France, on a regular basis to do guidance-related research.

Chapter 10 (Ireland) was co-authored by Dorothy Clark, an American counselor who now holds a faculty position at an Irish university, and by Sean Beausang, an Irish practitioner of counseling and guidance.

The co-authors of Chapter 11 (the Netherlands) are Nathan Deen, originator of the first specialized counselor training program in his country, and by Lawrence Brammer, an American professor who cooperated with the Dutch program as consultant and visiting lecturer.

Chapter 13 (United Kingdom) is the work of two British authors. Catherine Avent is inspector of career guidance for the Inner London Education Authority. Audrey Newsome heads the counseling services at the University of Keele.

7

A COMPARATIVE OVERVIEW

Thomas J. Donahue

The guidance movement in Western Europe has its own roots. The publication of <u>Hereditary Genius</u> by Francis Galton in 1869, the opening of Wundt's Psychological Laboratory in 1879, the founding of the British Child Study Association in London in 1893, and the publications of Binet and Henri in 1897 are significant dates in the evolution of European guidance. (Pieron 1953) Likewise the contributions of Pestalozzi, Froebel and Heidegger are crucial to the philosophical foundations of guidance in Western Europe.

Despite the fact that Parsons traveled through Europe in order to share his experiences and get ideas from like-minded people abroad (Davis 1969), some consider guidance and counseling to be strictly an American institution. Others might argue that the history of guidance can be traced all the way back to the tribal medicine man. Was Diogenes the counselor of Alexander? Socrates the counselor of Aristotle? Could Thomas a Kempis, Theresa of Avila or Erasmus of Rotterdam be considered counselors?

Regardless of how one might answer these questions, it is understandable that there have been parallel developments on both continents. The development of the guidance movement is the direct result of an increasingly complex industrial society. Today's parents no longer feel that they alone are able to guide their children effectively.

This Chapter has been condensed from an essay written for the book, <u>Guidance in other countries</u>.

European traditions and values

When examining some of the traditions and values which affect the guidance movement throughout the world, Americans must be particularly careful of two pitfalls. The first is an ethnocentric or chauvinistic bias, a tendency to believe that Americans are the model, and other countries are simply catching up with America. In fact, other industrialized countries are developing guidance systems which are quite different from our own in administration, organization, philosophy and practice. The second pitfall to avoid is generalizing about European guidance programs from the English model which is closer to Americans because there is no linguistic barrier. Britain is an island and the British people, customs, and traditions should not be considered typical of the people, customs, traditions on the continent. In any case, it is difficult to generalize as to European traditions and values, and even more hazardous to compare overly generalized concepts such as openness, permissiveness, and homogeneity with American cultural traditions and values. On the other hand, unless some social concepts and generalizations are used, it is difficult to make comparisons. Six generalizations that affect the development of guidance are stated below:

1. Europe has a more easily identifiable class structure than America. Titles such as Prince, Lord, and Lady are still used, especially in those countries which still have vestigial monarchies. Members of the working class and leisure class find it easier to accept their respective roles in society and identify more closely with their economic class. Social mobility is not necessarily considered desirable, and often, almost insurmountable social barriers exist to protect the status quo. Obviously, such a social structure will have significant implications in the guidance process.

2. European students generally have a greater respect for adult authority figures that American students. This deference to authority is an asset to paternalistic guidance based on the trait-factor theory, but it makes counseling in the American sense far more difficult.

3. By tradition, Europeans tend to look up to their educators. Thus, student-teacher relationships are generally more formal in Europe than they are in the United States. For example, French students asked many questions about my role as a counselor when I chaperoned a group of tenth grade students on a visit to a French academy for a few days. My students reported that it was the unanimous opinion among the French students that none of them would talk with a guidance counselor about certain personal problems. The French students seemed rather incredulous that the German and American students would talk to an educator in such a fashion. Such cultural differences play a large part in defining the role and function of the counselor from one culture to another.

It appears that many Americans fail to accept, or even recognize, the U.S. class structure with its stereotypes by sex, race, age, geographic origin, etc., since social status is not tied as closely to parental origins as it is in Europe.

Ronnestad (1974), a professor of psychology at the University of Oslo, points out that the social-political system of the United States stimulates a great deal of social mobility. Decisions made by individuals influence their socio-economic status directly to a much greater extent than in Norway. The author maintains that the higher degree of social mobility coupled with cultural heterogeneity and the complexity of the labor market in the States make career choices much more difficult for American youth as compared with Norwegian youth. Thus, one may imagine, American students need more assistance in their career choices than most European students.

4. Americans seem attracted to change, novelty, and faddism. Europeans are more likely to evaluate a new concept, practice, idea, or product carefully before trying it. They are more apt to remain within their geographical region. They are more likely to have a Lebensberuf (life occupation) rather than a career which includes a variety of occupations. Since Americans make career decisions from three to six years later than European students, flexibility and uncertainty are increased for American students. On the other hand, the relative finality of the early decision European students make means that the choice must be satisfying and appropriate.

5. Separation of church and state is strictly an American doctrine. England and Sweden, for example both have a State Church. Most European countries collect a church tax along with income tax, allow religion to be taught in the public schools, and some countries support parochial schools with tax revenues. In counseling, reference to God as a loving being who cares about children who are neglected by those who should care is permissible. Religion can be a useful tool to a European counselor, but it cannot be used in a comparable way by the American counselor in a public school.

6. Many Europeans consider America to be a friendly but depersonalized, materialistic culture which is wealthy and technologically advanced, but behind in social welfare legislation and programs. In examining the U.S. national history they see and continue to expect rapid change, mobility, and lack of a firmly embedded social structure. For these reasons, some individuals (Harris 1974; Ziv 1974) feel that counseling and guidance are much more needed in America than elsewhere. They point out that the depersonalization and constant change bring about insecurity and preoccupation with mental health.

European education

Many of European educational systems are highly centralized.

Usually, the Minister of Education is politically appointed. The Minister is advised by a large number of professional educators who assist in developing policy decisions, educational laws, administrative structure and curriculum.

Educational policy usually plays an important role in European partisan politics. The party in power establishes national educational policy and may develop or reform the educational system as it sees fit. Although some countries do have county or state boards of education and others centralize educational decision-making power at the province/district levels, the most usual administrative structure is a linear relationship from the Minister of Education through the various levels of administration down to the teacher.

Such centralization and uniformity has both advantages and disadvantages. It also has implications for the addition of new programs such as guidance programs in the school. Large amounts of money and careful planning are required before any change is undertaken.

Although each national educational system is unique, the Common Market, The Council of Europe, The European Communities Commission, The Organization for Economic Cooperation and Development, and allied social, economic, and political forces are pressuring the Western European educational systems to fit a common mold. Educational and vocational guidance will no doubt play an important part in the rather flexible but unified European educational system which is beginning to form.

Students in European schools who will not go on to university or technical training are likely to enter the labor market as apprentices at a far younger age than average American students. Vocational and educational decisions are made by most students at age sixteen or much earlier. Some countries have cooperative school/work programs so that teenagers are able to attend school for one, two, or three days per week while working or learning a trade during the remainder of the week. The apprenticeship training can take place under the auspices of a company, a union, church, government institution, school or a combination of these. Usually the apprentice spends part of the week working and part of the week going to school. School work is both practical and theoretical, but applies directly to the trade the student is learning, whether the trade is tool and die making or chimney sweeping.

Only a small portion of the students at any age level (ten to fifteen percent) complete the college preparatory school's stringent graduation requirements. Some of these students enter the labor market directly rather than attend a university. University entrance procedures are highly competitive. In some countries, receiving a diploma from a college preparatory school means automatic admission to the university of one's choice, if space is available. In other countries, competition is the decisive factor determining university entrance, even after attaining the coveted college preparatory diploma. Not only is higher education free throughout most of Western Europe, but most students receive stipends to cover at least part of their room, board, and student union dues.

European students may receive supportive services, although frequently the services are provided by specialists who are not employed by the school. For instance, most European schools have school psychologists available to students and teachers in need of advice or diagnostic assistance. Usually the psychologist is responsible for several thousand students and has an office in the City Hall, or local school administrative building. Either they travel to the various schools in their jurisdiction, or students come to their offices. (Ingenkamp 1966) Social workers are available under a similar arrangement. Vocational counselors usually work in offices not directly associated with schools.

Some Europeans see American Schools as social welfare centers rather than purely academic institutions. In Europe, student services, continuing education, social, recreational, and athletic programs are available, but are more likely to be associated with the community, state government, or federal government, businesses, or special interest groups. Likewise, free health and dental clinics are sponsored by the government for school children. Such health programs are often administered by an institution other than the school. On the other hand, Norway and some other countries have dental clinics and either a dental hygienist or dentist in the school.

Concept of guidance

For the most part, guidance in Western Europe is vocationally oriented. The educational system and labor market are not geared toward long-term, flexible career goals which Americans generally take for granted. Guidance in Switzerland, for example, is primarily concerned about short-term employability and needs of the labor market. (Stauffer 1974) Vocational choice in Europe is simpler because (1) students generally restrict their choices to occupations within their own socioeconomic class; (2) the choice is made at an earlier age; and (3) there is generally a smaller range of occupations from which to choose.

Vocational Guidance Centers throughout most of Europe will probably continue to be located outside of the schools, since most countries have found this arrangement to be very practical. (Davey 1955; Kieslinger 1967; Stauffer 1974) Guidance in these institutes is primarily a response to the manpower needs of a fluctuating economy. Little theoretical work regarding the gradual development of career choices has been done in Western Europe. (Köster 1977) All vocational guidance counselors in these centers are very familiar with the labor market, its current needs, and projected needs. Vocational test batteries and informal occupational tests are used to assist vocational guidance counselors.

In general terms, guidance in West-European schools follows predominantly one of these two patterns: (1) counselors are perceived as academic advisors of the students, particularly in matters of selecting educational goals and in transfers from one type of school to another; or (2) counselors are expected to serve as mental health professionals in the school. Additionally, a significant psychometric emphasis is detectable in some countries. The eight categories of tests most frequently used, for instance in Sweden, are: (1) school readiness; (2) tests of emotional retardation; (3) diagnostic tests for learning disabilities; (4) psychological and psychiatric tests for difficult children; (5) language tests; (6) school aptitude tests; (7) diagnosis of right- and left-handedness; and (8) tests designed to equalize grading of teachers in various subject levels.

Educational research is a relatively recent phenomenon in Europe and is not always considered part of the counselor's role. Education research takes place in or is organized by centralized institutions such as the Max-Planck Institut für Bildungsforschung in West Berlin. Research also takes place in universities and teacher training institutions. More comparative studies are being done in Europe than in America.

Without doubt, Europeans are less likely than Americans to accept a new educational procedure on its face value alone. Perhaps this is due to a conservative nature or perhaps it is due to the fact that in a centralized system, innovations must be cautiously approached or chaos may result. Educational research, innovation, and documentation have made great strides in Western Europe during the last twenty years. Undoubtedly this trend will continue.

Summary

Since European traditions and values differ from American traditions and values, it is understandable that the philosophy and techniques of guidance are also dissimilar. Various services for children and young adults, including vocational guidance, are more likely to be located outside of the school setting in European countries than in America.

Guidance in Western Europe developed independently of the guidance movement in America. Because the world in general and the labor market in particular have grown in complexity, educational reforms are taking place in practically all European countries. The reforms are likely to result in a more unified Western European educational system which will probably incorporate some form of comprehensive secondary school and will place major emphasis on educational and vocational guidance.

European educators and guidance leaders seem to devote relatively more energy and resources to comparative studies than do their American counterparts. While all countries have their unique problems in developing guidance services, comparative studies can often provide a fresh approach based upon the experiences of others.

References

Davey, H. La structure des services d'orientation professionelle: Leur evolution administrative et financiere. B.I.N.O.P., 1955, 11, 26-39.

Davis, H. V. Frank Parsons: prophet, innovator, counselor. Carbondale: Southern Illinois University Press, 1969.

Harris, R. From England... Personnel and Guidance Journal, 1974, 53, 47-49.

Ingenkamp, K. H. Die schulpsychologischen Dienste in der Bundesrepublik Deutschland. Weinheim: Beltz, 1966.

Kieslinger, A. Zwanzing Jahre Berufsausbildung in der Bundesrepublik Deutschland. Bielefeld: Bertelsmann, 1967.

Köster, U. Schullaufbahnberatung und schulpsychologische Beratung. Darmstadt: Wissenschaftliche Buchgesellschaft, 1977.

Pieron, H. La place de l'institut dans l'histoire de l'orientation professionnelle. B.I.N.O.P., 1953, 9, 6-28.

Ronnestad, M. H. From Norway... Personnel and Guidance Journal, 1974, 53, 52-53.

Stauffer, E. From Switzerland... Personnel and Guidance Journal, 1974, 53, 53-55.

Ziv, A. From Israel... Personnel and Guidance Journal, 1974, 53, 55-56.

8

FEDERAL REPUBLIC OF GERMANY

Victor J. Drapela

The Federal Republic of Germany is a major European power with a population of over sixty million. Its present geopolitical stature grew out of the post-war occupation zones of Germany controlled by the Western allies: the Americans; the British; and the French. The Federal Republic has a President as Head of State; a Chancellor as Head of the Government; it has two chambers of Parliament--the "Bundesrat" (upper chamber) and the "Bundestag" (lower chamber). The occupation zone once controlled by the Soviet Union is now the Marx-ist-socialist German Democratic Republic, frequently referred to as East-Germany.

A brief note on history

It should be pointed out that the division of Germany, although unnatural and imposed by international power politics, is perceived by most Germans as a fact of life to be accepted, at least for the present. In historical perspective, Germany was a unified country for a relatively short period of time, between the years of 1871 and 1945. Yet prior to the bond of common statehood, German Länder (states) existed side by side with many cultural, political, and economic contacts that finally led to the German Confederation (1815-1866). The cultural cohesiveness of German population groups was al-ways close. Learning, music, and literature were mutual bonds that linked them culturally while the proverbial "Tüchtigkeit"(efficiency and perseverance) linked them in the realm of economy and of applied sciences.

At the end of World War II, Germany lay in ruin. When traveling through the devastated Munich in September of 1945, I had difficulties imagining that the city could come back to life within a decade or two. But contrary to expectations, the "Wirtschaftswunder" (economic miracle)--stimulated by the Marshall plan--took place in an unbelievably short time. Reconstruction of the country has been accomplished with a view to the next century, yet with a clear appreciation of the historical monuments of the past. One of the most fascinating examples of this comprehensive urban planning policy is the city of Cologne.

German society after World War II

Dahrendorf (1967), writing from the perspective of a German social scientist, offers revealing insights into the gradual changes that occurred in his society after the demise of the Nazi regime. At first, few Germans admitted to being overly authoritarian and rigid--traits that have been traditionaly ascribed to them by many foreign observers. Rather they perceived themselves as orderly, thorough, reliable, gifted, ambitious, and hard-working. The merits of soldierly attributes that were admired by past generations were downplayed among people exhausted by war and facing starvation.

Nevertheless, the ingrained authoritarian tendencies, though publicly disavowed, lingered in German society even after the war, particularly in family life and in prevalent views on government and politics. While in the 1950's industrialization and technical modernization of the country raced forward in a framework of democratic institutions, the social fabric of Germany did not change significantly. This was made evident by the great voter appeal of authoritarian political figures, e.g., Adenauer; by the attitude of women who, in the German tradition, saw their primary roles as homemakers, child rearers, and church organizations workers; to a lesser degree, by attitudes of blue-collar workers most of whom were willing to accept a social position characterized by "being kept in one's place."

As a result of the backlash to the Nazi past, Germans were rejecting all reminders of the defamed regime, especially its emphasis on centralized government structures and its tampering with family life. They expressed their need for structure and continuity by a return to "proven German virtues." High on the list were orderly family relationships (frequently acted out in a truncated family whose breadwinner had been killed in war or was still in captivity); a return to religious customs and active church membership; emphasis on states rights within the federal structure.

However, even during the postwar decade subtle attitudinal changes were emerging, particularly among German youth, that led to increasingly independent behavior--at first in urban areas, later even in the countryside. The global youth unrest that followed in the 1960's did not have a quick response in Western Germany--in comparison to the neighboring France--but its eventual outcome has been more permanent and, on its fringes, radical and violent.

Schalk (1971) considers the present generation of German youth lacking in discipline, hypercritical, and almost belligerently independent. Young Germans tend to ridicule traditional symbols of the Establishment, such as public officials, school teachers, and college professors. On the whole, though, the attitudinal changes of German youth had a positive effect on the nation. More than half of the present West-German population is less than forty years old; thus, the attitudes of German youth of a decade ago are reflected in the prevalent values of the bulk of citizenry. The young adults have matured and mellowed, yet they have retained much of their openness to new ideas. Blind obedience is passé and so is narrow nationalism (the neo-Nazi groups, although attracting attention, are relatively insignificant). Politically, the German electorate, with the voting age lowered from twenty-one to eighteen years, has shifted to a position left of center.

However, one characteristically German trait which has special significance in the context of this Chapter has survived. It is the highly competitive involvement of both students and their parents in educational pursuits. A German scientist calls it an "almost hysterical regard for academic learning." Even socially liberal parents are apt to push their children beyond their ability and without regard for their vocational goals and academic motivation. According to statistical projections for the 1978-79 school year, one in every three West-German students below the age of sixteen is expected to suffer from symptoms of "Schulangst" (fear of school) and about 14,000 school-age youngsters are expected to attempt suicide during the year. (New York Times News Service 1978)

New educational policies

For many past generations the German school system was the chief bulwark of unbending authoritarianism. Thus the lingering image of the school as a formidable institution of power is, at least partly, responsible for the anxiety reaction experienced by so many students today. In reality, however, the German school system has undergone major changes in the area of educational policies, and to some extent, in structural patterns.

Since World War II, the official policy statements on education emphasize these objectives: (a) maintaining the high standards of instruction; (b) applying democratic principles and processes within the educational system and in individual schools; (c) helping youth become independent and self-directive; and (d) stimulating an awareness of interdependence among nations, particularly European nations.

It must have been difficult at first to implement these objectives in classrooms controlled by teachers with traditional attitudes of German pedagogy. But since then, new teaching personnel entered the field and helped bring educational practices in line with the stated policy. In recent years, the union of teachers, "Erziehung und Wissenschaft" (Education and Science), has become quite vocal in proposing new educational approaches and influencing policies. For instance, it

> has demanded a reduction in the size of classes in primary schools (Grundschulen) and continued reforms despite the decline in pupil numbers in the Federal Republic of Germany. Erich Frister, chairman of the GEW (teachers' union--Ed.), stressed to journalists in Bonn that the drop in the birthrate is providing an ideal opportunity to shape the "Grundschule" in such a way that it would be no longer a selection institute for the distribution of pupils among secondary schools, but a place where children could experience the joy of learning without fear and performance pressure. (<u>Bildung und Wissenschaft</u> 1978, p. 138)

Educational policies are frequently discussed in the media and in the legislative chambers at the federal and state level, with significant input provided by parents of school children. Björn Engholm, Parliamentary Undersecretary of State at the Federal Ministry of Education and Science, stated in a recent debate the need for a school

> which encourages the individual to practice freedom at an early stage, to assess himself and others and to become fit to tackle his own life's problems as well as those of society. (<u>Bildung und Wissenschaft</u> 1978, p. 157)

Besides the ongoing reforms of the school system, another topic frequently aired is the need for an international awareness of German people, especially youth. Hildegard Hamm-Brücher, Minister of State at the Bonn Foreign Office, called for the renunciation of "national egotism" in favor of "intercultural creativity" in all sectors of public life. In a parallel development, the Conference of Ministers of Education of all German States (Länder) agreed on a program toward "expansion of the European spirit among children in school:"

> The intention is to develop among the up-and-coming generation an awareness of what Europe has in common. Youngsters should thus learn within social studies, history, geography, and foreign languages to assess the position of both their own country and other peoples within Europe. Intensified exchanges are intended to enable teachers and pupils to gather practical experience alongside their theoretical knowledge about Europe. (<u>Kulturbrief</u> 1978 (9), p. 16)

The German educational system in flux

Traditionally, the educational system of Germany comprised a uniform four year curriculum in the primary school ("Grundschule"), several curricula at the secondary school level differentiated in terms of content and length, and post-secondary curricula in universities and other institutions of higher education.

The system of secondary schools is described by German educators as a "three-pillar structure" with these separate options: (a) the "Hauptschule" (main school) is primarily for blue-collar workers, for people who want to acquire the minimal knowledge and skills needed for adult life; (b) the "Realschule" (intermediate school) which provides technical and business education for mid-managerial and upper-level skilled workers, with a curriculum of six years, two more than the "Hauptschule;" and (c) the "Gymnasium" (preparatory school for universities) which trains the elite--professional and upper-level managerial people, with a curriculum of nine years leading to the "Abitur" which qualified the graduate for entry to university studies. Whereas German universities have been known since medieval times for their academic variety and curricular flexibility, the curricula of the secondary schools were mostly "cast in bronze" with virtually no choices to be made by the students.

Furthermore, the basic decision as to whether a student would enter the main school, the intermediate school, or the college preparatory school had to be made when the student was ten years old. Though children have matured more rapidly in recent years than in past generations, it is hard to imagine that a ten-year old youngster could make an independent choice of such importance. In most instances, the child would have no opportunity to choose, since decisions of this kind were typically made by parents, with some input by the teacher, based primarily on previous academic performance of the student. In case the performance was not sufficient and the parents were determined to have the child go the more prestigious route, special tutoring was usually arranged for.

Only in recent years an alternative secondary education model has been introduced which would offer a greater flexibility during the decision-making period and offer choices to the students themselves. In this experimental program, the "three-pillar" schools are being combined for four (or five) years in a single cooperative school ("Kooperative Schule") known by its abbreviation "KoS" which provides a two-year period for further educational decisions:

> Classes Five and Six are to form an "Orientierungstufe" independent of any particular type of school...to provide a fairer means of pupil assessment in regard to future school career. (Bildung und Wissenschaft 1977, p. 170)

Supporters of this educational policy aim at expanding the system of cooperative schools to make them available to all pupils in grades five through ten. They hope to replace the "three-pillar system" at the intermediate level of education by a new institution identified as "comprehensive school."

At present, the issue is being hotly debated and all schools using the cooperative model operate strictly on an experimental basis. Their operation is under constant public scrutiny. The main argument in favor of the new model is based on the need for allowing more time to students who may be "late bloomers" and stimulating a higher degree of self-directiveness in choosing educational goals. Opponents of the cooperative (and comprehensive) school reject the need for a two-year orientation period. They feel that it will add to the pressure for academic excellence over a longer period of time. They also feel that the quality of curricula in the more prestigious schools will suffer:

> The "amptutation" of Realschulen and Gymnasien, the "obliteration" of Gymnasien by severing the Oberstufe (upper level) from the Mittelstufe (mid-level) is rejected as is the mass concentration of pupils in gigantic schools with all their--proven--disadventages. (Bildung und Wissenschaft 1977, p. 170)

Eventually, individual States will have the final word on the course of secondary education within their boundaries reflecting conservative or innovative preferences of their electorates.

Emergence of school guidance

Guidance as an aid to students in planning their academic programs was not needed in the highly structured school system of the past. Yet, German teachers have always assumed an informal guidance role, particularly through personal interest in the welfare of their students--offering them advice far beyond the realm of school work. This was generally considered to be part of the teacher's professional involvement and such assistance was expected by students and their parents alike.

Arnhold (1976) traces the origins of formally established educational guidance and psychological services to the "Schülerkontrolle" (pupil control) organized in some schools prior to World War II. Its functions involved monitoring school attendance; handling truancy cases in cooperation with parents and, at times, with police; issuing permission for students to be excused from classes if they had mastered the particular subject beyond the desired target level. In 1953, the "Schülerkontrolle" was renamed "Schülerhilfe" (pupil assistance). This was the actual beginning of pupil personnel services in German schools.

The scope and quality of guidance services in the educational
system of the Federal Republic are still uneven, depending on the
support of such programs by the State governments. Heller (1974)
gives special recognition to the growth of educational guidance in
the State of Baden-Württemberg and considers it "a model for parallel
systems in other States of the Federal Republic." (p. 2) Frequently
mentioned as a pioneer and leader of the guidance movement in schools
is the State of Hamburg. (Martin and Wehrly n.d.)

At the federal level, the Conference of Ministers of Education
adopted in 1973 a resolution entitled "Beratung in Schule und Hoch-
schule" (Counseling in schools and institutions of higher education)
which makes educational guidance the responsibility of all States in
the land. In addition to helping students select curricula that appear most suitable for attaining their vocational goals, educational
guidance is to assist students in overcoming personal problems and
offer help to teachers and schools. (Reichenbecher 1975)

There is an evident relationship of the school reform movement,
particularly with regard to the new secondary education model, and
the emergence of guidance services in schools. The volume charting
the envisioned structure of comprehensive schools published in 1970
by the Council of Education ("Deutscher Bildungsrat") makes also an
appeal for the use of guidance counselors in schools. (M. Hoffmann 1975)
No matter how the basic structure of German education may evolve, the
erstwhile rigid uniformity is no longer acceptable to the present
generation. It is safe to say that the existing guidance services
will be substantially expanded and that guidance counselors and school
psychologists will deal increasingly with emotional problems of youth,
particularly those that are school-related.

The concept of school guidance

While admitting that guidance as a professional activity has
had no precedent in German pedagogy, Heller (1975, 1976) nevertheless
offers proof of a considerable interest in guidance, by his three-
volume handbook with contributions by some fifty authors. A detailed
analysis of the guidance concept is presented along with operational
applications envisioned in Germany and based on experiences gathered
in other countries.

Guidance is perceived as an overall helping effort that facilitates decision-making processes and stimulates personal growth. Various specialized services, e.g., educational, personal-social orientation, or psychological evaluation, are encompassed within the guidance framework. Heller (1975) lists four principal guidance functions: (a) the social-integrative function aimed at unifying efforts
of students, teachers, and parents and at promoting a new relationship of school and community; (b) the economic function which pre-
vents waste of resources by clarifying optimal educational routes for

91

the attainment of chosen vocational goals; (c) the augmentative function which increases scholastic achievement by facilitating and clarifying the interplay of students' abilities, interests, motivational, social-cultural, and environmental factors; and (d) the self-enhancement function which assists individuals to grow and mature as persons through life-long striving that has been initiated at an early age.

Guidance services are to be available to students, their parents, and their teachers at any stage of the educational process. However, they are considered to be most crucial during transitional periods, when important choices have to be made, e.g., at the end of primary school education; in the fifth and the sixth grade of the comprehensive school (orientation level); and prior to the entry to post-secondary education. Also a transfer from one school to another or relocation from one regional system to another require adequate guidance interventions, particularly when a student moves from the traditional to the new, experimental structure, or vice versa.

In the area of personal-social problems, the suggested guidance involvement includes diagnostic work and short-term counseling. Both preventative and problem-solving or remedial counseling are handled by guidance personnel. (Rosemann 1975) Whenever severe personality disorders appear, long-term therapy is to be provided by referring the client to another helping professional or agency.

Various counseling approaches seem to be in use among German guidance professionals, but no clearly developing trends are discernible about a preferred theoretical orientation. In one of the chapters of the earlier mentioned handbook edited by Heller, Martin (1975) discusses the merits and limitations of three major counseling strategies—the trait-and-factor, the client-centered, and the behavioral—and briefly mentions psychoanalytical, existential, rational-emotive, and gestalt approaches. He cautions against the temptation of embracing a single theoretical model blindly and urges German guidance workers to arrive at a personal theory that would reflect their perceived counseling goals, values, and other philosophical and empirical considerations, e.g., the role of counselors in society, the rationale of the helping process, envisioned counseling outcomes, preferred methodology, etc. Cultural and historical perspectives must also be taken into account.

An indication of emerging trends in German guidance methodology may be the apparent psychometric emphasis in professional literature. Psychological tests are extensively used in guidance work for appraisal and prediction of individual behavior and academic performance, for planning and justification of institutional reforms, and for evaluation of the relative effectiveness of guidance services. The repertoire of German psychological test instruments is impressive. Langfeldt-Nagel and Langfeldt (1976) list close to one hundred standardized tests available on the market. They were developed with appropriate norms and their coefficients of validity, reliability, and internal consistency are adequate. Testing is done to measure achievement, intelligence, aptitudes, interests, motivation, personality traits, adjustment levels, and other variables, e.g., the level of anxiety.

Although data-oriented, German guidance literature rejects all implications that the individual should conform to a narrow behavior pattern that is found "close to the mean." For instance, H. Hoffmann (1975) recalls the principle of Piaget that social adjustment is not a process of submission to environmental pressures. He proposes, instead, a double responsibility for the counselor in fostering social adjustment of students: (a) to help students understand the world they live in, particularly the school environment which provides security and structure and sets certain limits; (b) on the other hand, to influence the school system and make it more responsive to the legitimate needs of the student population; this involves providing sufficient elbowroom for personality development which is the basic right of every young person.

These general principles are supported by public policy statements. The German Council of Education recognizes that on occasions conflicts would arise between the interests of individual students and the needs of society. The Council does not expect educators or counselors to solve such problems. Rather counselors through open communication with students can help clarify the issues involved in the conflict and thus alleviate the conflict situation. (Reichenbecher 1975)

Educational guidance personnel

School guidance activities are carried out by school psychologists who generally do not teach and by teacher-counselors ("Beratungslehrer") who have a combined teaching and counseling assignment. School psychologists have received a complete academic training in their specialty, while teacher-counselors are qualified educators with additional in-service training in guidance. Martin and Wehrly (n.d.) observe that at present there is little or no commitment on the part of German universities to initiate formal training of counselors. Only part-time courses are available, the most promising of them being a two-year course offered by the University of Tübingen extension service. M. Hoffmann (1975) reports that plans for the integration of specialized guidance curricula within teacher education are being formulated.

The disparity of training between school psychologists and teacher-counselors seems to be a source of tension. The fully trained psychologists generally supervise activities of the teacher-counselors. This is being resented, particularly by teachers in the college-prep "Gymnasien" who feel that their independent academic

93

status is threatened.   (Martin and Wehrly n.d.)

Arnhold (1976) offers statistical data on current guidance personnel as well as projections of future needs. The school psychologist--student ratio was 1:15,000 in 1975 and is expected to be 1:5,000 in 1980. The teacher-counselor--student ratio was 1:3,000 in 1975 and is expected to be 1:1,000 in 1980. An "enormous demand for personnel" in the field of educational guidance is expected in the years to come.

Vocational guidance: A separate program

Educational and vocational guidance are institutionally separate in Western Germany. This may reflect the former absence of guidance services in the traditional school system which related to the world of work but marginally. Traditionally, vocational choices were made in German society with a view to entering an apprenticeship or securing employment. Consequently, vocational orientation and advice on job opportunities were perceived to be the functions of employment agencies.

The area of vocational guidance has been entrusted by law to the Federal Employment Institute ("Bundesanstalt für Arbeit"), a self-governing public body with a high degree of autonomy in its operation. The governing board of the Institute, "Verwaltungsrat," is composed of equal numbers of representatives from the ranks of employees, employers, and governmental or public agencies. The Institute has been skillful in publicizing its services and offering ongoing information on the labor market both through the mass media and through its own widely circulated publications. The information presented here has been provided by the Institute.*)

Organizational purpose

Under the provisions of the Employment Promotion Act
the Federal Institute bears the sole responsibility for
vocational guidance, including the placement of apprentices. It is obliged to advise juveniles and adults on
the choice of a trade or profession before entering employment, and on all questions concerning professional
advancement after entering employment. It gives special

---

*) Acknowledgement:

Several passages will be quoted verbatim from a booklet, Federal Employment Institute of the Federal Republic of Germany. Copyright 1975 by the Federal Employment Institute, Nürnberg. Passages quoted by permission of the copyright holder.

attention to the guidance of juveniles from secondary
and special schools, technical schools, vocational training centres, polytechs, and universities. The Federal
Institute also assists those who wish to change their
profession or have the ambition to advance in it, as
well as persons returning to civil life after completion
of their military service. Special care is devoted to
the vocational guidance of those who are physically and
mentally handicapped. It takes into consideration the
individual wishes and personal circumstances of persons
seeking advice. At the same time it takes into account
the situation and development of the labour market and
of various occupations.

The principal function of the vocational guidance service is to give information to juveniles and adults as
well as individual advice on vocational questions (individual guidance). This individual advice is supplemented
by information concerning different occupations (vocational information). Once a decision as to vocation has
been made, the guidance service assists in finding training facilities (placement of apprentices). Where necessary, moreover, it provides organisational and financial
assistance in order to ensure vocational training (vocational training incentives)... The vocational guidance
service fulfills its functions impartially and free of
charge... (Federal Employment Institute 1975, p. 26)

The Institute has been operating an extensive networks: nine
State centers; 146 local and 538 branch offices in Germany; and
twelve liaison offices (delegations) abroad. The latter were of
particular importance during the period of massive recruitment of
foreign workers. While vocational guidance of the Institute is available to any person in the labor market, it serves most the lower
75% on the socio-economic scale, those in need of vocational training
or retraining (particularly through apprenticeships), and those looking for jobs. It is less likely that, in normal circumstances, members of the professions would use the services.

Prevalent procedures and methods

All potential graduates of secondary schools receive in the
final stage of their education an invitation to request vocational
guidance services in terms of: (a) an interview with a vocational
adviser; (b) informational literature on various occupations; and
(c) a booklet that contains a comprehensive, self-administered inventory to help individual students assess their achievement, interests, values, etc. The actual guidance is done often in the course
of one interview which is more advice-giving than counseling-oriented.
In case of indecisiveness on the part of the client, a referral for

additional vocational interviews, psychological assistance, or medical evaluation are made:

> Decisive factors in the solution of a vocational problem
> are the mental and physical condition of the applicant,
> his age, education, preliminary vocational training,
> social circumstances, ambitions and special interests.
> The vocational adviser can make use of psychological
> opinions and consider them in his advice. Parents are
> free to ask the school to pass on a rating about the
> person seeking advice to the vocational guidance service.
> If the information so obtained is still insufficient to
> enable arrival at a clear judgement, a test can be car-
> ried out with the consent of the applicant by an employ-
> ment office psychologist, or an employment office doctor
> can determine the physical capacity. The conversation
> between vocational adviser and the person seeking advice
> is to prepare the decision; the final decision is, how-
> ever, in the hands of the person or his parents or guard-
> ians. (Federal Employment Institute 1975, p. 29)

Conclusion

In the relatively short span of its existence, German guidance
has experienced a rapid growth. The marked attitudinal changes of
the German population as a whole and the developments within the
school system from unitary, fixed patterns toward pluralistic structures were, no doubt, supportive to the guidance movement.

Two independent systems of guidance services exist side by side.
The vocational guidance that emerged within the official employment
agency operation is extensive and well organized throughout the country. It not only provides assistance in vocational decision-making,
but offers occupational training, placement, and financial aids as
well. Its basic orientation is pragmatic; its approach to helping
people, comprehensive; and its method, directive. Psychological variables are not ignored, but practical, economic facts are considered
more relevant for the client's vocational choice.

The educational guidance service is newer, less developed, less
organized, and still in search of its professional identity. By
the same token, it is less constrained by precedents or institutionalized policies. Rather than trying to settle problems of students,
it emphasizes clarification of issues, presentation of various options available, and stimulation of clients toward self-directiveness.

In the interest of the total person, there is need for close
liaison between educational and vocational guidance, i.e., between
schools and employment agencies. It will be quite interesting to
see in what form such a liaison will develop in Western Germany.

References

Arnhold, W. School psychology in Western Germany: Past-present-future. In Catterall, C.D. (Ed.) Psychology in the schools in international perspective, Vol. 1. Columbus, OH: International School Psychology Steering Committee, 1976, pp. 29-36.

Bildung und Wissenschaft (Inter Nationes, Bonn-Bad Godesberg), 1977, 1978.

Dahrendorf, R. Society and democracy in Germany. Garden City: Doubleday, 1967.

Federal Employment Institute of the Federal Republic of Germany. Nürnberg: Federal Employment Institute, 1975.

Heller, K. West Germany: Educational guidance work. Newsletter of the APGA International Education Committee, 1974, 1 (3), 2.

Heller, K. (Ed.) Handbuch der Bildungsberatung. Stuttgart: Klett, Vols. 1 and 2 1975, Vol. 3 1976.

Hoffmann, H-V. Beratung fur Modellschulen. In Heller (1975), pp. 549-569.

Hoffmann, M. Zur Situation der Beratungslehrerausbildung in der Bundesrepublik Deutschland. In Heller (1975), pp. 275-288.

Kulturbrief (Inter Nationes, Bonn-Bad Godesberg), 1978 (9).

Langfeldt-Nagel, M. and Langfeldt, H-P. Testverfahren für die Bildungsberatung. In Heller (1976), pp. 751-804.

Martin, L. R. Ansätze zu einer Theorie der Bildungsberatung. In Heller (1975), pp. 407-427.

Martin, L. R. and Wehrly, B. Counseling, school, and society: Interdependent systems. The example of the Federal Republic of Germany. Unpublished manuscript, not dated.

New York Times News Service. German school anxiety pushes children to suicide. Tampa Tribune-Times, 1978 (December 10), 36-A.

Reichenbecher, H. Bildungsberatung in der Bundesrepublik Deutschland. In Heller (1975), pp. 41-73.

Rosemann, B. Perspektiven der Bildungsberatung. In Heller (1975), pp. 351-364.

Schalk, A. The Germans. Englewood Cliffs, NJ: Prentice-Hall, 1971.

Suggested readings

In addition to the other English titles listed in the references, it should be noted that the periodicals

Bildung und Wissenschaft and Kulturbrief,

dealing with educational and cultural issues in Germany, are published in English. They can be obtained by writing to

Inter Nationes
Kennedyallee 91-103
D-5300 Bonn 2
Federal Republic of Germany.

9

FRANCE

E. L. Tolbert

The French people are characterized by individuality, respect for the opinions of others, and a demand for the same attitude for their own way of thinking from others. Hard work, frugality, and valuing property are widespread attitudes. The home and family occupy an important place in French society and parental influence is strong. Cultural traditions exert a pervasive influence on all aspects of life and are particularly heavy in the educational system. "The French school child, intellectually the most 'occupied' in the world, has as much work in school as his parents do at the office or factory." (Gambiez 1973, p. 99)

The French educational system is authoritative and highly centralized in order to implement the national policy of equality of all French citizens. (Gambiez 1973) Until recently, the educational system has relied heavily on rigorous examinations that in theory placed prestigious governmental and private-sector occupations on a competitive and democratic basis. In practice, however, the competition has been mainly among those of middle and upper class families. Those at lower socio-economic levels have not received occupational and educational guidance and preparation to permit them to compete effectively. (Wanner 1973)

Since 1968, however, education in France has been changing drastically, as planners have been taking into account the changing characteristics of the population and attitudes toward education. (Wanner 1973, a) Recent modifications include new provisions for technical and continuing education and for the education of the socially and culturally disadvantaged. (Wanner 1973, b)

Changing attitudes and values

Education has an extremely high status in France. Pupils are highly motivated to move up the ladder as far as possible; to some extent, educational attainment per se is more important than the career to which it leads. University education leading to the professions is the most sought after and the trade and technical levels are frequently short of students. This is certainly not a unique situation, but amounts to one that will have to be dealt with, particularly in view of current economic trends. Steps, including new legislation, are being taken to enhance the prestige of the trades and technical areas and to change attitudes about the status of different types of education.

Occupational values are changing, not so much in relation to the importance of work as to the conditions of work. There is a demand for more autonomy, more humanistic working conditions, and feelings of significance and achievement. At the same time, the career occupies a central role in the individual's life--a reflection of deep-seated values. The fact that the family plays a significant role in career decisions enhances the importance of guidance, education, and work.

The educational system

Figure 4.1. illustrates some of the choice points in the French educational system. The highly centralized system consists of a series of stages, with compulsory attendance ending at age sixteen. The first cycle of secondary school is quite similar for all except for those experiencing difficulties; these pupils may be transferred to technical and trade courses. Thus, while age thirteen is an important choice point, age fifteen is the most critical. Following age fifteen, pupils may go to technical school, prepare for apprenticeship, or select courses on which they will be tested in the "baccalaureate" examination taken at age eighteen. These examinations, comparable to those at the college sophomore level in the U.S., are the entrance requirements for all programs of higher education. Figure 4.1. indicates the variety of programs that are available.

Careful planning is extremely important because many choices are irreversible. For example, at age fourteen or fifteen, the pupil decides on areas to be studied for the major examination, the baccalaureate. This is a critical point because the courses taken and the grades obtained will determine the future educational career of the individual. (ONISEP 1973,b) Apprenticeships may be entered at age sixteen, or at age fifteen if specific preparatory classes have been completed. (ONISEP 1973,a)

Major choice points are covered by extremely detailed and clear

100

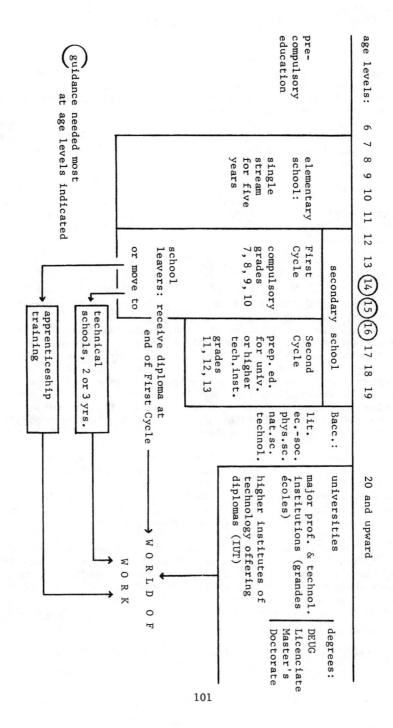

ORGANIZATION OF THE FRENCH EDUCATIONAL SYSTEM

Figure 4.1. Compiled from Long (1973), Organization for Economic Co-operation and Development (1972), and other sources.

101

information. Publications are readily understood by parents--an
important aspect, as parents play significant role in pupils' educational and career plans.

Some major modifications have been made in the French educational system in recent years. Following the "explosion of 1968"--
as it is referred to--changes have been made mainly in higher education; the impact on secondary school career guidance is not too vis-
ible. But new post-high school programs increase the need for career
guidance at both secondary and higher levels; inevitably the impact
will be felt. In addition, the 1971 legislation specifies a "national obligation" for continuing education and training, and provides--
among other things--for paid educational leaves for training. Programs such as these call for services to be available for workers'
and students' career development. The 1971 legislation adds a significant new dimension to career education in France, and with current extensive opportunities in apprenticeships, technical training,
and universities, appears to provide career education for anyone who
can qualify.

Guidance services

Guidance in France has had a long history, beginning early in
this century, about the same time as in other European countries and
the U.S. More closely associated with education than is typical for
other Western European systems, it is characterized by a highly centralized organization, heavy involvement of parents in the guidance
process, and services at critical educational choice points. Guidance
personnel are based outside of the school in an elaborate network of
offices covering all sections of the country. Directed by a national
office, all aspects of services are related. The key person is the
career counselor (counseiller d'information et d'orientation) who
provides the face-to-face guidance.

The guidance service is directed from the ministerial level and
policies emanate from this level. At the national level, the guidance
department, INETOP (Institut National d'Étude du Travail et d'Orientation Professionnelle) is in charge of counselor education, research,
guidance information, and practical experience. As this is not part
of guidance services, it is not shown on the figure.

ONISEP (Office National d'Information sur les Enseignements et
les Professions), which prepares information on education and work,
is interministerial and has ready access to information of other relevant departments. There also is a special department housed in
ONISEP for the study of occupational trends, needs, changes in jobs,
and the like. A professional journal, L'Orientation Scolaire et
Professionnelle, is published regularly.

Figure 4.2. shows the regional, departmental, and local divi-

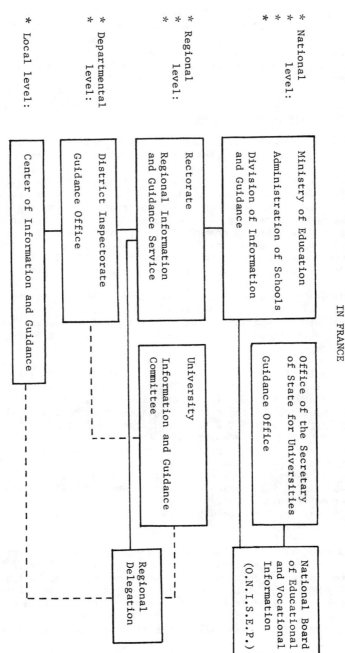

THE ORGANIZATION OF INFORMATION AND GUIDANCE SERVICE
IN FRANCE

* National
  level:

* Regional
  level:

* Departmental
  level:

* Local level:

Ministry of Education

Administration of Schools

Division of Information
and Guidance

Office of the Secretary
of State for Universities

Guidance Office

National Board
of Educational
and Vocational
Information
(O.N.I.S.E.P.)

Rectorate

Regional Information
and Guidance Service

University
Information and Guidance
Committee

Regional
Delegation

District Inspectorate

Guidance Office

Center of Information and Guidance

Figure 4. 2.

103

sions; all operate under national policies and are inspected regularly. While such policy indicates what is to be done, for example,
that counselors at the local level should emphasize economic information about occupational trends and needs, there may be variations in
the actual day-to-day procedures according to the counselor's preferences.

What the guidance worker does

Major responsibilities are visiting schools in the district
served by the guidance office, giving talks to pupils in groups, and
holding individual conferences if requested. Pupils may be referred
if problems are suspected. Group counseling is sometimes provided.
The counselor helps to set up an annual "career fair" in each district and regularly provides career information to the school. Depending upon the setting, counselors may do considerable work with
adults who need help in changing jobs or in obtaining training for
advancement. Placement and follow-up, however, are not carried out,
although counselors maintain contact with pupils while they are in
the educational system, including college and university.

Guidance could be characterized as more scholastic tha career-
related, reflecting the close tie-in of educational and training
programs with occupations. Entry into a particular educational program, of which there is a very large number, actually determines the
later occupation.

School visits are made to each institution about every two
months. The staff of the career guidance office in each district or
province (usually around five professionals) have this responsibility.
Evening meetings are the rule; parents are invited and usually turn
out in large numbers. The talks to large groups are primarily information giving, and a question-and-answer format is used. If some
of those attending have specific questions, special small-group meetings may be scheduled and information may be provided in greater
depth. At these meetings pupils and parents are provided with extensive printed information indicating courses available and admissions requirements. Pupils at ages thirteen, fourteen, and fifteen
participate, but contacts with pupils may begin as early as ages
eleven or twelve.

School visits are also made at regular intervals to review
pupils' progress and plans. This review consists mainly of looking
over records which contain very detailed information about plans,
school achievement, intelligence and aptitude data, and health.
Pupils may be called in for conferences if problems are detected.
These reviews of records continue all through the public education
program, and there is a follow-up on the job or in post-secondary
education.

Individual and group counseling are provided both at the school

and in district career guidance centers. The counseling process
tends to resemble a teaching relationship, utilizing occupational
psychology principles and emphasizing occupational requirements.
The usual procedure is as follows:

    (1) an introductory interview of a half-hour or more in length
in which interests and plans are discussed;

    (2) one or more testing sessions which may include measurements
of intelligence, personality, and motor skills;

    (3) a physical examination, primarily to determine what kinds
of work could or could not be done, based on physical ability (several decades ago, when many pupils went to work at age fourteen, a
vocational guidance physician was quite important in specifying what
the pupil could or could not do; now, with about 90% of pupils continuing on to further education, the doctor occupies a less commanding position);

    (4) an interview in which counselor and counselee discuss the
results of data collection and review plans. Parents may be present.

    The procedure provides the counselee the opportunity to make
his or her own decisions. Even if a decision does not appear to be
a good one, e.g., it will lead to choosing an overcrowded occupation,
the counselee has the freedom to choose. At the same time, the
counselor has the responsibility of helping to test the realism of
the choice and to assist in identifying alternatives if the original
plan does not work out. Parents play an important part in those
choices, but they tend to allow substantial freedom. Data on manpower needs are available, but the counselor does not act as an agent
of manpower policy.

    Placement, as was pointed out, is not a part of the counselor's
work. Pupils are referred to an employment service which helps job
seekers find specific openings. Employment offices are located in
each of the districts mentioned above, and a sharp division is maintained between guidance and placement services.

    A frequently used large-group guidance activity for information
giving resembles the U.S. "career day" or "career fair." Local employers who participate inform pupils and parents about jobs in their
establishments. These meetings tend to emphasize professional level
jobs and relatively little attention is given to trade and technical
areas. Counselors are aware of this imbalance, but can do little
about it as practically all pupils, with the backing of their parents,
want to enter the professions.

    Group counseling, involving self-exploration, affective aspects,
and the like, has received relatively little emphasis, but counselors are being provided preparation for this type of work (in-service
programs will be discussed later). With the building of competence
and with the interest expressed by counselors in learning how to
conduct group counseling, more assistance will very likely be provided by this technique.

Career guidance is also provided for adults who are out of school, even though the main emphasis is on pupil assistance. The focus is upon those who are out of work or changing jobs.

Some career guidance is provided by school personnel, but it seems to be primarily offering educational and occupational information, with a rather heavy emphasis on advice on choice of school programs. The counselor serves as the school psychologist in staff meetings where educational decisions about pupils are made. There is a tendency for counselors to handle the more serious problems, while lesser ones are taken care of by school personnel. The method of operation is more like consultation than a team approach; even so, teachers play a very limited role in career guidance.

Preparation of counselors

One of the functions of the National Guidance Department (INEOTP) is preparation of counselors and in-service programs for updating competencies or building new ones. There are eight major preparation centers in the country, one in Paris and seven in other sections. The Paris center is the model for others.

The preparation program is two years in length and is the same at all centers. There is considerable emphasis on psychology and sociology, and a thorough preparation in occupational requirements and trends, economic aspects of the labor market, and labor legislation. Part of the final year includes supervised experience in a career guidance center.

Admission to the preparation program is open to two types of applicants: (1) those who have completed two years of university work and who have received the DEUG diploma (Diplôme d'Études Universitaires Générales), the equivalent of the Bachelor's degree in the U.S.; and (2) civil servants who have the National Education Baccalaureate and less than five years of service, and those who meet other similar types of qualifications. The second option provides for more flexibility than the former. Women are on an equal status with men in the competitive admission process. Of about 1,500 to 2,000 applicants each year, 150 to 200 are accepted. No figures are available on the drop-out rate, but it is likely that most of those who enter the program complete it and take posts as counselors.

A systematic plan for updating skills and introducing new concepts brings together a hundred or so counselors each year for an intensive two-week short course. Recent topics covered are group counseling and research design and interpretation. Selection procedures are designed to identify those who can make the most effective use of the new material. Decisions on what to cover and on techniques to be used are made by the central office. Evaluations by those attending are very positive. This approach is quite impressive, for even though it introduces an element of uniformity (which may not be bad), it provides for almost instant nationwide infusion of new practices and concepts.

Control of admissions, so that graduates can find jobs, is relatively easy in a program of this type. Openings can be predicted and the number of counselors needed is used as a guide in determining how many new students will be admitted. Even so, there are not nearly enough counselors available for secondary schools, let alone for expansion into higher education for much needed services. In all, there are about 2,500 counselors in France, and about 500 in the Paris area.

In the first cycle of the secondary school (to age of sixteen), a ratio of one counselor attached to a Centre d'Information et d'Orientation to 1,000 pupils is planned. In these schools there is also one part-time career teacher per 600 pupils, one classroom teacher with guidance functions per 30 pupils, and an information specialist per 600 pupils. ONISEP provides information to school personnel. Much of the counselor's work is with young people nearing the end of lower secondary education (about fifteen to sixteen years of age) to make them aware of choices. (Reubens 1977)

While some are of the opinion that with adequate information, pupils can make effective and satisfactory plans, some counselors have expressed the importance of a developmental emphasis to this author. Super (1974) comments on this trend, but takes note of the conflicting emphasis on providing manpower for the nation's requirements.

Use of special materials, technology, and information

One of the most impressive features of the career guidance services is the extensive use of well designed booklets prepared by ONISEP for pupils and parents. These booklets, aimed at the key choice points in the educational system, clearly show the options, the requirements for admission, and the occupations or occupational fields to which options lead.

One particularly unique feature of the work by CEREQ (Le Centre d'Études et de Recherches sur les Qualifications), an inter-agency department, is the follow-up of workers to determine how well the individual utilizes the preparation which he or she has had. There is a real concern about the relevance of education and training for work. In addition to making its own surveys and predictions, CEREQ collects and synthesizes data from other agencies. The budget is drawn from both the Ministry of Education and the Ministry of Labor; CEREQ provides data to all governmental agencies.

Very little use is made of technology in direct services other than the motion picture films and slides. While computer technology is not used with pupils and parents, it is employed in compiling the results of occupational surveys and research programs. These types of information are prepared by CEREQ; formerly, this function was the responsibility of the University Bureau of Statistics. CEREQ's functions portray quite well the types of information provided to counselors:

(1) prepare analyses of the industrial structure and the changing nature of occupations;
(2) study the needed qualifications for various occupations and prepare occupational descriptions;
(3) study ways in which occupations are changing, e.g., as a result of technology, and make predictions about needs in various fields of work.

In addition to occupational surveys which will provide information about needs in various sections of the country, other projects are in process. For example, a book of occupational descriptions like the U.S. Dictionary of occupational titles has been prepared.

Current trends

The French guidance service appears to be moving in the direction of increased emphasis on occupational requirements, trends, opportunities, and assessment of aptitudes and abilities. National policy provides for a decision-making and career-planning type of assistance and encourages research and occupational data collection to support that approach.

A second trend is the expansion of career guidance services into higher education. The need is recognized. Judging by the development of services over the past forty or fifty years, it seems reasonable to predict that it will be accomplished in a decade or so.

A third trend is to prepare career counselors who can work at all levels rather than specifically in secondary schools. New programs of work-study for the employed as well as needs in higher education support this trend. The legislation already mentioned, which requires employers to pay workers for time off to prepare for advancement or changes to new jobs, emphasizes the importance of career guidance. The new universities which have been established following the "1968 revolution" also require career guidance.

The energy shortage and related economic conditions will likely increase the need for career guidance for the unemployed and for those whose jobs are being phased out. If there are large-scale dislocations, extensive programs of guidance and retraining will be imperative. There may be an increased emphasis on insuring that pupils know which occupations are overcrowded and which are short of workers. There are some indications that counselors may, to some extent, be expected to <u>control</u> the numbers of persons entering various types of preparation to avoid large-scale unemployment.

International cooperation

Correspondence to foster international cooperation is favorably regarded, although there is some concern about the language barrier. Exchanging ideas is regarded more favorably than a consultation approach; those in career guidance feel that they have as much to offer as to gain.

Exchange of personnel also appears to be favorably viewed, although language would be even more of a problem. Very little financial support is available at the present time. If financial problems were solved, it appears that plans could be developed for an exchange of persons to spend brief periods of two or three weeks in national and local offices. The exchange persons, however, would need to have enough competence in written and spoken French to communicate with colleagues and pupils.

Much of French research deals with problems quite similar to those studied in other countries--prediction of performance, assessment of occupational aptitudes, and procedures for developmental guidance. As has been pointed out, research is the specific responsibility of a department of INETOP. Studies are also done in universities.

Summary

The French career guidance system has clear-cut, specific goals. Thus, preparation of counselors can be structured to enable them to meet these goals. Practice can be quite realistic. Evaluation can be precise. Accountability can be demonstrated.

Parents play an active role in the career planning of secondary school pupils; they are routinely included in group meetings at schools and may be present when counselors and pupils discuss career and educational problems. While the amount of involvement may appear excessive, the implementation of decisions depends, after all, almost completely upon parental support.

Preparation of career counselors is consistent from program to program and is centrally supervised. It is under the direction of the same agency that controls counseling centers, research programs, and in-service education. This organizational plan makes possible an excellent degree of cooperation among these aspects of career guidance. CEREQ not only conducts occupational studies but also collects and synthetizes information from other sources. Furthermore, it follows up workers to assess the relevance of occupational preparation. Some studies are quite intensive and detailed, and cover specific sections of the country where the need is greatest. These local and regional studies are related to the nationwide situation.

Career guidance is provided by an office outside of the school. Services are provided to out-of-school individuals as well as to pupils. While a developmental emphasis throughout the span of education is lacking, there are services available at choice points and counselors follow up pupils during the period of public education.

Occupational and educational information is designed for the major decision-making points in the educational and training sequence and clearly describes the options available to pupils. The publications are provided free of charge to pupils and parents, and question-and-answer sessions are used to explain the options and requirements.

In-service education has two goals. One is to increase counselors' competence. A second is to introduce new skills. (Conservatoire National des Arts et Métiers 1972-73) The program is sharply focused and intensive; it is practical help for on-the-job tasks.

Accountability permeates the guidance program. For example, parents take part in guidance activities and make judgments about their value. Pupils are followed up to determine the suitability of plans. The goals and objectives of the program are explicit; they are, to some extent, approved by all concerned. The criteria are "behavioral" and evidence is provided to indicate the degree of success in reaching goals.

References

Conservatoire National des Arts et Métiers. Institut National
    d'Orientation Professionnelle, 1972-73.

Gambiez, C. U.S. and French education: Some reactions of a French
    journalist. In Rosen, S. M. (Ed.) International/intercultural
    education reports. Washington: U.S. Department of Health, Edu-
    cation, and Welfare, 1973, pp. 98-100.

Long, J. Information and guidance services in France. The School
    Guidance Worker, 1973, 29 (1), 13-19.

ONISEP. L'apprentissage. Author, 1973 (a).

ONISEP. BAC. Author, 1973 (b).

Organization for Economic Co-operation and Development. Classifi-
    cation of educational systems in OECD member countries.
    Paris, 1972, pp. 9-76.

Reubens, B. G. Bridges to work. New York: Columbia University, 1977.

Super, D. E. The broader context of career development and voca-
    tional guidance: American trends in world perspective. In
    Herr, E. L. (Ed.) Vocational guidance and human development.
    Boston: Houghton Mifflin, 1974, pp. 63-84.

Wanner, R. E. A French approach to career education. Washington:
    U.S. Government Printing Office, 1973.

Wanner, R. E. Some French initiatives in educating the socially
    and culturally disandvantaged. Washington: U.S. Government
    Printing Office, 1973 (a).

Wanner, R. E. A French approach to career education. In Rosen,
    S. M. (Ed.) International/intercultural education reports.
    Washington: U.S. Department of Health, Education, and Welfare,
    1973, pp. 15-24 (b).

The titles listed here are also suggested for additional reading
on guidance in France.

10

REPUBLIC OF IRELAND

Dorothy M. Clark and Sean Beausang

Ireland, an island of 32,524 square miles, lies to the west of Great Britain on the fringe of the European continental shelf. Its greatest length is 302 miles and its greatest width 189 miles. No part of the country is more than seventy miles from the sea.

The constitution of Ireland which was approved by a plebiscite on July 1, 1937 and came into operation on December 29, 1937 declares Ireland to be "a sovereign, independent, democratic state" and declares the national territory to be "the whole island of Ireland, its islands, and the territorial seas." It is important to know, however, that there are six counties in the north under the rule and educational system of Great Britain. This chapter will be concerned with the twenty six counties known as the Republic of Ireland.

Ireland is a parliamentary democracy. It has two houses: The "Dail Eireann" (House of Representatives) is composed of members elected on the system of proportional representation. The "Seanad Eireann" (Senate) is composed of 60 members of whom eleven are nominated by the "Taoiseach" (Prime Minister) and the others elected from panels of candidates representing various vocational and cultural interests. The elected President is Head of State and the Prime Minister is Head of Government.

Irish society

The texture of Irish society has changed radically over the

last twenty years with a rapid increase in the pace of industrial development and the emergence of its European identity which is the result of its EEC membership. Ireland joined the European Community in 1972 after a national referendum in which 82% of those who voted were in favour of membership. Agriculture, still the most important industry, received a massive boost as a result of EEC membership and the continuing expansion in industry has generally resulted in a more affluent and prosperous society. Discoveries of oil and gas around Ireland's coastline in recent years have generated a spirit of national optimism. However, unemployment remains a major problem and presently over 100,000 are unemployed, about 9% of the work force. In spite of the economic changes in Irish society, and allowing for an increasing European awareness, an adherence to traditional Catholic values and standards still remains. This is especially obvious in legislation where the family is consistently seen as the vital social unit, and divorce and abortion are still illegal.

Education in Ireland

The Irish education system is one of the most developed in Europe. Its origins can be traced back to the old bardic schools of the pre-Christian era and to the monastic schools of the Christian era. Over the years, schools have been seen as vitally important agencies for the promulgation of religious and political values, and for hundreds of years of English rule, both church and state attempted to exercise cultural dominance through the educational structures.

In 1831, forty years ahead of England and most other countries, an Act establishing a "national system" of education in Ireland was passed by the Westminster Parliament. The primary school system of today is the direct result of this Act. In 1878 the Intermediate Education Act established a loose structure for second-level education. Only the 1930 Vocational Education Act was another major developmental step for Irish educational structures. This Act empowered local vocational education committees to make provision for vocational education in their areas.

The modern education system essentially operates with the cooperation of various "aids". Few schools are owned and operated by public authorities. Primary and post-primary education is mainly denominational both in ownership and management. Primary schools serve children from five years to twelve years (approximately). The schools operate on a parish basis and are managed by committees which are controlled by church interests, both Catholic and Protestant (95% of the Irish population are Catholic). At the post-primary level, most schools (serving 68.9% of all second-level pupils) are optional and private, mainly owned and managed by religious orders even though the majority of the teaching staff consists of lay persons. Vocational schools enroll 24.4% of second-level pupils. These

114

schools are wholly public institutions; owned, operated, and maintained by vocational education committees with the emphasis on technical education. The remainder of the students are enrolled in
"comprehensive schools" (the first was opened in 1966) and "community schools"(established in 1973). These schools are managed by
committees and are often non-denominational in character.

Educational participation is almost 100% at primary level and
at second-level to the age of fifteen (the minimum school-leaving
age). Ireland's school enrollment rate for fifteen to seventeen
year olds (56% approximately) is higher than in most EEC countries,
but participation at third-level is relatively low (about 12%). The
second-level cycle normally runs from age twelve to age seventeen.
Since 1966 second-level education has been free.

The curriculum in Irish schools is decided by the Department
of Education through its inspectorate in consultation with teaching
bodies and the universities. There is a common primary school curriculum and the second-level courses are largely determined by the
Department of Education examinations: the Group Certificate (taken
mainly by pupils in vocational schools at the age of 15), the Intermediate Examination (taken at the age of 15 or 16), and the Leaving
Certificate Examination which is taken at the end of second-level
education. Entry to third-level education is mainly decided on the
basis of performance in the Leaving Certificate and, since slots
in third-level education are very limited, students are under considerable pressure to "perform".

Guidance services in Irish education

In 1960 the first psychologist was appointed by the Dublin Vocational Education Committee to institute a guidance service for the
city's vocational schools. In 1966 the Department of Education established the School's Psychological Service to initiate a guidance
service in schools throughout the country. The Department of Psychology in University College, Dublin, initiated the first Irish
course for guidance personnel in 1967. This one-year course was
open to qualified teachers with three years of experience. In 1968,
in order to provide at least some career guidance for as many pupils
as possible, the Department of Education established a system of
short summer courses to train guidance teachers. These courses were
phased out in 1971. From 1972 to 1976 the Mater Dei Institute in
Dublin provided a one-year course to train additional guidance teachers. The National Council of Guidance Services came into existence
in 1973 to promote guidance and counselling. In 1976, to encompass
the new title of "guidance counsellor", the name was changed to the
Institute of Guidance Counsellors. Current membership of the Institute is approximately three hundred, spread over eleven branches
throughout the country.

About 50% of the 840 second-level schools have a guidance coun-

sellor. It is estimated that at least 100,000 students still have
no access to guidance and the schools in rural areas are especially
disadvantaged. A school must have at least 250 pupils to qualify
for a guidance counsellor and, although a second guidance counsellor may be appointed in schools of 600 or more, few have been appointed. As a result, caseloads are generally unrealistic, and depending on the size of the school, it is common for a single guidance counsellor to have to take care of 500 students. At present
there is no provision for the employment of guidance personnel at
the primary school level. Within higher education, the appointment
of counsellors in two of the five universities has only recently tak-
en place.

The vast majority of Irish guidance counsellors are employed in
the post-primary sector, although a small number work with the National Manpower Service, a state agency which provides a career placement service. In order to qualify as a guidance counsellor in Ireland, one must be eligible for registration as a second-level teacher, as defined by the Registration Council. In most cases, therefore, guidance counsellors have a primary degree which takes at least
three years to complete, have obtained the Higher Diploma in Education (a post-graduate teaching qualification) and have undertaken a
one-year course in guidance and counselling. Normally at least three
years teaching experience is required before a teacher can be accepted
for guidance training. The main supplier of guidance counsellors is
University College, Dublin, offering the Diploma in Careers Guidance.
Certain British courses in guidance and counselling are also accepted.
Also, honours graduates in psychology who have completed teacher training are recognized as guidance counsellors. The registration body
for guidance counsellors in second-level schools is the School Psychological Service of the Department of Education.

Guidance counsellors are employed in schools on the same basis
as teachers. Although a specialist member of staff, a counsellor is
very much part of the staff group and must teach a formal subject or
undertake group guidance for at least three hours per week. The
working week of most second-level teachers in Irish schools rarely
exceeds twenty-two hours per week of school-based work; the minimum
requirement is eighteen hours. Guidance counsellors are free to arrange their own timetable, except for the three-hour class contact
requirement. Physical resources for guidance and counselling are
generally unplanned and most guidance counsellors have to make do
with a small office and a couple of filing cabinets. In the newer
schools provision has been made for guidance suites. The vast majority of guidance counsellors have no specific secretarial assistance and have to make use of the school's general office. Standardized record systems are almost unknown.

The role of guidance counsellors

The concepts of guidance and counselling are still quite new to the Irish educational scene and there is still a considerable degree of uncertainty regarding the role of the guidance counsellor. While career work remains an important part of the work of all guidance counsellors, the emphasis varies from one guidance counsellor to another. Much depends on the individual guidance counsellors' concept of their roles and on the background and training. There are no directives by the Department of Education for guidance counsellors, except for the formal three-hour class contact requirement, and the way guidance counsellors spend the day is largely a matter for themselves and for the school principal. Some principals are inclined to use guidance counsellors as extra teachers and class-contact time can sometimes be as much as ten hours per week.

Guidance and counselling in Ireland is mainly concerned with assisting second-level students in curricular decision-making. A general objective would be to ensure that the students are following the courses most appropriate for them and, where they are able to choose, making sure that they are aware of the alternatives and of their own strengths and weaknesses. The guidance counsellor tries to get to know pupils, their families and interests, in order to build up relationships of trust and openness. The counsellor's task can be divided into three main areas: personal, educational, and vocational guidance. It is difficult to set limits for each of these areas and there is undoubtedly considerable overlapping of objectives.

During the school day pupils are free to approach the guidance counsellor on any matter. Not too much stress is placed on "problems", however, as this would indicate that the guidance counsellor's task is dealing with pupils who are in trouble. If necessary, referral can take place to psychologists of the School Psychological Service or to the psychiatric services of the local health board. Educational guidance is seen as a vital part of the guidance counsellors' role. Their function is to develop an awareness in the pupils of the implications of the school curriculum and courses.

Psychological assessment at a basic level is a normal part of educational guidance. Intelligence tests and aptitude tests are administered fairly extensively. Most of the tests used are either British or American in origin. However, St. Patrick's Research Centre in Dublin has standardized the Differential Aptitude Tests for an Irish population and Cattell's HSPQ has recently been standardized for Ireland by the Department of Education. St. Patrick's Research Centre has also produced its own battery of achievement tests in Irish, English, and Arithmetic which together with a verbal proficiency test are designed for use in primary schools.

Vocational guidance becomes a priority during the latter years of the post-primary school. Guidance counsellors will usually set up a career library in the school so that students may have access to job information. Counsellors may also organize careers seminars for the students with speakers from third-level institutions and from industry. Preparation for job interviews is also a task which is commonly expected of guidance counsellors and in some schools interviews are simulated on videotape. While job-placement is the responsibility of the National Manpower Service, many guidance counsellors try to establish links with local industry and actively seek out positions for their students.

While most of the tasks of the Irish guidance counsellor have been mentioned above, the emphasis on each area will vary according to the needs of individual schools and pupils. Also, guidance counsellors find their list of duties becoming longer each year to include any area of responsibility which is not immediately claimed by other members of the school staff. It is now considered "normal" for guidance counsellors to take responsibility for liaison with parents, to deal with disruptive pupils referred by teachers, to arrange visits to industry as part of the career programme and to co-ordinate the school's approach to pastoral care. The fact that the guidance counsellor's role is not clearly defined is seen as an advantage by most guidance counsellors. Many, however, would be in favour of a "code of ethics" for guidance and counselling in Ireland. The Institute of Guidance Counsellors is presently drawing up a discussion document to establish minimum guidelines and standards for the profession.

A number of agencies provide informal counselling opportunities for young people who have left school. Youth clubs, staffed mainly by adult volunteers, are quite common throughout the country and provide programmes of social activities as well as afford members the opportunity of contact with adults who care. "Contact", the first Irish "open door" type of counselling agency for young people, was opened in Dublin in 1972. Young people may visit the centre, staffed by psychologists and social workers, during office hours with or without an appointment. In the larger towns, the Samaritans organization which seeks out the lonely and the suicidal also provides a counselling service for the general population and its services are becoming increasingly popular with young people. On a nationwide basis, marriage guidance services are provided by the various churches.

Summary and projections

The freedom guidance counsellors have to arrange their own schedule (apart from the minimum "three hours of formal teaching per week") indicates, along with the requirement of at least eighteen hour-work per week, an opportunity to develop a program without requirements "structured from above." The fact that physical resources are generally unplanned might be considered a clue as to the esteem in which counselling services are held. Because newer schools are provided with guidance suites, it appears that a higher regard is developing.

The first Irish course for preparation of guidance personnel

118

was initiated in 1967. The young guidance profession has had the advantage of basing its programs on values particularly suited to the Irish culture and has not become addicted to either testing or recordkeeping.

What of the future? There are many possibilities. One of the influences may be Ireland's membership in the European Economic Community. There will probably be an increasing dialogue among professionals of member countries. The contacts resulting from exchange of information and of ideas may lead to the adoption or adaptation of programs and methods suited to situations in which there are parallel elements. There is, in addition, the possibility of directives and uniform standards. In regard to professional exchange, the question of reciprocity will no doubt be considered, since educational preparation differs somewhat from country to country.

Another factor influencing the future will be the trend toward development of community schools. It is likely that committee management and parental influence may lead to efforts to provide guidance services at all educational levels. The introduction of guidance service at primary level is of vital importance as it would afford a preventive approach to problems before remediation is needed at second level.

How will counsellors be able to meet the above and other needs? Perhaps some research into qualities essential for guidance personnel would result in a second look at present requirements and some effective changes could be made. In Ireland, counselling is closely tied up with teaching and career guidance. The future will probably find the profession broadening its scope and refining its functions, thus eliminating some of the role-conflicts occasioned by teaching assignments.

Guidance counsellors themselves are seeking to define and clarify their roles. They believe eventually to initiate services on the primary level, to extend service on second level, and to initiate service on third level.

Presently, two of the five universities are about to employ a guidance counsellor. Only one counsellor each! It is time for the profession to develop and adopt a set of standards, proclaim its role and its responsibilities and exert proper influence on the Department of Education policies.

Suggested readings

Akeson, D.H. The Irish education experiment. London: Routledge and
   Kegan Paul, 1967.

Beausang, S. The adolescent subculture in the Irish context. Career
   Guidance and Counselling (Journal of Institute of Guidance
   Counsellors, Ireland). Summer 1977.

Bradley, M.K. Counselling past and present: Is there a future?
   Personnel and Guidance Journal, 1978, 52, 42-45.

Department of Foreign Affairs. Facts about Ireland (Third edition).
   Dublin, 1972.

Horgan, J. Education in the Republic of Ireland. In R. Bell et.al.
   Education in Great Britain and Ireland. London: An Open University Source Book, Routledge and Kegan Paul, 1973.

Moran, M.E. Future dimensions of counselling. Career Guidance and
   Counselling (Journal of Institute of Guidance Counsellors, Ireland). Summer 1977.

National Youth Council of Ireland. Irish youth directory. Dublin,
   1978.

Tussing, A.D. Irish educational expenditures past, present and
   future. Dublin: The Economic and Social Research Institute,
   1978.

11

THE NETHERLANDS

Nathan Deen and Lawrence Brammer

The Netherlands is a highly industrialized, densely populated, and highly literate European country. It is renowned for its maritime feats, geographic discoveries, engineering marvels, and literary-artistic achievements. Once a great colonial power, the Netherlands consists now of a cluster of maritime provinces on the North Sea. Its people are passionately committed to personal freedom and a democratic political system. The economic and political scene is dominated by a constant tension between forces moving the country in a socialistic direction and those pushing for maximizing private enterprise and individual choice. While maintaining an intense commitment to individual values, there is also a long tradition of social concern for the less fortunate in all parts of the world. This concern is manifested in the Netherlands by numerous social services, educational programs, and traditional neighborliness and hospitality. Life styles vary considerably, although unifying threads persist in the Dutch passion for sports, both spectator and participant, and devotion to the arts and horticulture. Sports clubs, folk arts, plant shows, and museums abound. While nominally a secular society, a Christian culture predominates. Many schools and colleges are controlled by the churches.

Netherlands' education

Since the bulk of this chapter is devoted to school counseling, a brief description of the Dutch educational system is provided. Compulsory education begins at age six; but most children begin kindergarten at four. Elementary education covers six years, followed by four to six years in secondary schools. There are specialized secondary "Atheneums" or "Gymnasiums", university preparatory programs of six years. In addition, there are comprehensive high schools and vocational training schools. A recent innovation is the middle school which aims at comprehensiveness and covers a broad, late childhood age range. This program should replace a "bridge year" that was introduced earlier to ease the transition from elementary to secondary programs. Students proceed through the system in groups called "classes" or "forms", although repetition of a year is possible for those not making sufficient progress.

Schools are classified as public or private (parochial), and all are government financed. One third are Roman Catholic; one third are Protestant; and one third are public. With central funding, all schools are financed equally without regard to local economic status. All systems stress cognitive achievement and are very subject-centered. In the traditional secondary school, a student must cope with twelve or thirteen subjects at one time. Grading distributions tend to follow a bell-shaped curve.

Netherlands' schools are going through great philosophical and structural changes. Much discussion is underway among school personnel at all levels about objectives, organization, and methods to carry out designs proposed by the Ministry of Education for the next twenty years. (Ministry of Education 1974) Much of the change is underway already, creating stresses and needs for new roles and skills. There is a shift from rigid tracks to more flexible and individualized programs. There is also a flavor of human development mixed with the traditional mastery of subject disciplines. Educational change, therefore, is taking place in four areas:

(a) Changes in organization emphasizing continuous progress and coordinated programs with fewer breaks from kindergarten through secondary years. Instituting middle schools required a shuffling of previous ideas about maturation and comprehensiveness, for example.

(b) Shifts in content toward more comprehensiveness and diversity of offerings is apparent. Social, affective, and cultural content and skills for surviving in society are emphasized, along with academic enrichment and vocational skills. More optional subjects are offered now in secondary school than a few years ago.

(c) Changes in teaching methods and conceptions of the learning process are underway, especially in elementary education. Variety, individualization, and student responsibility are the key words. Objective testing is more accepted.

(d) The need for more specialized counseling services is being felt. The conditions of ferment in the educational system, broadening of educational and career choices, and increasing complexities of survival in the larger society created acute needs for specialized

122

counseling functions. One difficulty in the system currently is to help all school personnel perceive this need for counseling more clearly.

These educational changes reflect needs students will have for coping with the rapid social changes underway in Netherlands' society. While there is still a huge gap between the ideal reform plan and actuality in the schools, there is considerable trust in the Netherlands that the educational system will prepare students effectively for the world they must inherit.

Non-school counseling services

While much of the developmental student counseling is done informally in school settings, the bulk of the formal helping services is provided by the private sector or by government bureaus. The health care system provides much of the service to severely handicapped, while counseling and clinical psychologists offer private service to families. Some commercial agencies provide guidance and placement to all age groups. Most of the career counseling and placement services, however, are performed through the Vocational Guidance Bureaus financed and managed by the Ministry of Labor.

Informal support groups

The Netherlands experienced the socially disruptive events common to all European societies during the industrial revolution of the 19th century. Extended rural families broke up, parents moved to the cities, and neighborhoods with their carefully nourished support systems and self-help capabilities diminished. Churches maintained some vehicles for help and international self-help movements among youth such as the YMCA and YWCA, spread worldwide. Yet these traditions for informal help had to be reestablished in the modern Netherlands. Government policy has been fostering reestablishment of this spirit and of a structure translated as "neighborship." This movement is needed, especially in the cities, to counteract the destructive consequences of anonymity. To facilitate development of this "neighborship", special community workers are prepared through institutes in the Social Academies. In most cities, crisis centers are emerging that offer a refuge for the lonesome, help for drug addicts, and support for others in need. These centers sometimes are run by volunteers.

Counseling and guidance in schools

Pedagogical centers are national structures serving the three segments of Dutch education--Public, Catholic, and Protestant. While they do not offer counseling activities directly, they provide some research services, in-service training, and general coordination of services in the guidance domain.

Regional school support centers offer services to all local schools in the region, regardless of religious affiliation. These services include special help, primarily with developmental and remedial learning problems. Psychological and medical help are among these services, but they are limited largely to elementary schools; general counseling is not offered. Some secondary schools have psychologists, however.

Career counseling is offered through specialized counselors ("deans") in technical schools; but the bulk of career counseling is performed by the Labor Ministry bureaus described above, or by the deans of students in the general schools.

Most schools have student deans who perform general guidance coordination duties, see problem students, and provide some career guidance. These are guidance-teachers who have little or no special counselor training beyond a short course in career guidance. They tend to be overburdened with duties for which they have had little preparation.

Teachers perform many general counseling duties and some are selected for special assignment as "mentors." These special teachers monitor individual student growth and perform many broad guidance functions. Much of their service is performed through groups and student activities.

The specialist counselor

A new, unique counselor model has emerged among national models of school counselors, in that these counselors were asked to create their own roles in their schools. The current training model is to select teachers who have special interest in counseling and who have the endorsement of their teaching colleagues. These teachers attend a special counselor education program for half time over a school year. They return to their schools to establish specialized individual counseling programs, which, in many schools, do not yet exist. Their additional functions are to coordinate many informal teacher-counselor activities performed by mentors and student deans into a cohesive school guidance program. While there are commonalities among these programs, there are wide differences due to unique school histories and politics. Special interests and talents of the counselors contribute to this variability. In some schools, a group program predominates; in others, an individual counseling service is primary. Some counselors perceive the installation of a comprehensive guidance assessment program as their principal objective. Others see their roles as initiators, facilitators, or coordinators, rather than providers of direct service.

124

Another unique function of these counseling specialists is that they have prepared themselves also as curriculum consultants. This role comes about in part from their background as teachers, but preparation for this consulting function is included in their counselor education program. The rationale is that they often obtain their credibility and acceptance from teachers through providing their helpfulness to those teachers. Similarly, counselors obtain some skills in organizational development and change methodology in the counselor education program. Thus they enhance their acceptance with administrators by working on school organization problems which interfere with student development. These specialist counselor trainees find, in addition, that they must facilitate school changes to make counseling a viable enterprise in their schools. This function requires special change agentry skills and interests.

Since the idea of a specialist counselor was new to Dutch schools, a goal for the counselor preparation program was to gain recognition for the counseling function, without diminishing the jealously guarded counseling functions performed by many of the generalist-teachers. This new program injected systematic and professional elements into a loosely performed vital educational function, while preserving the essential interrelationship between education and counseling. In the five years of its existence, the program graduated over two hundred of these counselors. Their impact is such, that at this moment, the Government plans to remodel the training of "school deans" after the counselors' training program and spread training programs to a number of Teacher Training Colleges over the country.

Counselor education

Until 1975 counselor education in the Netherlands consisted of occasional short-term workshops for teachers on special topics, such as youth and drugs, and some in-service work in career education. Some counselors trained in psychology departments at the universities found their way into schools; but most of these students performed special clinical services such as student assessment, assignment of the handicapped, and some treatment of emotional disturbances.

The idea of specialist counselor emerged during the national planning for change in education which took place in the early 1970's. The Ministry of Education funded an experimental program in counselor education in the Pedagogical Institute of the University of Utrecht. (Deen and DeVries 1978) This program was started in the fall of 1975, with 27 students selected from schools widely distributed over the country. They spent half time at the Institute and half time at their schools, for one academic year. Their expenses for training and substitutes were borne by the Ministry. At the time of this writing, the fourth class is proceeding through the program. Institute staff members follow up regularly through visits to school sites. The Institute also convenes assemblies of graduates for eight days a year to update and extend their training.

The general philosophy which guides this specialist counselor program states that:

(1) counseling and guidance activities ought to be integrated with the whole school program and must be a basic element of school policy;

(2) the counselor's role description should come from general agreement in the teachers' assembly, since this is where local school power resides;

(3) the needs of pupils are the ultimate rationale for all guidance services;

(4) guidance programs are instruments of innovation rather than promotion of the status quo;

(5) the training should reflect a balance between content- and person-centeredness;

(6) counseling requires training in attitudes and skills to create a helping relationship; and

(7) counseling should emphasize a preventive rather than a remedial approach. (Deen and DeVries 1978)

The program of 38 weeks reflects the philosophical assumptions stated above. The program, therefore, consists of an educational cluster (theories and practices of education, needs and status assessment, change and innovation). A second cluster is youth studies (sociology of youth, developmental psychology, careers, and life cycles). The third cluster is counseling (group dynamics, practicum, counseling theory). A supporting cluster includes communication theory, observational methods, referral to agencies, developing guidance structures, and topics of special interest. The program includes individual conferences with staff, writing position papers, and developing cooperative projects. The students work together intensively and, as a result, develop into a close-knit supportive group. They return to their individual schools to apply the principles and methods learned in the Institute. Thus, the work is very experimental, with a close interplay between theory and practice. Much attention is given to the counselor's development as a person, as well as to the development of skills and concepts. Modern media are used extensively for modelling of skills and giving video feedback about their counseling with students. Participants are encouraged to develop their own theory and style of counseling.

Evaluation of the training program and performance of the students is a central feature because of the experimental nature of the program and its funding. Several evaluation modes were used, including a continuous process evaluation by staff and students, formative evaluation every two and a half weeks by staff, and summative evaluation at the end of the year where students and staff give detailed evaluation and conduct two-day discussions of the training outcomes. Students ranked the elements of the program in terms of value for their work. Counseling practicum, group dynamics practicum, and counseling theory emerged as the top three components, in that order. A part of the summative evaluation was an in-depth study by an external evaluator at the end of the second year. Interviews with the counselors, their colleague teachers, principals, and students were conducted to determine what the counselor trainees were doing differently from the pretraining period, and how their results were perceived by the school personnel. In addition, questionnaires were completed on many aspects of counseling programs in their schools. The focus was on the impact counselors were making in their schools as a result of the training program. The findings indicated that the counselor education program at the University of Utrecht was fulfilling its mission extremely effectively, judged by changes students were effecting in their schools, and their favorable reception by colleagues. It appeared that the model of the specialist counselor-consultant being produced in the training program was a useful addition to traditional as well as new school organizations. (Brammer 1978)

Organizations for counselors

Psychologists have an organization to serve their professional needs and special theory interest groups, such as behavioral and transactional, have their organizations also. Until recently, however, no group existed to serve the needs of the specialist counselor in schools. Graduates of the program described above have established an active counselor organization which has the potential of becoming a major association for school counselors of all types. The government has recognized the group officially.

Summary

While informal counseling has been a part of the Dutch educational scene for a long time, the idea of the specialist counselor-consultant is a new arrival in secondary schools. This unique model stresses direct helping service to students, coordination with other school staff doing counseling, and provision of consulting services to teachers and principals committed to constructive educational change.

Counseling functions are in a state of flux due largely to the
monumental changes in philosophy, structure, and method in the
schools. The experimental counselor education program at the
University of Utrecht appears to be a viable model in secondary
schools for the foreseeable future. Other countries might profit
from this strategy for change in counselor roles and the conduct
of training by counselor educators in the Netherlands. To produce
the specialist counselor program, they studied models of counseling
around the world and then designed a program uniquely adapted to
Dutch educational needs and politics of the nineteen seventies
and eighties.

References

Deen, N. and DeVries, D. Counselor education in the Netherlands.
    International Journal for the Advancement of Counseling, 1978,
    2, 146-171.

Brammer, L. M. The making of a Dutch school counselor: One
    American's perspective. International Journal for the Advance-
    ment of Counseling, 1978, 2, 172-188.

Ministry of Education and Science. Contours of a future education
    system in the Netherlands--A summary. The Hague, 1974.

128

12

SWEDEN

Victor J. Drapela

Sweden is a Nordic country known for its high standard of living, its policy of neutrality, and the liberal attitudes of its people. Due to its geographical location, the country has had relatively little immigration in the past. Thus, the Swedes have retained, to a high degree, their typical features--tall body built, blond hair, and blue eyes. The vast countryside is generally unspoiled, and most people enjoy the outdoors: hiking and boating, during the summer; skiing and skating, during the winter.

Genesis of modern Swedish society

Swedish society has undergone dramatic social changes in the first half of this century, moving from a traditionalist, conservative mentality to its present liberal values. It is well to remember that since the days of the Protestant Reformation, the religious organization to which all people in the country had to belong was the State Lutheran Church. A newborn baby automatically became a member of that Church. Although (since 1860) allowed to embrace another religious creed, Swedish citizens were not free to withdraw from the State Church. This archaic law was abolished only after World War II. Needless to say, the State Church wielded considerable power and exercised a rigid control over the behavior of the people. Most clergymen supported the concept of a strict law-and-order system and emphasized the validity of patriarchal prerogatives of employers vis-à-vis the uneducated workers. The Church feared democracy and opposed its spread while trying to prop up the vanishing social system of the past.

As a result, a massive secularization process began among wide population groups. People had become increasingly alienated from the Church establishment which they identified with the **upper** social strata and explored alternative philosophies of life. However, they retained their Church membership, since it is to their advantage in many practical life situations. For instance, local parishes are issuing birth certificates for all people, no matter what their credal affiliation, and there is a widespread feeling that formal withdrawal from the Church may complicate matters, when a person needs documents while applying for a job or for a driver's license. (Fleisher 1967) At present, most people in Sweden feel no commitment to organized religion and hold liberal views on philosophical and ethical issues. Sexual relations before marriage are generally accepted, and so are divorce and cohabitation or motherhood without marriage. A typical Swedish family is small (because of the widely used birth control methods) and many young mothers work. This is possible because of the wide network of public child-care centers in the country. (Myrdal 1968)

The attitudinal changes of vast population groups were stimulated by parallel economic developments in the country that directly affected the traditional structure of Swedish rural society. As industrialization increased, a steady migration from the countryside to the cities diminished the ranks of farmers, timbermen, and fishermen. The center of gravity in national affairs--cultural trends, social customs, and political clout--shifted from the rural population to industrial workers in the cities. There was a phenomenal growth of labor unions (at present about 95% of workers hold union membership), as the Social Democratic Party grew to prominence in national politics. Emphasizing social reform within the democratic context rather than Marxist dogma, it was the ruling party of Sweden for several decades.

This policy of socialist pragmatism has generated a system of advanced welfare programs. They include comprehensive medical care; maternity and child care; housing subsidies for low income families; and generous retirement benefits that run at over 50% of the worker's pre-retirement income. By the same token, Sweden is also known for its high taxes. The current tax structure diminishes income differences while providing various insurances for the lower income groups who would not secure them, if the decision were theirs alone. (Fleisher 1967)

The educational system

The present structure of public education in Sweden came about through a series of school reforms in the 1950's and the 1960's. Compulsory education is provided for youth from seven to sixteen

years of age in the nine-year "comprehensive school." In the first
three grades, classes are limited to twenty-five pupils. After that,
the number of students permitted in a class goes up to thirty. A
foreign language, English, is taught from grade three on and a second foreign language may be added in the seventh grade. As will be
explained later in detail, vocational guidance is an integral part
of the curriculum with emphasis on practical job experiences. Elective subjects are introduced in grades seven and eight, and in the
last grade students are helped to arrive at a basic vocational decision. They have an option to continue their education in secondary school or to enter the world of work.

Almost 90% of Swedish youth take advantage of the opportunity
for additional education in the "upper secondary school." (Melldén
1976) At this level, about twenty programs of study are available
within an integrated system that has three main tracks: (a) the
"gymnasium" which is a preparatory school for university studies;
the "continuation school" (fackskola) which trains students for
intermediate levels of responsibility in the fields of social work,
business, and technical occupations; and the vocational school
(yrkesskola) which prepares students for skilled technical occupations. After graduating from continuation school or from vocational
school, students can take additional courses in adult education centers (vuxenutbildning) which are municipally administered. (Husén
and Boalt 1967)

Educational philosophy

The Education Act of 1962 envisioned a school system in which
young Swedish citizens would not only acquire skills but also fully
develop their personhood. The school is to teach respect for every
student as an "individual human being." Teachers should cooperate
with the "neighborhood" in which its students live, be it rural or
urban, i.e., with interested individuals and with public institutions
of the community. The entire concept of the Swedish school is guidance-related and pupil-centered, as can be seen from these officially
proposed aims of education in the comprehensive school:

(1) Guidance and care: pupils should feel accepted and stimulated to grow in all areas of personal development.
(2) Acquisition of study skills: pupils are to learn how to
work independently and methodically, how to integrate knowledge and
respect truth.
(3) Skills in language and mathematics: these have to be perceived as basic instruments for widening one's knowledge.
(4) General education: pupils are to learn how to live successfully in a democratic society and acquire an adequate degree of
cultural consciousness and an ability to assess the needs of life.
(5) Esthetic education: this involves art appreciation for
personal enrichment.

(6) Practical skills: pupils should acquire a balanced attitude toward life by learning manual skills in addition to theoretical insights.

(7) Vocational training: on the basis of their talents, pupils
should receive vocational guidance to be assisted in their personal
career planning.

(8) Health education: this involves information on physical
and mental health, on health habits and outdoor activities.

(9) Social education: the class being a "collective," helps
students develop social skills applicable in society at large, i.e.,
the community, the nation, and the world.

(10) Development of personality: this is the most urgent task
which involves the growth of students as individuals. (Husén and
Boalt 1967)

An interesting--and in some quarters controversial--feature
in Swedish schools is the compulsory sex education from first grade
on. The topics are gradually expanded and eventually include the
biological understanding of sex organs, sexual maturity, nocturnal
emissions, masturbation, menstruation, pregnancy, and child birth.
Later yet, family relationships, contraception, and venereal diseases are discussed. (Fleisher 1967)

Personal-social guidance in schools

The pupil-centeredness of Swedish school policy implies that
teachers themselves are to assume a major guidance role, particularly in the areas of values, social consciousness, and self-awareness
of their pupils. Teacher training emphasizes the need for innovative methods in classroom work and for research interests by teachers regarding the student population. (Husén and Boalt 1967) A
relatively high degree of flexibility is required on the part of
teachers which facilitates their professional role as developmental
guidance practitioners.

In their guidance functions, teachers are aided by school psychologists some of whom meet with groups of classroom teachers on a
regular basis and provide a sort of in-service training. Individual
counseling, particularly in problem situations, is the responsibility
of school psychologists who use a variety of therapeutic approaches.
This service is still being developed. The present ratio is 3,000
students to one psychologist. (Melldén 1976)

Comprehensive and upper secondary schools are served by "pupil
welfare teams" that deal with issues of general welfare of the student population and with individual cases of students in need of
special assistance. Each team consists of the school administrator,
a classroom teacher, a remedial teacher, a study and vocational guidance advisor, the school physician, the school nurse, the school psychologist, and a social worker. These teams usually meet on a week-

ly basis and their meetings are called "pupil welfare conferences."
At such conferences, the team reviews current school concerns of a
general nature and makes decisions on how to handle individual cases
presented for discussion. Remedial treatment is agreed upon and a
follow-up later assesses the effectiveness of the treatment. (Melldén 1976)

Vocational guidance in schools

A close liaison exists in Sweden between educational and employment authorities. Vocational guidance in schools is organized jointly by the Labor Market Board and the National Board of Education.
Here are a few notes on the development of this partnership:

> Various local experiments in the field of vocational
> guidance were launched during the early decades of the
> present century. During the twenties and thirties, un-
> employment created a particularly acute need for voca-
> tional guidance for young people. In 1924 the first
> youth employment exchange in Sweden was set up by the
> Employment Service in Stockholm. Several more soon
> followed in some of the major cities. These exchanges
> provided referral services for young persons under 18 to-
> gether with vocational guidance...

> Organizational co-operation on vocational guidance in
> schools was established at an early stage between em-
> ployment offices and schools. At first, this concerned
> only elementary school pupils, but by the 1940s it had
> also come to include lower and upper secondary schools,
> girls' high schools and folk high schools.

> As part of the school reforms of the 1950s and 1960s es-
> tablishing the nine-year experimental school which pre-
> ceded the present nine-year comprehensive school, special
> careers teacher appointments were successively introduced
> to provide vocational guidance...(National Labour Market
> Board of Sweden 1977, pp. 9-10)

These career teachers usually received their training in an employment agency setting. (Fältheim 1959) Eventually, their job title has been changed to "study and vocational guidance advisor."
This change is tied in with the 1971 decision of the Swedish Parliament (Riksdag) to introduce a new program that would combine the
teaching of subject matter with career guidance. The program was
fully operational by 1974. It is known by its acronym SYO and can
be found in virtually all curricula, especially at the upper secondary school level. (National Labour Market Board of Sweden 1977)

While SYO follows a more academic route to career guidance, an-

other--concrete--occupational experience mandatory for Swedish youth
is the "practical vocational guidance" (acronym PRYO) during the
last two years of the comprehensive school. All students in grade
eight have to spend three weeks in some job training and all ninth-
graders have a two-week compulsory PRYO job training experience scheduled for the fall term which, in some instances, can be extended to
36 days. "PRYO is jointly organized by schools and employment offices.
The employment offices are responsible for the acquisition of PRYO
(job) places, the schools for the placement of students." (National
Labour Market Board of Sweden 1977, p. 16) In future years, PRYO
job experiences will be provided even for younger children in grades
one through six.

Vocational guidance through employment offices

The policy of close liaison between educational institutions
and employment offices has helped young workers become acquainted
with governmental guidance services that could be tapped later. A-
mong Swedish labor market strategists and guidance experts a great
deal of emphasis is placed on vocational orientation for the general
public. This is done through lectures to various groups and through
radio and television programs. Printed information can be found in
the press and in special publications that inform the public on newly developing trends in the labor market.

However, since Swedish employment philosophy emphasizes the
value of every individual as a person, the need for vocational
counseling on a one-to-one basis is recognized as an important process in the delivery of vocational guidance:

New entrants to the labour market are often uncertain of
their personal capabilities in relation to education and
working life. Special efforts are needed, e.g., on behalf
of pupils who have curtailed their schooling or whose academic merits are not sufficiently competitive.

The same uncertainty is often shared by re-entrants to
the labour market, e.g., housewives who want to go back
to work but whose qualifications, if they have any, are
out of date. Many of these women need detailed assistance with their occupational and educational choice...
(National Labout Market Board of Sweden 1977, p.13)

The standard sequence of employment counseling follows these
steps: (a) preliminary interviews that clarify personal data and
analyze strengths and limitations of the client; (b) information
on educational and occupational opportunities available for the
client in proportion to his or her interests and abilities; and
(c) additional helping processes that aid the client in career planning. These include psychological tests or consultations with other

institutions and agencies, particularly with regard to training or re-training opportunities, financial assistance, etc.

When needed, social agencies and medical facilities are used for referrals. Swedish guidance personnel work in close liaison with a network of institutes that specialize in occupational psychology. Most of the institutes are privately run and work under contract with public employment offices. Psychological testing is seen as an "auxiliary" service. Thus, aptitudinal test scores are not "accorded any decisive significance" by themselves but are taken into consideration only as one of many tools employed in the guidance process.

Group work is not widely used and is mostly restricted to information giving, to interpretation of data that are of interest to a number of individual clients, and to discussions of common concerns within a client population. (National Labour Market Board of Sweden 1977)

Guidance personnel in employment offices

Employment counselors in Sweden are recruited among people who themselves had been exposed to the world of work and had practical job experience. About 60% of the present personnel involved in vocational guidance have earned degrees at universities or colleges specializing in social studies. Many other counselors have done some college work but entered the job market prior to graduating and earning their degrees.

Employment office supervisors have been training their guidance personnel on the job. The first year of employment offers the novice counselor a variety of theoretical and practical learning experiences. Additional in-service training is provided for more experienced counselors at regular intervals and lasts usually one week at a time. (National Labour Market Board of Sweden 1977)

References

Faltheim, Mr. Guidance and counselling in secondary school as related to various school systems--Sweden. In Husén, T. (Ed.) <u>Differentiation and guidance in the comprehensive school</u>. Stockholm: Almqvist & Wiksell, 1959, pp. 153-161.

Fleisher, F. <u>The new Sweden.--The challenge of a disciplined democracy</u>. New York: McKay, 1967.

Husén, T. and Boalt, G. <u>Educational research and educational change</u>. New York: Wiley, 1967.

Mellden, A. L. School psychology in Sweden. In Catterall, C. D. (Ed.) <u>Psychology in the schools in international perspective</u>. Columbus, Ohio: International School Psychology Steering Committee, 1976, Vol I, 87-101.

Myrdal, A. <u>Nation and family: The Swedish experiment in democratic family and population policy</u>. Cambridge, Massachusetts: M.I.T. Press, 1968.

National Labour Market Board of Sweden. Vocational guidance in the labour market administration. <u>Bulletin--International Association for Educational and Vocational Guidance</u>, 1977, <u>31</u>, 9-21.

These publications are recommended for additional reading on the subjects of Swedish society and guidance.

13

UNITED KINGDOM

Catherine Avent and Audrey Newsome

Society and economy

The United Kingdom of England, Wales, Scotland and Northern
Ireland has a population of fifty-five million living in the second
most densely populated area in Europe. The four parts of the Kingdom
derive from historical factors and have certain pronounced differences in their educational systems and laws. Basically, the United
Kingdom is a democracy headed by a hereditary monarchy and generally
considered politically stable and socially comfortable. Economically,
it has been in decline by comparison with its major industrial competitors and considerable attention is being paid to this at the present
time because it was the first country to industrialise, some two
hundred years ago, and can still quote many examples of technological
innovation but has not been as successful as West Germany, Japan, and
the United States in capitalising upon these inventions in order to
produce manufactured goods cost-effectively. The importance of this
economic factor is that the land and sea surrounding the United
Kingdom can only provide food for approximately half the population,
so that it is necessary to import foodstuffs and raw materials for
industry, these imports being paid for by exports of manufactured
goods and the demonstrably successful financial institutions in
banking, insurance and brokerage associated with the City of London.
The United Kingdom was heavily involved in World Wars I and II, and
suffered considerable destruction of property and resources, many of
which have only slowly been rebuilt.

There are distinct differences in traditions between four
provinces of the United Kingdom. Many readers in other countries

are aware of the problems of the province of Ulster which is predominantly Protestant, having been settled from England 400 years ago, but with an increasing population of Roman Catholics whose sympathies are frequently with the Irish Free State. The Welsh have tenaciously preserved their own language which is entirely different from English (and cannot be understood by English people) and have in recent years become increasingly conscious of their own cultural traditions, although for legal and administrative purposes England and Wales have been one nation for centuries. Very few Scots speak Gaelic but a Scottish Nationalist movement has made rapid progress in the last twenty years, not unconnected with the presence of vast oil resources under the North Sea off the north coast of Scotland, thereby making possible a degree of economic independence which some nationalists hope to extend into political independence from England. At present, all four provinces elect Members of Parliament on a simple majority vote system, the constituencies being devised to provide a reasonable measure of equality of population. There are 625 Members of Parliament. The second chamber, the House of Lords, consists of hereditary peers who undertake to attend the House and take part in legislative activity, together with those men and women of distinction in all walks of life who have in recent years been elected to life membership of the House of Lords.

New social developments

A recent feature of UK society has been the immigration of some four million persons from those parts of the world which formed the British Empire, notably the Caribbean Islands, East and West Africa, and the Asian states of India, Pakistan, Bangladesh and Sri Lanka, together with a considerable number from Malaysia and Hong Kong. What was a relatively homogeneous society of white Christian northern Europeans has become demonstrably multi-ethnic, particularly in certain large centres of population where immigrants have tended to congregate.

Changes in life styles are apparent in the United Kingdom, as in most European countries. There is less respect for law and order and the old values associated with' property. Class distinctions are less prominent; the increasing liberation of women and their entry to practically all forms of paid employment has been paralleled by the ready availability of the contraceptive pill and abortion, as a result of which there is a marked decline in the population of children, with severe consequences for the teaching profession. The generation gap in ethos and attitudes makes for particular difficulties for older workers in the fields of education, health and counselling, in that they have to be conscious of changing attitudes on the part of adolescents and young adults towards their own future and the ways in which they plan their lives. In addition, the advances of the welfare state and a relatively generous provision of social security payments has much reduced the old concepts of competitive educational achievement which stimulated entry to occupations which provided economic security and social status. There is far less difference in the disposable income of professional people and shop-floor workers as a result of the eroding of differentials in pay structure and the harsh incidence of taxation. This also has notable consequences for education and guidance. The universal access to television and ready availability of convenience foods and household appliances has changed domestic patterns, but the United Kingdom does not have such a pronounced increase in numbers of people pursuing full-time education as can be seen in some other countries.

Elementary and secondary education

Education in the United Kingdom is compulsory from the age of five until sixteen. A recent drive to combat adult illiteracy might indicate a low level of general literacy, but the UK would generally be regarded as a country with total literacy, though many adults who left school at the minimum age have difficulty in coping with the demands of modern life. There are education authorities coinciding with the major local government boundaries, but there is no central control of the curriculum in British schools. Independent fee-paying schools are permitted and many of them have an international reputation for the academic quality of the education they provide. Only about five per cent of the population receive education in fee-paying schools but there is an interesting educational feature in the United Kingdom--the provision of schools which are wholly maintained out of public funds but which were established by trusts that are in many cases church-related. There are Roman Catholic schools, Church of England schools, and a few schools for Jewish and Free Church members. The significance of this is that parents can choose, if they live in an area where there are such schools, to have their children educated under the aegis of a particular religious denomination. In all schools, there is provision in the legislation by which public education is provided for the day to start with an assembly which is in varying degrees intended to have some religious significance. There is no system of saluting the flag or any other daily patriotic gesture. Religious instruction in county-maintained schools is normally undertaken according to a syllabus which has been agreed by representatives of religious denominations; despite the increasingly multicultural nature of the population it is still predominantly Christian.

Many areas provide nursery schools for children between the ages of three and five, but they are not obligatory. From five through ten, children pursue primary or elementary education, in many cases with a break after the first three years, and at eleven in England and Wales and twelve in Scotland, children proceed to secondary schools of varying titles, but not fully comprehensive in their educational provision. Such schools have academic and general tracks and, in many cases, a vocational or technical element introduced in the later years of the pupil's career at school.

There are no compulsory subjects, but most secondary school pupils study English, mathematics, science, humanities, aesthetics, practical subjects, and one or more foreign languages. French is normally the second language, but in schools with a strong academic tradition, there may well be classes studying German, Spanish, Russian, Latin and Greek, as well as French.

The Scottish system differs by being more broadly based and more comparable to that in an American high school, but in most cases an examination set by an authority external to the school is taken by two-thirds to three-quarters of the pupils at the age of sixteen. For the past two decades, there have been two separate examinations, the General Certificate of Education, which is taken at the age of sixteen at Ordinary Level and at the age of eighteen at Advanced Level, the latter providing the required qualification for entry to universities, polytechnics, and other forms of higher education. In Scotland, the Higher Certificate is taken at the age of seventeen and many Scottish students proceed to university a year younger than their English counterparts, but most undertake a four-year university course, rather than three, which is normal in England and Wales.

Schools which are maintained or aided by the education author-ities are required to provide 200 days of instruction in the academic year which runs from early September until mid-July, with breaks at Christmas and Easter and shorter breaks in the middle of each of the three terms. The semester system is not used and the three-term pattern is continued into higher education, with certain exceptions for students on co-operative programmes. British secondary schools vary in size from small schools of some 450 pupils to a small number of large schools of 2,000 pupils. The average is probably between 1,000 and 1,500 pupils. Traditionally, secondary schools have been single-sex, but increasingly boys' schools and girls' schools are combining into co-educational schools.

The statutory school-leaving age of sixteen means that all young people are faced with a mutually exclusive decision which has to be taken at that stage in their lives: whether to remain at school for the last two years, known as the sixth form; to transfer to a further education college for full-time education which could be parallel in content with that available in school, but could also be biased towards a particular occupation or industry; or to leave school and hope to find a job. For those that remain in high school until the age of eighteen, about one-third of the total, there will be choices between strictly academic programmes in which three-quarters of the instructional time will be devoted to the study of three, often closely-related, subjects, such as chemistry, physics, and mathematics, or English, French, and history; or there may be a two-year course designed to equip students for office work, including stenography and typing skills; or there may be programmes of general education, some of it of a remedial nature, if students are below the level of achievement of their peers. There is no system of promotion by grades, but only by age, so that within each class or group the students are likely to be of the same age, however much their attainments may vary. Most schools operate some form of setting or streaming by ability and attainments up to the age of fourteen, but mixed-ability teaching, as it is called, is widespread during the earlier years of secondary school courses.

University studies

Entry to university in the United Kingdom is competitive, in that it depends upon the achievement of required standards in certain subjects in the public examinations. It is not possible to buy admission to a university if it cannot be achieved by the entry examinations. A generous system of financial grants enables students to have a university education, if they qualify for it. Tuition is generally free and the tradition of residential university study away from home is widespread. Provisions are made for financial assistance to enable students to choose from any one of the university institutions, payment being made according to parental means. Fourteen per cent of the population currently have a university education.

University education is provided in fifty-one institutions, entry to which is conducted by a computerised mechanism, whereby the student can choose from five institutions and the selection of the students is entirely in the hands of the university or college faculty. Universities are private in the sense that they are not controlled by state or local education authorities, but a large proportion of their income is derived from Central Government funds and the financing of students, from public funds. In addition, there are thirty polytechnics which approximate the American state universities and offer degree level education, the degree being awarded by the Council for National Academic Awards and not by the individual polytechnic. A further group of institutions of higher education or colleges (mainly developed from institutions for the training of teachers) together with colleges of technology and commerce, art and agriculture, make up a total of some 500 institutions of tertiary education.

Many students in Britain are obliged to choose their careers and associated university courses at the age of sixteen when they choose the subjects to be taken in the last two years of secondary school. In order to be a dentist, it is necessary to major in sciences, for example, and there is no provision for those who have taken languages and humaniteis in school to take an engineering curriculum in a university. The degrees are to a greater extent vocational than in the United States. It is not common for an intending doctor to take a bachelor's degree in anything other than the pre-medical sciences, although it is not impossible to do so. Undergraduates study law, engineering, veterinary medicine, architecture, etc.

Guidance and counselling

The structure of the educational system, therefore, imposes a need for guidance and counselling at the stages at which students are faced with choices. If they are to qualify for entry to a profession, it will be necessary for them, in most cases, to have achieved a certain level in the public examination in certain subjects. The first choices are made when students are aged thirteen and have to decide which subjects to take in the two years of preparation for the public examination at the age of sixteen. There are twenty-two possible subjects and no student can normally take more than ten. Students are encouraged by those who advise them to take a broad range of subjects, including arts, sciences, humanities, and practical subjects. So educational guidance begins at that age, although there will have been informal guidance at earlier stages when pupils may have learning problems in certain areas of the curriculum. Educational guidance continues at each stage at which students are faced with a choice from various curricular options or have problems in achieving the standard they have set for themselves in a particular subject. Obviously, those students who have identified learning or personality problems will receive intensive help from the child guidance services, educational psychologists and counsellors, but all students have to make choices from the provision available within the school and most receive some guidance, even if only at a relatively informal level.

At the age of fifteen to sixteen, a formal system of vocational guidance operates, whereby students are helped individually to make the necessary educational decisions in the light of their vocational consequences. This is desirably, but not always, preceded by a two- or three-year programme of careers education embracing self-awareness, educational and occupational awareness, decision-making skills, and the necessary techniques for acquiring information on the possible next stages, and "marketing" themselves for it. Schools with well-developed careers education programmes will have several teachers sharing this responsibility under a department head, with the same status in the school as the head of a major subject area, such as languages or science. The students should have had the opportunity of taking interest inventories and aptitude tests, undertaken projects on the occupational structure of the area, perhaps been exposed to a series of films and television programmes, visits to colleges and places of employment, large-scale careers conventions and exhibitions. Other schools may pay only limited formal attention to vocational information and careers education, leaving this to the regular visits from officers of the careers service,

142

which is a branch of the local education authority administration and which operates a careers information and guidance service for all schools in the area, including, where required, placement introductions to employers and some follow-up supervision of young workers.

Counselling in the accepted American sense is still very limited in the United Kingdom. Some large schools have appointed trained counsellors who may first meet with groups of students at the age of thirteen or fourteen and arrange to be available for individual interviews at any stage thereafter. Counsellors as such are unknown in primary schools. There is a long tradition of what the British call "pastoral care" whereby teachers with a particular interest in student affairs may be asked to take responsibility for a group of as few as fifteen students or as many as 360 in a year group, or what is termed "house" which is an arrangement taken over in the day schools from boarding schools where pupils live in houses of 50 to 100 students. These teachers may have some disciplinary responsibilities and only a limited concept of counselling, though quite effective in dealing with the simpler day-to-day problems of relationships between students and their homes, their teachers, friends, etc.

The counselling profession

With the development of comprehensive schools in the last fifteen years, educational authorities have recognised the need for a more professional approach to students' problems in secondary schools and, as a result, the profession of school counsellor has been established. Only a minority of schools have been able to appoint a counsellor, since there are only a few one-year postgraduate training courses available for this area of specialisation. At the college and university level, it has been common for some fifty years for persons to be appointed to take account of students' health and welfare, including residential accommodation, and for careers and appointments services which first developed at the end of the 19th century in some of the older universities. To a great extent, these last were primarily job placement facilitators and it could be claimed that only in the last twenty years have universities made adequate provisions for the mental and physical health and welfare of students and for services to cope with their emotional and social needs.

School counsellors are usually highly regarded members of the school staff. They aim to be full-time counsellors, but in many schools have found themselves obliged to undertake some normal teaching duties and in other cases, to combine the job of counsellor with that of careers adviser. The facilities provided for them to do their job vary, but they now have their own professional association and they undertake to a considerable degree mutual help and in-service training to combat the isolation which pioneers in this profession had undoubtedly suffered.

143

There are now more opportunities for teachers to train as counsellors on a full-time professional basis by means of a post-graduate course than there are for careers teachers, many of whom have to be content with short in-service training courses of a week or less, part-time evening programmes and weekend or vacation courses offered by their own association or the Institute of Careers Officers.

Counsellors generally regard themselves as more concerned with individual counselling than with group work, although many undertake the latter and do so essentially in a non-directive way, aiming to assist students to cope with their problems and not proposing solutions for them. An intelligent, knowledgeable and caring approach based upon a deep understanding of the attitudes and circumstances of young people are regarded as paramount. A willingness to take the young persons' views on their future or problems at their face value, and not to make judgments, are regarded as vital, together with a recognition that the environment into which young people are going from the education system is changing rapidly. Some students' problems cannot be easily solved, but students can be helped to face their problems and to weigh alternative solutions. Similarly, students themselves choose appropriate courses of higher education or career, but they need help in deciding the effect that this will have on their total future life style.

There is much less reliance upon test procedures in the United Kingdom than in the United States, although tests are widely used by educational psychologists in dealing with problems of educational or personal maladjustment and in identifying needs for special educational provision on the part of students with learning difficulties or behaviour problems.

There are one-year full-time and equivalent part-time training courses for careers teachers and careers officers; counsellors in educational settings have a one-year postgraduate course and for educational psychologists the course frequently lasts two years. A psychology degree is required for educational psychologists, but not necessarily for careers teachers, counsellors, or student personnel workers in higher education. In addition, there are specific training opportunities outside the educational field in, for example, marriage guidance and mental health. The newly-established British Association of Counselling provides a meeting point for people engaged in counselling activities in varying settings which could be religious, medical, educational or those of social work.

Informal guidance and counselling

It is well known that much guidance and counselling takes place on an informal basis and that parents are, generally speaking, more influential than other adults on the destiny of young people. Youth organisations exist in large numbers, some of them church-related and some of them international, such as the Boy Scouts. Young people look to television and magazines for ideas and information, when considering their role in society, and it has to be recognised that, whatever formal system of educational and vocational guidance and personal counselling may be offered within a school or college, the most likely people to influence young adults are their friends and the teachers of their favourite subjects. The academically successful can frequently point to the teacher who first inspired them with a love of music or literature or biology or whatever the subject that they ultimately decided to major in for their higher education or to use as the basis for training for a particular occupation.

Conclusion

In the last twenty years, great strides have been made in the United Kingdom in the professional recognition of guidance and counselling as responsibilities of the education system. American professors were invited to start the first two counselling trainings in the universities of Keele and Reading and there is still much dependence upon American literature and research in this field. Some initial prejudices against counselling can be said to have virtually disappeared with the development of comprehensive secondary education, with the consequent wide range of choices and options and therefore a need for young people to have guidance in making educational decisions. Careers education hardly existed in the 1960's and by now it has merited full-time specialist training for teachers undertaking this function. Universities look to their careers and appointments services to provide far more than mere job knowledge for students. In many institutions, a multi-professional team has been established to help students establish a social, sexual, and occupational identity as self-directive, mature individuals.

Suggested readings

Avent, C. <u>Practical approaches to careers education</u>. Cambridge: CRAC, Hobsons Press, 1978.

Craft, M. and Lytton, H. <u>Guidance and counselling in British schools</u>. London: Edward Arnold, 1974.

Hughes, P. <u>Guidance and counselling in schools</u>. Oxford: Pergamon Press, 1971.

Jackson, R. <u>Careers guidance: Practice and problems</u>. London: Edward Arnold, 1973.

Kline, P. <u>The psychology of vocational guidance</u>. London: Batsford, 1976.

Law, W. and Watts, A. G. <u>Schools, careers, and community</u>. London: Church Information Office, 1978.

Newsome, A., Thorne, B. and Wyld, K. <u>Student counselling in practice</u>. London: University of London Press, 1975.

Proctor, B. <u>Counselling shop</u>. London: Andre Deutsch, 1978.

Vaugham, T. <u>Education and the aims of counselling</u>. Oxford: Blackwell, 1977.

Weir, D. and Nolan, F. <u>Glad to be out</u>. Edinborough: Scottish Council for Research in Education, 1977.

THE SOVIET UNION
AND COUNTRIES
OF THE SOCIALIST BLOC

After the collapse of the tsarist regime in Russia, the Union of Soviet Socialist Republics has emerged as champion of a new social-political program in government and economy. ' However, in the twenty years from the October Revolution in 1917 until World War II, the huge colossus extending from the Ukraine in the West to the shores of the Pacific in the East remained an enigma. Ideological fervor competed with pragmatism. The country underwent dramatic developments, a civil war, economic setbacks, many internal crises.

Then, in 1945, Germany surrendered to the Allies and the Soviet Union, having overcome its greatest challenge, rose to the rank of a world power. As soldiers of the Red Army stood on the shores of the Elbe River and occupied all Eastern and the major portion of Central Europe, a new geopolitical entity emerged. Originally defined as a sphere of Soviet influence, the large geographical area did eventually turn into a socialist bloc. In the West it is known as the Soviet Bloc and it consists of a number of countries with a Marxist form of government.

These "people's democracies" are bound together militarily through the Warsaw Pact and economically through the Council of Mutual Economic Assistance (CMEA). Czechoslovakia, the German Democratic Republic, Hungary, Poland, and Romania are the principal members. Yugoslavia which also has a socialist form of government is only marginally associated with CMEA action plans and generally follows an "independent road to socialism." Most of the nations are Slavic, although other national groups--Germans, Hungarians, Romanians, etc.--add variety to the ethnic structure. Culturally,

147

socially, and economically, the countries have diverse backgrounds, but more than three decades of Soviet influence have produced a common denominator, a degree of generic if superficial uniformity. Therefore, the present Section is not subdivided according to national boundaries but rather in terms of topical units.

While surveying guidance within Marxist-socialist society, the author paid particular attention to attitudes of socialist professionals who have molded the minds and the behavior of young people throughout the Soviet domain. All of them profess a strong ideological preference. They view themselves as "dedicated builders of communism." Their missionary zeal has been at times benevolent and persuasive, at other times, highly directive or manipulative. If élan and vigor can be found among socialist youth, they were attained through intense ideological shaping. If conflicts and philosophical skepticism are cropping up within socialist society, they have come about because Marxist guidance has failed to reach the people, particularly the young.

To penetrate the complex structure of life in socialist society, the author who is a native of Czechoslovakia and lived, for a time, himself within the socialist system, analyzed past and current guidelines issued for communist youth leaders and educators. These sources reveal the envisioned goals and the preferred methods of Marxist programs. The author also reviewed the stated outcomes of Marxist guidance efforts and compared them with his personal observations during several trips to East-Central Europe in recent years. For documentation which, in view of the rather unique character of Marxist guidance strategies, had to be detailed he used primary sources published in the Soviet Union and in other socialist countries of Eastern Europe.*)

---

*) Acknowledgements:

In the chapters comprising Section Five of this volume, several passages are quoted from the following publications covered by copyright:

Great Soviet Encyclopedia. (c) 1974 by Macmillan Educational Corporation. Reprinted with permission of Macmillan Educational Corporation.
Soviet Education, 1977, Volume 20, Number 2. (c) 1978 by M. E. Sharpe, Inc., Publisher. Reprinted with permission of M. E. Sharpe, Inc.
Education, Training, and Vocational Guidance in Socialist Republic of Yugoslavia. Copyright 1976 by Republic Self-Managerial Interest Association for Employment, Zagreb; and Yugoslav Federation of Vocational Guidance Associations, Belgrade. Reprinted with permission of both Institutions.

Chapter 14 describes life in socialist society. Societal dynamics and environmental influences that are taken for granted by people living there but are usually not fully understood by outsiders have been spelled out. From the social-political milieu crystallize ideological, educational, and vocational guidance policies. These are presented in Chapters 15 and 16 along with programs, methods, and achievements of socialist guidance.

The "upbringing of youth" is carried out by "societal institutions" and the Communist Party of each country has the final authority in planning and supervising all programs. One must remember that the Communist Parties operate in close liaison, and that the decisions of the Soviet Communist Party wield particular influence throughout the socialist bloc.

14

MARXIST-SOCIALIST SOCIETY

Victor J. Drapela

Russian peasants: From serfdom to revolution

There is no doubt that tsarist Russia was among the most backward countries of Europe prior to World War I. Her people were at
the mercy of a despotic government. The overwhelming majority, uneducated and superstitious peasants, lived in primitive hamlets,
seeking mutual protection against the harsh elements. The long
Russian winter brought life in the rural regions to a virtual
standstill. Without the most elementary public services, without
an adequate school system, cut off from communication with the outside world, the Russian "mushik" (small man) had little opportunity
for advancement.

The chief aid for survival was the inborn tendency among peasants to cling to each other. Group patterns were predominant in
village life. Most field work was done on a communal basis. Wor-
ship in the local Orthodox church was structured as a group process
with maximum participation by the congregation, even in the ritual
of public confession and spiritual rehabilitation of the sinner.
The ready acceptance of collectivist patterns under Marxist rule
was facilitated by the prerevolutionary life style of Russian peasants.

The state of virtual slavery may have bred apathy among the
masses, but in some individuals it sparked revolutionary ideas.
Uprisings by the "Decembrists" in 1825, by university students in
the 1880's, and by Saint Petersburg (now Leningrad) metal workers in

151

· 1905 under the leadership of an Orthodox priest, Father Gapon, have
set the stage for a major upheaval. People knew that they had nothing to lose. The military disasters and the economic failures in
World War I finally provided the spark that ignited the fuel of dis-
content. After the collapse of the tsarist regime and a brief administration by a middle-of-the-road government, Lenin and his com-
rades assumed power on November 7, 1917. The Union of the Soviet
Socialist Republics was born.

In March, 1918, the new regime signed a separate peace treaty
with the Central Powers (Germany, Austria-Hungary and allies) at
Brest-Litovsk. A few months later, a new Soviet Constitution was
adopted, and in March, 1919, the Communist International was founded.
In Lenin's view, the International was to work toward the destruction of capitalism and the establishment of proletarian dictatorship throughout the world.

As mentioned earlier, the beginnings of the Soviet system were
less than auspicious. Because of a civil war and of serious economic setbacks, the Soviet leadership temporarily retreated from its
doctrinaire Marxist policy. Along pragmatic lines, it supported an
intensive economic rehabilitation to consolidate its power. In January, 1924, Lenin died and the Party accepted Stalin as the undis-
puted ruler of the Soviet Union. From 1928 on, drastic industrialization and collectivization campaigns took place. Millions of
"kulaks" (small landowners) were removed from their farms. Next
came a series of purges among Party workers and military officers
(the Tukhachevsky affair) which greatly weakened the Soviet defen-
sive posture and led to disastrous defeats of the Red Army in the
first months of Hitler's military assault. However, the stubborn-
ness of the Soviet people and the savagery of the Russian climate
eventually broke the back of the Nazi intruders.

The brief summary which follows describes the first decades
of the Soviet state from the official communist perspective. It is
typical of such statements by its ideological emphasis, its optimistic tendency, and its boasting of Marxist-socialist accomplishments.

On October 25, 1917, a new era was opened in the history
of mankind, when the working class in Russia, led by the
Communist Party and Lenin, founded the first socialist
country in the world.

The young Soviet Republic was faced with the immensely
difficult task of building up, in an enemy-surrounded,
backward country, a society that was the dream cherished
through long centuries by all the oppressed and down-
trodden in the world: a society for which the fighters
of the Paris Commune in 1871 and the fighting squads of
workmen of Krasnaya Presnya in 1905 gave their lives;
which was scientifically substantiated and elaborated

by Marx, Engels, and Lenin, the great teachers and leaders of the proletariat.

The workers and peasants of Russia fought a three-year severe battle with the home counter-revolutionary and interventionist forces. The price of devastation and economic dislocation was paid for the hard-won victory. Few as they were, the factories and plants were locked in silence, the war-ravaged fields lay fallow, there was a scarcity of food, clothing and fuel.

Is it possible to begin building socialism in a ruined and pauperized country? The skeptics did not realize that the building of socialist society had already begun; that the foundation stone had been laid when the first decrees of the Soviet Government gave the people possession of the land and its mineral wealth, of the factories, plants, banks, and railways; that the abolition of private ownership of means of production was the greatest of all strides ever made towards the elimination of the exploitation of man by man...

The Soviet society's tomorrow is not just a dream. It is already assuming tangible form. Construction on a magnificent scale is under way on the infinite expanses of the Land of the Soviets, in its cities and towns, in the heart of its forests and steppes, and along the banks of its mighty rivers. The Soviet people, led by the Communist Party, are realizing Lenin's program of building a communist society. (U.S.S.R. today and tomorrow 1959, pp. 8-9)

East-Central Europe: A battlefield of nations

Significant differences exist between the historical background of the Soviet Union and the countries that comprise the Soviet Bloc. While the people of Russia had lived--first under the Tatar yoke and later under their own despotic rulers--in isolation from the rest of Europe, the nations of the present socialist bloc had been for generations exposed to various cultural experiences, and at times, suffered from overexposure to European power politics. These factors have to be taken into consideration when assessing the present cultural climate in the two geographical units. While the emergence of the U.S.S.R. attracted a fair amount of interest to the roots of Russian civilization, the kaleidoscopic history of Soviet Bloc countries was little known in other parts of the world.

East-Central Europe had been for centuries a crossroad and a battlefield between East and West. One of the first confrontations was linked, paradoxically, with the Christianization of the Slavic tribes. Since German missionaries, along with the message of faith, brought the threat of military conquest from the West, many Slavic rulers turned to the Byzantine Emperor both for religious doctrine and political protection. Eastern culture had made at first significant inroads, but its weight gradually diminished. Western influences predominated later, especially under the rule of the Hapsburgs. At one time or another, most of the countries of the Soviet Bloc were provinces of the Austro-Hungarian Empire.

The Hapsburgs provided political stability and relative security in East-Central Europe for many generations. True, they were opposed to national self-rule in the provinces, but their repressive policies were tempered by the lighthearted "Gemütlichkeit" and the characteristic inefficiency of the Austrian bureaucracy.

Nationalist movements in the area suffered probably more from other quarters. The rule of the Russian tsars in eastern Poland made the Austrian government look, by comparison, quite benevolent. Western Poles were exposed to intensive and systematic Germanization by Prussia. The Balkan peoples were for generations harassed by the Turks who, at times, ruled the entire area. This produced an atmosphere of violence which was as characteristic of the land as its scenic grandeur. For the Serbians, guerrilla warfare virtually became a way of life. Even after the establishment of the more lenient Hapsburg rule there was no lasting pacification of the Balkans.

East-European people have acquired some common characteristics forged by the need for survival. While foreign armies marched in and out of the area, the majority of people felt like pawns rather than participants in the events. This feeling of detachment was intensified by the prevalent social system of the time. The administration of local affairs was in the hands of feudal overlords who combined a degree of paternalism with petty capriciousness. In some cases they served as a protective buffer against the absolutist policies of central governments, but at times they exploited their subjects without mercy.

Under these conditions, the common people have developed a refined art of coming to terms with the powers that be, while outwitting the system and scoring a few points. The emotional outgrowth of this constant struggle has been a mixture of overt melancholoy and guarded gregariousness. In musical terms, a typical example of this emotional profile is the Hungarian "czardas." Beginning with halting, woeful themes, it grows to a crescendo of joy and ends in a brief intoxicating triumph. Even serious composers of the area have been attracted to the folk music, and many of them looked for inspiration to the tunes of village fiddlers and mountain shepherds. The people in East-Central Europe like to sing and dance.

Much of what has been said about music applies as well to other folk art. It is low-key, but an unmistakable feeling of joy permeates the hand-painted decorations in rural homes and the hand-sown festive costumes of the peasants which vary in design from one district to another.

As feudal structures weakened and the emerging power of the burghers made itself felt, a more formal cultural life with nationalist overtones sprung up in the cities. It is well to remember that urban and country life styles in East-Central Europe have greatly differed, not only in terms of work, housing, and communication facilities, but even more in the degree of cultural sophistication--and cynicism. While many cultural leaders of East-European nations were born in tiny hamlets, they were stimulated to greatness in the urban atmosphere to which they naturally gravitated.

At the end of World War I, President Wilson became convinced that an equitable settlement of "East-European affairs" was a prerequisite for lasting peace. In 1918 he proclaimed the fundamental principle of self-determination for small European nations. Thus, by the end of World War I the stage was set for the foundation of new sovereign states where in the past the Austrian Eagle ruled.

Each of the small independent nations had its own internal problems, but their eventual downfall was brought about by their mutual mistrust and hostility. The issues at stake were old territorial claims and conflicts over minority enclaves. In the Hapsburg Empire the various nations mingled to such a degree that it was impossible to draw their new boundaries without prejudice to some historical or ethnographic consideration.

In most of these newly created countries, an important social force was the middle class, with typical petit-bourgeois values and strong nationalist tendencies. The ranks of this socio-economic stratum were augmented by members of the erstwhile nobility, many of whom had lost their wealth along with their titles, and by bright, ambitious climbers from the lower socio-economic class who succeeded in business or in government service. A significant phenomenon was the political involvement of members of the academe (e.g., Masaryk). Family traditions and local customs were universally considered of significant value. While the middle class of Czechoslovakia embraced Western democratic and liberal traditions, Poland and Hungary kept many of the remnants of the feudal era, particularly a commanding posture of the church in public life.

The status quo was not to last long. In the 1930's the Nazi movement usurped power in Germany and spread terror throughout Europe. In 1938 Austria was occupied by German troops and in the fall of that year England and France signed the Munich agreement, allowing Hitler to dismember Czechoslovakia. The spectacle of two major Western powers sacrificing their own ally to Nazi dictatorship had a devastating impact on East-European morale. Less than a year later the Continent was at war.

The Nazi conquest of the area in World War II inflicted serious damage on all socio-economic strata. The middle class suffered the most, particularly in Poland, whose intelligentsia was exposed to a program of systematic decimation by the Gestapo. This explains the weakness and apathy of non-communist parties at the time when Soviet power entered the region.

The Soviet social order

When in 1917 Lenin took over the government of Russia, he proclaimed a socialist state based on the teachings of Marx and Engels which he adapted to Russian conditions. A proletarian revolution leading to a classless society was set in motion. Under the leadership of the Communist Party, all means of production were seized and transferred from private to public ownership. A new ideology was formulated and its acceptance made mandatory: the "scientific philosophy of life" known as "dialectic materialism," logically linked with atheism. In the view of socialist writers, dialectic materialism is the most advanced system of thought, since it blends theory and practice: "Deducing theory from practice, it subordinates the former to the interests of the revolutionary transformation of the world." (Great Soviet Encyclopedia 1974, Vol. 8, 188)

From the very beginning, strict discipline was imposed within Communist Party ranks and was also applied to the general population.

> Monolithic unity and iron discipline of the ruling Communist Party are crucial conditions for the Communist Party to exercise its leadership role in the dictatorship of the proletariat. These conditions played a decisive role in ensuring the victory of socialism in the USSR, and they continue to play an important role as the entire people's state struggles for the construction of communist society. Iron party discipline does not exclude but assumes criticism and self-criticism within the party, class consciousness, and voluntary submission. Party discipline is indissolubly linked with the ideological unity of the proletarian party. (Great Soviet Encyclopedia 1974, Vol. 8, 290)

Respect for authority has always been strong in the minds of Russian peasants, and there is no trace of democratic traditions in the Russian national heritage. Thus, the authoritarian framework of the new, socialist state was quite acceptable to most people who considered it an improvement over the tsarist regime. True, only 53% of the U.S.S.R. population are Russians, but Soviet people in general are fascinated by assertive, unbending leaders both at the national and at the regional and local levels. Although they may personally feel threatened by such leaders, Soviet people consider them to be symbols of their country's power, and they are proud of them. Smith (1976) met several individuals throughout the Soviet Union who

156

spoke proudly of Stalin ("We knew where we stood with him") many years after he had been publicly declared guilty of abuse of power and of cruelty.

Another feature of the socialist order, enforced collectivism, has also found acceptance among the Soviet population. As was earlier mentioned, communal living patterns were an established tradition among Russian peasants. Communal decision making was institutionalized during tsarist times in the village "mir." The "mir" was a formal gathering of heads of families who collectively decided matters affecting the village. Hingley (1977) points out that, owing to some special genius of the Russian psyche, the rulings made by the village "mir" were invariably unanimous. The principle of majority and minority as they exist side by side in a pluralistic structure is foreign to the Russian mind.

Under communist rule, collectives have been mandated as the basic structural units in all settings: educational, occupational, and recreational. Their emphasis was on work output and on ideological integration. In the view of Makarenko (1951), a collective is

in its ideal form an organization of mutual responsibility, self-governing and self-determining, within which the individual first learns the meaning of moral principles and in their observance finds the security he needs to mature. (p. 64)

In a more recent definition by Hyhlík (1964), the collective is perceived as an organized, supervised, coordinated, and evaluated group. It is specifically charged with promoting socialist ideology and revolutionary zeal. General characteristics of a collective are: (a) shared goals; (b) organization; (c) discipline; and (d) in some cases, symbols, e. g., badges.

To maintain the momentum of ideological indoctrination, the Communist Party kept training cadres of bright propagandists who would have the skills of presenting the official doctrine in an interesting way. Kalinin (1950) formulated the issue as follows:

You can teach Marxism-Leninism in two ways: in the creative way, and, I would say, in the abstract way.

What is the difference between the creative way, which is a particularly difficult one, and the abstract way? To teach in the abstract way means to take a book, mark off "from here to here," make your pupils read it and then to question them about what they have read. This method yields the least results, both as regards teaching and as regards propaganda and agitation. The more abstract the propagandist or agitator is, the farther his thoughts are from concrete things, the less will be the impression he creates . . .

157

Present time teachers of the fundamentals of Marxism-
Leninism are faced with the enormous task of improving
teaching methods, of mastering the creative method of
teaching this highly attractive subject. (pp. 465-466)

Some realities of Soviet life

While the propagandists were doing their job, real life in the
U.S.S.R. did not always follow their script. In theory, Soviet society is classless, but a closer examination of its structure will
uncover a different picture: a privileged elite; a comfortable
managerial middle class; a large stratum of skilled and semiskilled
industrial workers; and the mass of peasants who live in rather
primitive conditions throughout the vast countryside.

It has been stated earlier that urban and rural life styles
differed in Eastern Europe. In the Soviet Union, the contrasts are
huge. Popov (1977) admits that unsatisfactory conditions exist in
agricultural settings where over 70% of workers are involved in
dull, heavy manual labor. Consequently, many peasant youth are unwilling to stay in the countryside. They make every effort at securing some job in the city in order to get a permit to live there.
At present, only 3.55% of agroindustrial workers are below the age
of 30. The rest are older, almost exclusively peasants (98.9%) of
whom more than half are women. In most cases (78%), their education is limited to primary grades plus ten days or less of on-the-
job training. (Prudnik 1978) A shortage of qualified agricultural
personnel is a major problem of Soviet economy.

An important social institution in the Soviet Union is the
family. Parents are reminded that, along with their children,
they form a basic unit of socialist society and that a loving concern for children in the spirit of collectivism is their primary
duty. (Makarenko 1954) Love for children is certainly a typical
characteristic of Soviet parents. Both mothers and fathers spend
much time with their children and freely express their affection.
(Bronfenbrenner 1970)

Children get additional attention from their grandparents,
many of whom live in as part of the family. There are other, practical reasons for this widely spread custom; for instance, family
shopping. In Soviet society, it requires a great deal of time and
effort to shop for food and clothes. If the grandparents are willing to go to various stores during working hours and stand in line
for hard-to-get items, their sons and daughters gain more leisure
time, when they return home from work.

Most Soviet women are gainfully employed. This does in no
way preclude their having a family, since the Soviet state provides free nursery and kindergarten facilities. Belova (1972)
studied preferences of Soviet women with regard to family size.

158

The concept of zero population growth (childless marriages) was rejected outright. Thirty-three percent of the women favored having
two children and 45% opted for three children. In regard to ethical standards of family life, a gradual "liberation from religious
influences" has taken place. Younger people are reported to be
less religious than older ones. The higher the educational level
of the family, the more pronounced its atheistic attitude. Religious families are said to be generally less educated and socially
isolated. (Vasil'evskaia 1975)

While religious life may be vanishing in the Soviet Union,
the strong need for emotional release, linked in past generations
with Orthodox liturgy, has remained. Like most Slavs, the Russians
enjoy singing and dancing. But their feelings have greater inten-
sity: their melancholy is profound and their joy borders on aban-
don; the strength of their marching songs is overwhelming.

Most Soviet people harbor very deep emotions about World War
II, the "Great Patriotic War," as it is officially known. It was
during that critical period of history that a new Soviet value perspective emerged: a blend of Marxist socialism and of Russian nationalism. Even the minorities (about 47% of the population)
shared the feelings of pride. Because of the War, ethnic patri-
otism and Marxist politics have become compatible. The Soviets
perceive themselves as a "great, heroic people" to carry out a
revolutionary mission.

The old xenophobic attitude toward outsiders who may corrupt
the natural health of the Russian character is reinforced by
ideological arguments of the Communist Party. Western, pluralistic
patterns are considered chaotic, and multi-party democracies are
seen as tools of the rich.

It is this reasoning by which the average Soviet citizen jus-
tifies the need for securing a large geographical area on the western frontier where fraternal socialist countries would serve as
guarantors of the homeland's safety.

The emergence of the socialist bloc

The Great Soviet Encyclopedia (1974) links the victory of the
Red Army over Nazi Germany with the emergence of socialist states
in East-Central Europe--a claim that is undoubtedly correct:

In a bloody and destructive war the Soviet Union de-
fended the socialist achievements, and the most advanced
social system protected its freedom and independence.
"The victory of the Soviet people in the war confirmed
that there are no forces in the world that can stop
the forward development of the socialist society"
(Program CPSU, 1969, page 17) . . .

A major consequence of the Soviet victory and of the
mighty revolutionary movement that developed at the end
of the war and in the first few postwar years was the
emergence of the world socialist system. The peoples
of Albania, Bulgaria, Hungary, the German Democratic
Republic, the Democratic Republic of Vietnam, China,
the Korean People's Democratic Republic, Poland
Rumania, Czechoslovakia, and Yugoslavia embarked on
the path of socialism. (Vol. 4, 349)

In the first years after the communist takeover, many people
of the region lived in a state of consternation. Even communist
activists who aided the Soviet expansion were frequently incarcer-
ated and some even executed (e. g., Slánský, the first secretary of
the Czechoslovak Communist Party). An explicit moral code of
Marxist-socialist behavior was promulgated, and individuals were
required to attend sessions of ideological indoctrination. During
such sessions and on other occasions, they were asked to engage in
ideological self-criticism and in "comradely" criticism of each
other, both public and covert. Many non-communist intellectuals
sought survival by volunteering for menial jobs in which they were
not exposed to the threat of ideological purges.

After Khrushchev publicly denounced Stalinism as a deviation
from true Marxism, many of the harshest features of the police state
were repealed. However, the people were not quick to forget the
years of terror and their response was generally cautious. As
years passed in relative tranquility, gradually a new mood emerged
among large segments of the population, particularly among young
intellectuals, artists, and writers (paradoxically, the chief consumers of Marxist ethical guidance). It was a shift from ideological orthodoxy toward independent thinking and value judgements.
During the Dubček-led experiment of "socialism with a human face,"
a surprisingly large number of people openly defied the status quo.
They opted for personal integrity at the expense of corporate
approval--a phenomenon that Brzezinski (1970) considers symptomatic
of the late 1960's on a global scale.

The Soviet leadership took a dim view of such ideological ex-
perimentation and suppressed it by military power. Its rationale
is offered below:

In the postwar years, as a result of a numerical growth
in the membership of Communist parties, some of whose
young members did not have sufficient theoretical training, the necessity of continued struggle for greater
unity within the Communist parties on a Marxist-Leninist
basis became evident. Right-wing revisionist elements
revived, with particularly grave consequences in Hungary
in 1956 and in Czechoslovakia in 1968. The struggle
against revisionists, who have sought--under the guise

160

of "free discussion"--to deceptively disseminate their anti-Marxist views in the Communist Party, remains one of the most pressing tasks facing the world communist movement. (Great Soviet Encyclopedia 1974, Vol. 9, 377)

It is well to remember that most "revisionists" were dedicated Marxists. They wanted to make socialism viable among people with a democratic tradition, whose values were primarily shaped by Western influences. Although of the same Slavic origin, the people of Czechoslovakia and the Russians were caught in a profound cultural conflict during the events of the late 1960's.

After the forcible liquidation of the Prague experiment in August, 1968, many Soviet Bloc citizens have become more cautious again. They seem to display two separate sets of behaviors which are quite unrelated--an overt attitude of cooperation with the system and a private pursuit of personal need fulfillment. The socialist system is accepted as an inevitable fact of life to be reckoned with, and laudatory remarks about the Party are made (and understood) by the average citizen as formal clichés assuring social respectability. However, the overriding concerns of most people are not ideological but practical: an adequate degree of privacy and freedom within the system, and material gain. Coveted symbols of privacy and mobility are a weekend cottage, a car or motorcycle, which additionally are manifestations of personal success.

Many middle class values have been retained by people living in the Marxist-socialist milieu. A degree of nationalism and a marked interest in pre-socialist cultural achievements of the ethnic region are linked with family traditions and social customs usually associated with the "bourgeois" past, e. g., kissing the hand of a woman. A survey conducted in an urban setting by Růžičková (1968) on teenagers' marriage ideals and expectations identified a number of traditional middle-class traits that seemed to be highly desired by the youngsters, e. g., physical beauty and housekeeping skills in the brides-to-be and moderation plus industry in the future grooms. The typical middle-class tendency of foregoing immediate gratification and saving money for deferred goals has been a virtual necessity in socialist society where credit buying is not prevalent. Idealistic Marxist writers have repeatedly complained about "socialist petty bourgeois types" whose ideological fervor is superficial and who exploit the system for private gain.(Jodl, 1964)

Philosophically, large segments of the Soviet Bloc population, especially the intelligentsia, drifted into apathy and skepticism which is, at times, openly admitted. (Kosík 1968) Since religious beliefs have been weakened among young people (with the exception of Poland), ethical nihilism has become widespread. As a result, some young people have adopted superficial attitudes,

161

while others search for a new meaning in life that may link their involvement in the "here and now" with a feeling of transcendence. It is well to remember that the capacity for uniting material concerns with a dose of mysticism has been typical of East-European peoples for centuries. (Chalupný 1973)

Although all East-European governments exert some political pressure on their population, the degrees vary significantly from one country to another. The reactions of individual nations are by no means identical. Some tried to change the system and, with the exception of Yugoslavia, had failed. Others do not argue with the system but quietly chart their own affairs with relative freedom from ideological premises which they accept in theory.

References

Belova, V. A. Family size and public opinion. Soviet Review, 1972, 13, 380-399.

Bronfenbrenner, U. Two worlds of childhood: US and USSR. New York: Russell Sage Foundation, 1970.

Brzezinski, Z. Between two ages. New York: Viking, 1970.

Chalupný, E. Realismus a mystika v české národní povaze. Svědectví, 1973, 12, 269-288.

Great Soviet Encyclopedia. (Translation of the 3rd Edition.) New York: Macmillan, 1974.

Hingley, R. The Russian mind. New York: Scribner's Sons, 1977.

Hyhlík, F. Duševní hygiena a vztahy lidí v kolektivu. In Doležal, J. (Ed.) Hygiena duševního života. Prague: Orbis, 1964.

Jodl, M. Mládež, hodnoty, politika. Literární noviny, 1964, 13 (41), 1, 3.

Kalinin, M. J. On communist education. Moscow: Foreign Language Publishing House, 1950.

Kosík, K. Naše nynější krise. Literární listy, 1968, 1 (11), 8.

Makarenko, A. S. A book for parents. Moscow: Foreign Language Publishing House, 1954.

Makarenko, A. S. The road to life. Moscow: Foreign Language Publishing House, 1951.

Popov, V. Increasing productivity of labor in agriculture. Soviet Review, 1977, 18 (2), 57-80.

Prudnik, I. V. Agroindustrial workers. Soviet Review, 1978, 18 (4), 31-65.

Růžičková, V. K otázce výchovy k rodičovství na základních devítiletých školách. Československá psychologie, 1968, 12, 360-369.

Smith, H. The Russians. New York: Quandrangle-New York Times, 1976.

U.S.S.R. today and tomorrow. Moscow: Foreign Language Publishing House, 1959.

Vasil'evskaia, N. S. A preliminary concrete sociological study of

attitudes toward religion in the contemporary family. <u>Soviet</u>
<u>Review</u>, 1975, <u>16</u>, 59-81.

15

GUIDANCE AS IDEOLOGICAL FORMATION

Victor J. Drapela

Traditionally, East-European school systems followed the dou-
ble-track model typical of all European education: college geared
preparatory schools for the elite and a basic literacy training for
the majority. While a degree of discrimination against lower socio-
economic classes existed virtually in all countries, the tsarist system made social discrimination a central theme of its educational
policy. Only two or three percent of youth were admitted to secondary schools, and special warnings were issued against admitting
to higher education children of coachmen, lackeys, cooks, and wash-
erwomen. At the end of World War I, Russia's illiteracy rate was
estimated at 75%.

The new Soviet regime took immediate measures to raise the educational standards of the population and got an enthusiastic response. Even ideological neutrals were thrilled by the challenge
and willingly cooperated with the Bolsheviks. On August 2, 1918,
Lenin, in a dramatic proclamation, opened educational opportunities to all Soviet people, children and adult. The policy of free
education for all has been so successful over the years that by now,
the Soviet Union has become a land of avid readers.

The Soviet school

In Lenin's view, literacy was not a goal in itself but a condition for communicating Marxist ideas to the masses. Thus, literacy was of vital importance for the success of the revolution. It

was the task of the new school to mold a dedicated socialist generation. Lenin declared the aim of the Soviet educational system to
be identical with the class struggle against the bourgeoisie. Schools
would not be allowed to remain politically neutral. They would have
to develop a distinct class character. (Arseniev 1962)

The conditions prevalent in the country after the revolution
required two types of schools operating side by side. Children and
adolescents attended primary and secondary schools with curricula
of seven (later eight) and three years, respectively, six days a
week. Adults had a chance to attend special classes offered mostly in the evening, after work. This policy of providing educational opportunities to Soviet people throughout their entire life span
has been retained to the present. Emphasis has been placed on technical and science curricula, particularly in vocational schools,
which frequently operate in factory settings. Advanced and specialized secondary schools, called "tekhnicums," are a very desirable
alternative for those students who are unable to get admitted to
universities which are fairly selective.

Ideological guidance: The concept

Leninist educational theory insists on the unity of curriculum
and ideological propaganda. The socialist world view must permeate
all academic subjects. The entire reality one lives in is to be interpreted by teachers and students in proper philosophical perspective. Students are continually exposed to the tenets of socialist
theory and are motivated, particularly by reinforcements within the
collective, to implement them in their lives. It is this highly directive adjustment process which Makarenko (1954) calls "socialist
character formation" that helps Soviet people, from their earliest
developmental stages on, come to terms with socialist society. The
Russians call this process "vospitanie," a term usually translated
as "upbringing." In reality, it is the very substance of all Marxist guidance.

The Great Soviet Encyclopedia (1974) gives the following interpretation:

Upbringing (is) the purposeful, systematic shaping of a
personality in preparation for active participation in
public, productive, and cultural life. In this sense
upbringing takes place as a process of organized, joint
activity of the family and school, preschool and extra-
curricular institutions, children's and youth organizations, and society as a whole. (Vol. 5, 406)

The fundamental principles of bringing up children and
young people in a socialist society are the connection
of upbringing with life and the practical work of build-

166

ing communism; upbringing in labor and in groups; the development of initiative and independent activity through tactful pedagogical guidance; the consistency, continuity, and systematic quality of upbringing; and consideration of the age traits of the students and an individualized approach to them. Various methods that correspond to these principles have been utilized. Methods of persuasion and exercises in the organizing of varied activities for the students have a particularly large place in the process of upbringing. Encouragement and punishment are other pedagogical methods. (Vol.5, 407)

Adults can also be subject to educational influences. The upbringing of adults takes place during their productive and social life and as a result of educational work conducted by Party, state, and social organizations and cultural and educational institutions (libraries, clubs, palaces and houses of culture, museums, lecture halls, and so on).

At the present stage in the construction of communism in the USSR, what is most important in ideological work is the "upbringing of all working people in the spirit of a high level of ideology and devotion to communism, a communist attitude toward labor and the public economy, a complete overcoming of vestiges of bourgeois views and morals, and a universal, harmonious development of the personality; and the creation of a truly rich spiritual culture" (Program of the CPSU, 1969, p.117). (Vol. 5, 408)

This type of ideological guidance has been entrusted to the teachers and other educators from preschool to adult levels. This seems logical in view of the required linkage between curriculum and ideological indoctrination.

Ideological guidance: The process

It was Lenin's wish that the dialectic method be used in all educational activities, particularly, since individuals readily responded to societal shaping. In their quest for growth, young people had to experience a series of attitudinal and behavioral confrontations what would stimulate their dynamic thrust forward, in the direction of socially appropriate behavioral goals.

According to this method, the point of departure is the "thesis" expressing an established value. It is challenged by the "antithesis." The resolution of the ensuing conflict leads to "synthesis." A new conceptual reality is born only out of conflict. Thus, the ideological guidance process follows a well-defined route:

(a) The educator and the class collective provide powerful motivation for the individual to improve for the sake of society and to be eager to change.

(b) The young person is made to realize his or her lack of knowledge and of appropriate behavior patterns. This is considered a necessary point of departure for all human growth.

(c) The ensuing state is one of contradiction between "thesis" (lack of appropriate behavior in the individual) and "antithesis" (demands of society for appropriate behavior). The individual who has been ideologically motivated in terms of "socialist ideal and duty" is now ready to interiorize the contradiction and to experience a creative conflict. This state is painful but challenging. Individuals try to solve the conflict according to specific conditions which exist within them.

(d) As a result of the conflict resolution, a change of behavior takes place. This is the final stage of the dialectic process-- "the synthesis." In some cases previous behavior patterns must be summarily rejected, e.g., when moving from antisocial to socially acceptable behavior. At other times, past behavior is retained in a modified version. Such gradual "dialectic becoming" is an ongoing process which is cyclically repeated. (Zehner 1961; Čáp 1963)

Obviously, this type of ideological guidance was not meant to produce homeostatic fulfillment of the individual. On the contrary, heterostatic challenges were considered an important condition for growth. Because of the "simplicity" of this method, Marxist educators felt that everyone could learn and improve socially as long as he or she had proper social motivation. It has been inferred that lack of progress was either caused by physiological factors or by ideological resistance. (Doležal 1958)

Personal need fulfillment has been consistently downplayed by Marxist ideologists, many of whom identify it with the "decadent self-indulgence of capitalist countries." Most needs, considered quite legitimate by counseling psychology in the West, are perceived as "whims of individualist types." Socialist persons fulfill their needs best by promoting the goals of classless society which then nourishes all of its members. (Doležal 1964)

Membership in socialist society is portrayed as an honor to be deserved rather than a situation to be born into. The Rogerian concept of "unconditional positive regard" for any person, no matter what his or her attitude, is considered absurd. To become mature members of socialist society, young people have to acquire a high degree of self-discipline, self-denial, and heroism. In Makarenko's (1954) view, heroism naturally emerges from the masses of Soviet people. If need be, the heroic acts of past generations will be repeated by Soviet youth in the future.

Socialist society claims to provide a high degree of freedom for young people. In the language of the Communist Manifesto, "the free development of everyone is a condition for the free development of all." This socialist freedom is contrasted with "unhealthy autonomy" claimed by people in capitalist countries. Sukhomlinskii (1961) interprets socialist freedom as a liberation from selfish cravings for material goods. There are other descriptions, some using a heavy dose of symbolism. However, most socialist authors seem to accept the following definition of freedom: A spontaneous, disciplined willingness to embrace societal guidance that provides benefits for all.

Collectivism and work ethics

Socialist ideological guidance cannot be fully implemented apart from collective life experiences. Two characteristics set off socialist youth collectives from youth groups as they exist in the Western world: mandatory membership and uniform ideological orientation. Class collectives in educational institutions have their goals plainly spelled out by their leaders, the teachers, according to current educational policies formulated by the Party. A definite goal hierarchy seems to emerge from the collectivist structure: Highest are the goals of socialist society; next in line, the goals of the collective; last are the goals of individual members who are to prove their ethical worth by subordinating their personal interests to the goals of society. (Koláříková 1962) Postponing or foregoing gratification in favor of societal needs is called by some Marxist educators the art of "delayed perspectives." (Čáp 1962)

Traditionally, the leadership in collectives has been directive. A core of ideological activists would form a supportive nucleus around a politically dedicated leader and help generate dynamics needed for behavior modification of less committed members. Two types of relationships among members are differentiated: "functional," i.e., objective and goal-oriented; and "personal-selective," i.e., satifying the personal needs of individuals. In the traditional Marxist view, the relative value of any collective is assessed by the nature of prevalent relationships among its members: they should be "comradely," but above all, "functional."

Marxist educators frequently point to the valuable guidance function of well-run collectives: a group can be steered more effectively than an individual, and group dynamics, in turn, have a powerful molding influence on the individual who has no choice but come to terms with the group consensus. (Matoušek and Růžička 1965)

A clear linkage exists between the collectivist life style and socialist work ethics. Marxist theory considers the two elements complementing each other and as such indispensable in the process of socialist character formation. The social value of a person is

169

determined by the quality of work he or she performs and even more by the person's work attitudes. Marxist labor theory has been anxious to remove the barrier between manual and intellectual work. It has also emphasized the need for the worker to willingly accept a job that may not be to his or her liking but that is needed by society. The worker should think with joy of the people who will reap benefit from the work performed. It is this vicarious satisfaction that promotes the ultimate need fulfillment in the socialist worker who feels driven by inner necessity to transcend egotistical desires. (Kolaříková 1962)

Ideological guidance in the socialist bloc

Since the late 1940's, when Marxist socialism got firmly established in East-Central Europe, all educational systems of the area have undergone a major revision. A virtual uniformity of curricula has been achieved. Education is free and compulsory up to the age of 14 (or 15). The comprehensive curriculum extends typically over 12 years of which 8 to 10 years are spent in the "basic" school and the rest in college prep or vocational schools. Universities, some of them venerable institutions, are rather selective. While in the past, ability of candidates was the primary prerequisite for admission, present applicants need to document their ideological commitment in addition to proven scholastic achievement.

A new organizational pattern of coordinated educational programs has been created by communist task forces of the various countries. Working in close liaison among themselves and with Soviet advisors, they formulated and enforced a unitary policy of ideological training based on the Soviet model. (Kienitz 1962)

Students were exposed to a massive campaign of reeducation about existing social systems. The basic theme repeated in many variations was the contrast between capitalism and socialism. By its very nature, capitalism was said to be pathogenic, producing egotism and greed in individuals, and thus splitting society from within. Conversely, socialism was portrayed as health-producing and uplifting, the ideal society to live in, well suited to the needs of youth, the wave of the future. (Doležal 1964) In socialist society, young people had a chance to fully develop their personalities by acquiring "noble character traits" typical of members of classless society. These traits were numerous and they were spelled out in detail. Typically, they divided into four categories:(a) ideological and ethical traits; (b) work-related traits, (c) social traits; and (d) self-attitudinal traits. (Rosina et al. 1963)

Since ongoing ideological indocrination became the focal point of all school work, the teachers—many of them typical middle class persons—had to be reeducated first. Professional literature of the 1950's published for educators was almost exclusively political propaganda. The ranks of teachers were searched for undesirable elements who resisted the new political trend. Since the process took place during the Stalinist era, the degree of intimidation and coercion was such that the morale of educators greatly suffered.

Educational psychology was especially singled out as undesirable. To understand this, we need to backtrack to the early years of the Bolshevik educational system in the U.S.S.R. Through the influence of Pavlov's research, a professional cadre was given the responsibility to offer psychological services to Soviet school children. The term "pedology" was used for this branch of applied psychology in educational settings. However, after a moderately successful period of work, pedologists were attacked on ideological grounds. They were criticized for using psychological tests and for accepting the "two-factor theory" which emphasized the social heredity and background as influencing children's behavior. (Bauer 1959) In 1936, the Central Committee of the Soviet Communist Party issued a decree on "pedological perversions" which amounted to an immediate ban of such activities. Psychological services in industry were stopped also.

In the socialist bloc, strong attacks against psychology were launched by the government-supervised media in the 1950's. Even some psychologists, to save themselves, joined in the criticism of past professional work. Bureš (1965) describes this period in vivid terms as a time when no one believed that psychology had anything to offer to the building of socialist society.

This period of intimidation was quite counterproductive to all attempted educational efforts, and paradoxically, weakened even the ideological indoctrination which it was to promote. While most workers in education and in the helping professions were caught in a dilemma of either jumping on the bandwagon of the new trend or getting fired, the young people of East-Central Europe who had some idea of democratic processes were generally unimpressed and some became outright skeptical. This was certainly the case among the liberal-minded Czechs.

In other East-European countries, traditional family values continued exerting considerable influence on the mentality of young people and blunted the efforts of ideological shaping. In Poland, the thrust was primarily religious in the Catholic tradition with strong anti-Russian sentiments. In Hungary, it was the fiery pride of Magyar nationalism. In Yugoslavia, where Soviet policies were openly defied, ethnic customs of the various regions assumed new importance in the federate government structure, with ensuing tensions among population groups.

After Stalin had died and his image had been publicly downgraded, the cruel atmosphere in the socialist bloc gradually relaxed. However, the damage inflicted on the educational process in general, and on ideological commitments of the younger generation in particular, was evident. The upheavals of the 1950's and the 1960's were not spearheaded by disgruntled middle-aged bourgeois survivors of the past. Rather they were led by young intellectuals who had been exposed to the counterproductive practices of rigid ideological guidance.

Nevertheless, the airing of ideological issues had some positive results for socialism. People in East-Central Europe were attracted to the social services and potential benefits that the new system had to offer--certainly an improvement over the past bureaucracies. This explains why even most dissenters and human rights advocates in the Soviet Bloc seem to opt for the retention of socialism in a modified form.

References

Arseniev, A. M. Über die Grundzüge der sozialistischen und kommunistischen Erziehung. In Kienitz, W. (Ed.) Das Schulwesen sozialistischer Länder in Europa. Berlin: Volk & Wissen, 1962.

Bauer, R. A. The new man in Soviet psychology. Cambridge: Harvard University Press, 1959.

Bureš, Z. Dvacet let československé psychologie práce. Československá psychologie, 1965, 9, 429-440.

Čáp, J. Psychologické základy vyučování a výchovy. In Tardy, V. et al. Psychologie pro učitelské obory. Prague: Státní pedagogické nakladatelství, 1962.

Čáp, J. Pedagogická psychologie. Prague: Státní pedagogické nakladatelství, 1963.

Doležal, J. K problému povahové uzavřenosti v žákovském kolektivu. Pedagogika, 1958, 8, 185-209.

Doležal, J. (Ed.) Hygiena duševního života. Prague: Orbis, 1964.

Great Soviet Encyclopedia. (Translation of the 3rd Edition.) New York: Macmillan, 1974.

Kienitz, W. (Ed.) Das Schulwesen sozialistischer Länder in Europa. Berlin: Volk & Wissen, 1962.

Koláříková, L. Struktura osobnosti. Sborník prací Filosofické fakulty Brněnské university. 1962, B-9, 65-80.

Makarenko, A. S. A book for parents. Moscow: Foreign Language Publishing House, 1954.

Matoušek, O. & Růžička, J. Psychologie práce. Prague: Nakladatelství politické literatury, 1965.

Rosina, J. et al. Obecná psychologie. Prague: Státní pedagické nakladatelství, 1963.

Sukhomlinskii, V. A. Výchova komunistického vztahu k práci a k společenskému vlastnictví. Pedagogika, 1961, 11, 10-30.

Zehner, K. Úloha pedagogické psychologie při přestavbě školy. Československá psychologie, 1961, 5, 119-125.

16

AN EMERGING SERVICE MODEL OF GUIDANCE

Victor J. Drapela

In the dichotomy of product- versus service-oriented activities, guidance clearly fits the service model. It deals with people, helping them in their quest for a contented and productive life in society. In this context, an important issue emerges: What is the basic commitment of guidance? Does guidance primarily serve the needs of a particular society by shaping individual members' behavior, or does it serve society in an indirect way, by concentrating on the growth of individuals who are essential components of all social groups?

True, Marxist theory does not admit the validity of such a distinction for its classless society where societal goals are expected to coincide with the need fulfillment of individuals. But in practice, the scale of priorities eventually tips one way or another. Certainly the type of Marxist ideological guidance, described in the previous Chapter, was clearly committed to socialist society. The needs of individuals were given only marginal consideration.

This leads to a basic question: Is a humanistic model of guidance, concerned primarily with the enhancement of individuals, acceptable in the Marxist-socialist system? Theoretically, the answer is yes. Marx, the revolutionary philosopher, considered himself to be a humanist. His favored dictum, "Nothing human is alien to me," is frequently quoted in socialist literature.

The present Chapter will offer information on current trends

175

in the Soviet Union and in the socialist bloc that will help readers form their own opinions as to the actual emergence of a humanistic, service-oriented guidance model in Marxist society.

THE SOVIET UNION

Even at present, societal needs are officially the exclusive
priority of Soviet guidance efforts. This traditional Bolshevik commitment is particularly evident from the constant references in educational literature to sources from the revolutionary era, some
fifty years ago. It is undoubtedly this high degree of ideological
dogmatism combined with centralized management of educational activities that cause the current problems in vocational and personal-
social guidance which are admitted by Soviet authors themselves.

Youth organizations

A comprehensive youth club program organized by the Soviet state
in its early years and virtually unchanged to this day approximates
somewhat the concept of guidance as a service to individuals. It
was designed to indoctrinate the young club members in Marxist ideology, but also to provide cultural enrichment, thus stimulating the
creativity of individual members. There are three officially sponsored organizations to serve youth from eight years on through early
adulthood. Children from eight to eleven years are eligible to belong to the Little Octobrists. The Young Pioneer Organization
serves youth from ten to fifteen years of age. The Komsomol counts
young people between the ages of fourteen and twenty-eight years as
its members. Membership is not compulsory, but there is a strong
social pressure to join.

Lenin's wife, N.K.Krupskaya, was personally involved in the organization and the early developmental stages of the Young Pioneer
organization. Here are some of her suggestions which are still frequently repeated today:

The Young Pioneer organization should see to it that
their members have every opportunity to share one another's experiences. That does not mean that they should
be "entertained," that they should have special shows
and matinees arranged for them. The thing is not to entertain them, but to make their organization's activities
lively and emotional...

The second factor making for unity is close friendship,
knowledge of how each lives and studies, and mutual assistance. The one who knows more should help the backward in his homework, the one who eats well should share
his food with the one who does not, the one who has not
got to do any household chores should help the one who

has. There should be well-organized comradely, mutual aid within the Young Pioneer organization.

The third factor is collective studies, reading excursions, wall newspapers, diaries, etc., etc. Here it is especially important not to divide children into active Young Pioneers who do everything, and are therefore overburdened,and passive who are not allowed to do anything...

And lastly, social work and application of the knowledge and habits acquired through collective work for the good of all. The question of choosing social work. The voluntary and conscious character of this choice, collective decisions, collective planning, correct appraisal of capability and capacity. (Krupskaya 1957, 120-121)

The Young Pioneer groups work closely with schools. In fact a certain scholastic achievement level is required for a child's good standing in the Pioneer organization. Educational hobbies, artistry, and mechanical skills are fostered along with revolutionary consciousness. Prominent figures of the Marxist movement serve as models of behavior.

The Young Pioneer organization is a step higher than the Little Octobrists. However, the principles of educational guidance are very similar in both organizations. They are to prepare youth for the Komsomol—the social and political "novitiate" for potential Communist Party members. The Komsomol uses the so called Lenin Lessons (based on actual episodes from Lenin's life) for educational experiences of its members. Young people who are effective Komsomol members, i.e., bright, docile, and resourceful, are in line for responsible positions in Soviet public life.

If they qualify at all, Komsomol members stand a better chance of being admitted to institutes of higher education. And since in theory, societal status in the U.S.S.R. is not linked to the prestige of one occupation over another, a promising Komsomol member who is not suitable for university training may qualify for a responsible public position by virtue of technical skills and ideological dedication. This explains why Marxist indoctrination is very intense at the level of Komsomol training. It would be redundant to list here the envisioned goals of this training. They are identical with the ideological guidance objectives discussed in the previous Chapter. The Great Soviet Encyclopedia (1974) spells them out in detail. (Volume 5, page 239)

Chistiakova (1975) reports that Komsomol groups provide ongoing vocational orientation for their members at special evening sessions. Career aspirations of youth and economic needs are discussed. Qualified spokespersons from industrial plants report on opportuni-

177

ties for employment in local industry and explain training requirements for career advancement in various fields. Komsomol groups are
also keeping in close touch with youth employment commissions of the
region. Placing a dependable Komsomol person in a responsible position of a workers' collective is considered an aid to appropriate
ideological labor motivation of the entire group.

The Soviet concept of vocational guidance

The vocational orientation projects in Komsomol groups are informal and unsystematic which is fairly typical of all vocational
guidance in the U.S.S.R. Although an official decree was published
in 1969 "On the vocational guidance of youth," no vocational guidance network has been organized in the years that followed. Kotliar
(1974) complains that a large percentage of young people make their
career choices without professional assistance, influenced by random circumstances.

Most people entering the world of work have no information on
the nature of their prospective jobs. Ottenberg (1978) reports that
only 4% of 20,000 interviewed young workers in Leningrad, Sverdlovsk,
and Khabarovsk gave an affirmative answer when asked whether they had
any prior knowledge about the nature of the job they were to be given.
He feels that an "encyclopedia of occupations" needs to be published
in the Soviet Union as a guide to youth making vocational choices.

There are no specially trained professionals identified by official Soviet sources as "guidance counselors." Those mentioned as
being involved in vocational guidance are teachers (Krevnevich
1973),Pioneer "mentors" (Smirnov 1972), Komsomol leaders (Chistiakova 1975), and factory foremen (Litviniak 1976). No guidance or
counseling skills are required of these persons by educational or
employment authorities. Some of the teachers in charge of vocational guidance have received a brief training course of twenty to
thirty-six hours on proper methods of offering occupational information. (Eichberg 1975)

These conditions will not seem surprising, once we realize that
vocational guidance in the Soviet Union is totally devoid of counseling activities. In fact, it is not more than a general orientation
on current manpower needs along with appeals to the graduating students to fill the quotas. Soviet authors emphasize these points:

(1) Teachers are to promote labor ethics and get students involved in work brigades during their vacation time, e.g., through
school forestry programs, landscaping certain city areas, or working in state enterprises, to impress upon them the satisfaction of
working with one's hands. (Ivanov 1976)

(2) Teachers are to observe evident abilities of students,

their apparent liking for a particular job, and their vocational interests in general. Each student's behavior should be purposively shaped with due concern for the developing personality and taking into consideration the needs of national economy for specific personnel. (Krevnevich 1973)

(3) The present top priority is motivating young people for blue collar occupations, since of the seven million new workers that will be required every year in the 1970's, five million will have to enter blue collar careers. (Krevnevich 1973)

(4) There are graduating students who do not sufficiently appreciate manual work and have a leaning toward work "with a humanistic direction." Some of them avoid socially productive labor for a period of time. Special attention has to be given to such individuals and they need to be placed in productive jobs. (Kochemasov 1977)

How do "unideological" career expectations develop among Soviet youth? The answer may lie in the fact that parents have generally a greater influence on their children's career planning than do the teachers. And oblivious of Marxist theory about the equality of all occupations, parents may try to push their children into more prestigious occupations that require college training. The teenagers readily accept this career orientation and dream about becoming scientists, educators, or medical doctors. However, at graduation time from the secondary school, they find themselves channelled into blue collar occupations.

Although the concept of vocational guidance is now frequently used in Soviet literature, it should be clear that it has its own, peculiar meaning. Occupational information is offered, but the career choice is not left to the person entering the world of work. Rather the career decision is made with the young worker according to societal needs by those who represent socialist society.

Personal-social guidance, lack of counseling

The absence of counseling that is evident in vocational guidance is equally apparent in the process of "character formation" of Soviet youth. In theory, the socialist environment itself, by the power of its ethical principles, forms noble personality traits in its young members, and collectives are the societal tools for helping socialist youth overcome all personal problems. Thus, individual counseling would seem counterproductive, since it would conceal the problems from the collective where they should be aired and resolved.

Undoubtedly, this collectivist approach to resolving personal problems has had some success among Soviet people. But there are indications that today, additional assistance on a more individual basis is needed in the Soviet educational system.

In August, 1974, a socio-educational study was published, in four installments, in the official paper of the Komsomol organization, Komsomolskaia pravda, which gives it a special significance. The author, Valerii Agranovskii, is a Soviet journalist who presents the case history of a fictitious youthful offender, Andrei Malakhov, arrested at the age of sixteen for armed robbery. The author explains the structure of his study thus: "My intention is simple: together with the reader, I shall follow our thief through his life, touching all the high points of his criminal destiny." (Agranovskii 1977, 15)

The author rejects the prevalent explanation of criminal behavior as a remnant of bourgeois attitudes:

> To explain the delinquent behavior of today's youth solely in terms of their past experience and the influence of the (pre-1917) bourgeois social environment, while disregarding the fact that not only these young people but their fathers and mothers were born under the Soviet regime, is no longer simply wrong, it is totally inadmissible. (Agranovskii 1977, 12)

He also questions the interpretation of delinquent behavior as an outgrowth of social deprivation. Andrei's parents are graduates of a higher technical institute, both working and well paid. But in spite of social respectability, the family climate has been impersonal. The boy had little chance to develop a close relationship with his father who was rather rigid and almost unconcerned about his son's problems. Andrei's teachers were proper, very loyal to their school. But they had no rapport with the boy and reacted to his misbehavior by endless lectures:

> Andrei spit on the floor? A talk. He stole a button? A talk. Did he think they were being unfair? A talk. Even after he began to "show contrariness and refused to talk"--that, too, is written in the daybook, though who can fail to sympathize with Andrei if he complained about so many of these talks! Evdokiia Fedorovna, with a pertinacity to be envied, wrote, "We had a talk about the need to listen diligently to what adults, and especially teachers, say"...
>
> Andrei listened submissively to Evdokiia Fedorovna and occasionally even nodded his assent, so as not to destroy the illusion that sometimes the wise and true words of the teacher were really reaching him. (Agranovskii 1977, 76)

The author notes that the most evident void in Andrei's upbring-

ing--perhaps the most crucial void as well--was the lack of warmth
and personal concern on the part of significant adults in his life.
The feeling dimension in Andrei's personality development was almost totally neglected. The boy had little opportunity to develop
a positive self-concept, a sense of his own worth as a person.

In an effort to generalize his observations, Agranovskii (1977)
quotes the Soviet psychologist, B. Anan'ev, who contends that "The
problem of achieving an optimal blend of feeling and intellect is
one of the most timely problems of Soviet schools." (p. 65) Instead of an exclusively collectivist education, Agranovskii (1977)
proposes a blend of collectivism and individualism, since collectivist education alone adapts children to society "at the expense
of leveling individuality." (p. 45)

It seems that Agranovskii (1977) has voiced concerns that are
shared by a number of educators in the Soviet Union. Ticktin (1977)
considers it "no accident" that the story was published in the Komsomol'skaia pravda:

> The Scientific Research Institute of General Problems
> of Upbringing, attached to the USSR Academy of Pedagog-
> ical Sciences, staged a discussion of Agranovskii's tale
> about Andrei Malakhov. Most of the participants, who
> were specialists in social education, shared Agranovskii's
> views and welcomed publication of his work; they also
> added several points that were a logical extension of
> the story. (Ticktin 1977, 9)

The article and the ensuing discussion conducted by Soviet experts have come up with a number of significant findings:

(1) The Malakhov case is no exaggeration nor is it an isolated case. There are plenty of Malakhovs who are clever enough to
keep their associal attitudes without openly violating the law.

(2) Youth in Soviet schools needs attention and assistance
not only at the cognitive level but also at the affective level.
Such an assistance should be offered both in groups and individually.

(3) There is a need to promote attitudinal and functional
changes among Soviet teaching personnel. The present authoritarian
image should be deemphasized in favor of an empathetic, supportive
role, with a focus on the developmental needs of youth.

These observations certainly point in the direction of a humanistic, service-oriented guidance model that would gradually
make use of personal counseling.

CZECHOSLOVAKIA, HUNGARY, POLAND

In the late 1950's, after the demise of Stalinism, a gradual development of applied psychological services took place in East-Central Europe. However, the ranks of psychologists have shrunk because of the long moratorium on professional training imposed by war and in the period of discrimination that followed during the "cult of personality." For instance, the Psychological Institute at the Comenius University in Bratislava that was established in 1958 had only five qualified professionals on its staff (today it has fifty). Furthermore, the accusations made against "pedology" in the Soviet Union two decades earlier still lingered in the minds of the remaining professionals.

A new blueprint

However, even in this climate, sporatic voices were raised in favor of systematic professional activities in the guidance field. An example was the outspoken essay of Bárta (1962) published by the Faculty of Philosophy at the University of Brno. It analyzed un-founded,mistaken opinions about guidance and counseling which were summarized as six prevalent myths: Psychological counseling is not needed because (a) deviant behavior will automatically disappear in communist society; (b) teachers have enough training to provide guid-ance; (c) psychology has no professional field of its own; (d) the ultimate solution lies in offering psychological information to the masses; (e) present-day psychologists can be likened to Soviet pedol-ogists who had been discredited in the past; (f) psychological coun-seling should operate outside of educational settings.

The author then made recommendations about the scope of guid-ance (educational, vocational, behavioral) and about the structure of such services within the socialist system. The first level was to be in-school guidance administered by counselors who would re-ceive a basic professional training. The second level was perceived as a network of guidance centers for referral purposes in more seri-ous cases. The third level was to be a system of clinical services available in central locations and staffed with fully trained psy-chologists. In retrospect, it seems that Bárta (1962) spoke for a large number of his colleagues who in the following years were able to implement many of his suggestions.

Emerging guidance services

In the mid 1960's it became clear that the rigidly ideological model of Marxist guidance was ineffective, and in some areas of East-Central Europe, even counterproductive. When in August, 1968, I in-terviewed officials in the Education Ministry in Prague, I sensed a great deal of frustration, bewilderment, and indecisiveness there.

182

The representatives of the educational system provided little factual information about developments in the schools. They spoke about "certain errors of the past" which they hoped to correct, but they mentioned no concrete operational policies.

It is significant that the crisis of credibility of the Soviet Bloc establishment (1967-70) roughly coincided with the reorganization of the guidance system in East-Central Europe. New Party and government directives for the use of guidance as a service for young people rather than mere indoctrination were issued during that period (e.g., in 1967 for Czechoslovakia; in 1968 for Poland). It took, of course, several years to implement them, even in the more progressive districts from which we have reports. (Svoboda 1976)

The present delivery of guidance services in the three countries follows this basic pattern: Many schools have counselors or teachers who received at least rudimentary training in pupil personnel services and who serve as coordinators of guidance (mostly vocational) in their respective schools and as liaison persons with guidance centers outside the school system. (Zalecki 1976) Regional and district guidance centers are staffed with professionally trained workers in the field of psychology, pedagogy, social work, and special education, with medical services available when needed. (Svoboda 1976) These centers are assisting the schools by providing consultations for teachers and parents, as well as appraisal and counseling services for students. Their function is both preventative and remedial. They work especially with retarded children, maladjusted children, or those having disabilities of any kind.

Guidance personnel

At first, classroom teachers were encouraged to volunteer for a brief in-service training experience that would qualify them for guidance work. Gericke (1975) speaks of locally organized workshops instructing teachers in practical guidance skills. This temporary arrangement was later systemized and expanded. Professional training curricula for counseling psychologists have been initiated in all three countries. They usually consist of two years of graduate study with emphasis on psychology, sociology, economics, and manpower management. Some psychology departments, unfortunately, see counselor training as only marginally related to their professional mission, although employability projections of psychologists in guidance are very favorable. (Svoboda 1976)

While reviewing Soviet Bloc literature, one has a distinct feeling that there is a lack of qualified personnel in the guidance field, especially at the mid-level of expertise. Better educated counselors and psychologists are often unwilling to relocate to provincial towns, although they are offered incentives such as above average apartments in new buildings.

At present, school counselors are generally limited to secon-

dary schools and the upper grades of the "basic" school. The main
reason may be their primary function in the vocational area although
in some places they are involved in problem-centered and developmental counseling also. While some fifteen years ago all guidance was
done on the basis of collective interaction, individual counseling
has now been introduced as a valid guidance approach in socialist
society.

A new guidance rationale

The recent developments in Soviet Bloc guidance are not only
at the organizational level, but also at the philosophical level.
At first glance, not much has changed in the overall picture. A
lot of doctrinaire rhetoric has remained in journal editorials and
in the required quota of ideological treatises within professional
literature. (e.g., Linhart 1973; Hodovský 1973) However, in the
same volumes one finds professionally significant work including unbiased attitudinal surveys. Comparative studies of behavior patterns
in socialist society and capitalist society are conducted without
the political prejudices of earlier years. (e.g., Kotásková 1972)
This does not mean that the present generation of guidance leaders
is less committed to Marxist socialism. It indicates a higher degree of professional sophistication by which a person can reconcile
a strong ideological preference with respect for alternative solutions elsewhere.

A pronounced psychological emphasis and respect for the individual typify the new guidance rationale. Individual behavior is
not perceived as a phenomenon to be manipulated but rather as a legitimate expression of a person who, in spite of the unitary ideology and social system, has unique traits that have to be recognized.
Koščo, Rapoš, and Rybárová (1974) identify the current guidance
approach as counseling psychology, a service to individuals throughout their entire life cycle. It is a many-sided helping commitment
which deals with important life situations, developmental episodes,
vocational or personal crises, readjustment to new circumstances,
and the process of aging and retirement.

Counselors and psychologists must pay particular attention to
the sequence of developmental processes in a person's life-span
("biodromálna psychológia"). They need to be well versed in the
following areas: (a) developmental personality problems of individuals; (b) balance of self-development and social interest; (c) helping individuals actively participate in the development of society
while maintaining their preferred life styles; (d) counseling individuals on making use of societal services; (e) counseling individuals on solving essential problems of life; (f) promoting individuals' self-enhancement and full personal satisfaction in the social
context. This involves coming to terms with the needs of oneself
and the requirements of a healthy development of society. (Koščo
1971, 1975)

The erstwhile insistence on practicing group guidance only within collectives has been undergoing changes also, even though the original terminology is being retained. Novák (1974) reports on remedial group work with boys who had severe behavioral problems. The group process he describes is very similar to the non-directive, group-centered model. The main emphasis is placed upon gaining self-awareness and developing a more positive self-concept.

Legislative policies for guidance services

A representative sample of legislative policies for guidance services in schools is the formal "Instruction of the Czech Ministry of Education" (covering the western part of Czechoslovakia) published in 1972. I am presenting here a summary:

(1) Educational guidance provides services to youth up to nineteen years of age, to schools, and social institutions caring for children. It helps solve problems of psychological and social development, with due respect for the individual's uniqueness. It pays particular attention to preventing and treating defects in the educational, psychological, and social areas.

(2) Guidance counselors are to be employed in all schools from the first to the ninth grade, in special education schools, and in the gymnasia (secondary, college prep schools). Certified counselors are to have a two year graduate training in guidance or hold certification in psychology, along with political and professional qualifications. They are to help classroom teachers promote a healthy social development and education of youth in cooperation with parents or legal guardians; help youth by professional means deal with personal, educational, and vocational problems; and consult with parents, agencies, the Pioneer and other youth organizations, the school physician, as well as with centers for youth guidance outside the school system. The principal is not to assign responsibilities to the counselor that are not consistent with the counseling function.

(3) The district guidance center is a back-up agency for the guidance counselors in schools. It offers consultation services; deals with learning and behavioral problems of youth; intervenes when parents exert an unfavorable influence on the child; evaluates youth for the school, for the courts, the police, and the district health organizations, if requested; sets up specialized instructional units, if needed; identifies gifted and retarded children; offers information on vocational and educational opportunities for youth in the district and advises counselors who are to guide and modify interests of youth; does vocational counseling for youth, particularly those whose vocational choice could not be settled in the school; and offers professional recommendations to the organs that are charged with occupational placement of youth. The district guidance center also directs the work of educational counselors, provides additional training for them, and informs the public.

(4) The regional guidance center supports and supervises all professional activities in the districts under its jurisdiction. It provides diagnostic and remedial services in cases that need special attention. It also does long-range planning of programs, particularly in vocational guidance, for the region. (Ministry of Education of the Czech Socialist Republic 1976)

Vocational guidance: An interface

Current professional thinking on vocational guidance in the three socialist countries stresses the linkage of healthy personality development of the individual during elementary school years and his/her readiness for vocational choice and job entry. Koščo (1976) advocates a full integration of educational and vocational guidance functions. Vocational maturity is defined by Rókusfalvy (1976) in terms of: (a) motivation (established interests, life planning, etc.); (b) behavioral self-directiveness (intellectual development, self-awareness, philosophy of life, etc.); and (c) performance prerequisites (adequate health, sense perception, and motor functions; will power; character traits related to learning and work; social adaptability). Vocational maturity also involves the ability of recognizing one's strengths and limitations, and of coordinating one's own striving with the demands of society and national economy. Any young person who has achieved such a level of maturity is able to make a free and independent vocational decision. (Zalecki 1976)

The vocational counseling process is to be carried out with concern for the individual and with recognition of the current priorities of national economy. These priorities are not in the form of informational data to be merely considered; they are spelled out as specific quotas for "worker recruitment and distribution" which are set by central planning authorities. They specify exact numbers of new workers required at various skill levels in the different sectors of economy. A telling example is the article in a professional guidance journal, Výchovný poradce, written by a manpower specialist from the Ministry of Labor in Prague. It deals with the "placement of fifteen year old youth during 1975" and reports on the degree of meeting the established quotas. Here is the summary of the grand totals in three basic categories:

Category	Quota	Reality	Quota met in %
Higher schooling	40,300 pers.	41,181 pers.	102.2
Apprenticeships	75,120 pers.	74,802 pers.	99.6
Unskilled labor	7,000 pers.	5,999 pers.	85.7

The author states that all fifteen year olds of both sexes were "apportioned and placed with no remainder." (Blažek 1976)

This ambiguous situation in vocational guidance is symptomatic of the entire guidance scene. It is a subtle, ongoing interface of the impersonal, bureaucratic dictum and of the humanistic commitment stated by the guidance profession. To what degree the commitment is carried out depends on individual counselors.

186

YUGOSLAVIA

The report on the current state of guidance in Yugoslavia
has been compiled from two authoritative sources。 One is a mono-
graph authored by Branka Brančić, Head of Vocational Guidance in the
Republic of Serbia; the other, a booklet edited by Dragan Tarbuk,
President of the Yugoslav Federation of Vocational Guidance Associations. Although committed to Marxist ideology, Yugoslav guidance in
many ways differs from the typical socialist model. A telling example:
Yugoslavs have been free to seek employment in Western Europe.

Development of guidance

Brančić (1970) explains:

In its initial phase, vocational guidance in Yugoslavia
developed within the framework of the employment service
which, in light of rapid economic development, directly
encountered problems connected with changes in the economic structure, manpower supply and demand, and with the
coordination of individual ablilities and job requirements。
The everyday practice of the employment service made it
evident that the employment process must take into consideration all factors which provide successful employment. It was for this reason that the employment service
accepted vocational guidance as an activity which greatly
contributes to the resolution of the cited problems。。。

Today, vocational guidance in Yugoslavia is recognized as
an activity primarily directed to and concentrated on the
individual, to solve his vocational problem in accordance
with his personal needs, inclinations, and abilities while
taking into consideration the needs and opportunities of
the society, to aid the individual in his self-actualiza-
tion。 As the vocational problem is faced by persons in
the course of schooling or new employment applicants, as
well as by persons already employed but who--primarily
due to changes in production technology and the structure
of the economy--must make a new choice of profession, un-
dergo retraining and adjustment, vocational guidance has
been recognized as an activity which unfolds throughout
the whole, active human lifetime. It has been accepted
as a uniform system whose professional work should be
carried out in the school, in the employment office, and
in the enterprise, and which assumes the acceptance of
uniform conceptions and constant cooperation from organizational, methodological, and operational aspects。。。

The focal point of developing vocational guidance in the
field of education in Yugoslavia is primarily directed

187

toward the elementary school and the gymnasium...

Efforts are made here to aid the pupils in attaining vocational maturity, to be ready to make realistic decisions in connection with occupational choice, and to prepare them for finding the best possible solutions for
eventual vocational problems. In contacts with parents,
the development of their viewpoints on the occupational
choice of the children is influenced, and occupational
information is offered to them. (pp. 2,3)

Principles of guidance

The recipient of vocational guidance is perceived as a person
to be aided rather than manipulated. Brančić (1970) presents a number of principles adopted by the Yugoslav guidance profession:

(1) Vocational guidance as a complex social and professional activity is directed toward the optimal development of an individual and the realization of his potentially strong points. It contributes to higher work efficiency and satisfaction on the part of employed persons
and to their more complete participation in self-managerial socialist relations through the labor process.

(2) Man's individual freedom, as the highest principle
of every humanism, must be present in occupational and
employment choice.

(3) Individuals have the right to professional assistance in occupational and employment choice, and this assistance is free of charge.

(4) Timely discovery of talented individuals and their
best possible guidance to those professions where their
contributions will be the greatest also represents one
of the more significant objectives of vocational guidance.

(5) Vocational guidance is neither terminated nor exhausted with the choice of vocational education or employment. Following the individual through the course
of vocational training and professional activity, his adjustment and stabilization in employment, and his improvement within the framework of his occupation represents another important feature. . . (p. 5)

Employment policy

Tarbuk (1976) offers information on the employment policy in the country:

> The right to work, the freedom to choose an occupation
> and employment, the right to material welfare during tem-
> porary unemployment, and satisfying the demands of the
> associated labor for manpower represent the basis upon
> which the national conception of employment is formed
> and developed...
>
> The social-political basis of the employment may be found
> in the documents of:
> the League of Yugoslav Communists;
> the Yugoslav Socialist People's Union;
> the Confederation of Yugoslav Trade Unions and pertinent
> organizations in the socialist republics and autonomous
> regions; and
> the Yugoslav National Assembly and the assemblies of the
> socialist republics and autonomous regions.
>
> The self-management of employment affairs is realized by
> and in self-managerial interest associations for employ-
> ment founded by associated labor. The associations are
> coordinators of employment activities in communes, auton-
> omous regions and republics throughout the country.
> They are composed of delegations of the basic organiza-
> tions of associated labor and the representatives of trade
> unions. Influence on the formation and implementation of
> employment policy is exerted through these employment as-
> sociations, which have their own elected assemblies.
> (pp. 24,25)

When explaining the structure of self-management in labor affairs, Dragan Tarbuk, during one of my visits in Yugoslavia, emphasized that the system rested on input from the rank and file rather
than on administrative edicts of a detached, centralized bureaucracy. In this way, programs affecting labor management are to originate at the same level where they would eventually be implemented.
The higher levels of Self-Managerial Association activities are
linked with mediation, clarification, and coordination of programs
proposed by the rank and file. I have attemped to explain this process by a diagram adapted from Tarbuk (1976, 26) with some additions
of my own to make it clearer for non-Yugoslav readers. See Figure
5. 1.

Guidance personnel

Brančić (1970) gives specific information on the staffing of
self-managerial employment offices throughout the country:

> The personnel staffs of local employment offices, which are

189

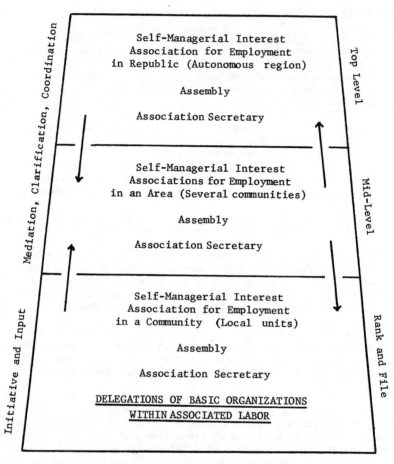

Figure 5.1. Diagram of the organizational structure used by
Self-Managerial Interest Associations for Employment.

engaged in occupational information and vocational counseling (as well as selection for the needs of enterprises) are composed of various profiles. Occupational
information in the employment office is implemented and
organized by a pedagog, although this also implies the
work of other experts who are in contact with the applicants. In addition to providing individual and group information (in some cases, only its organization) and par-
ticipating in the process of counseling, the pedagog
closely cooperates with the school in order to advance
this work as well as to organize school referral of pupils
for counseling.

In the process of individual vocational counseling, a
team of employment office personnel, composed of different professional profiles, contributes (each from his own
specialized field of activity) to the obtainment of an
overall picture of the applicant and to a prognosis of
his educational and work results. As the estimation of
the vocational potentials of an individual is based on
psychological and medical examinations, as well as investigations on the socio-economic and cultural background
of the individual, the composition of the counseling team
is usually as follows: psychologist; physician; pedagog;
and social worker. (pp. 7,8)

Vocational interviews

Tarbuk (1976) explains the typical sequence of vocational guidance processes through a series of interviews. The first is the
contact interview which provides information on the candidate for
a job and establishes a mutual understanding between the potential
worker and the employing institution. Next is the exploratory interview that follows the complete medical and psychological evaluation. It sums up the candidate's potential based on data which
have been gathered from various sources and from the candidate.

The counseling interview which is last in the sequence, is not
used for all candidates, but only for those who

failed to understand their problem in the course of the
working out, those with psychological or medical counter-
indications (or both) with regard to the desired occupation, and with those that persist in qualifying for those
occupations in which the community is not interested,etc.
Although this form of interview is called advisory, its
purpose is by no means to impose, let alone enforce an
advice on the candidate. The purpose of this interview
is only to help the candidate realize his problem once
more, allow him to solve it by himself and make the most
positive choice, both for himself and for the community.
(Tarbuk 1976, 41)

Professional organization

In 1956 the Yugoslav Association for Vocational Guidance was
founded and the following year the first issues of its professional
paper called Čovek i zanimanie (Man and occupation) were published.
In 1966, the Association was transformed into a broader Yugoslav
Federation of Vocational Guidance Associations serving professionals
in all the Republics of Yugoslavia. The organization is a member of
the International Association for Educational and Vocational Guidance. (Tarbuk 1976)

References

Agranovskii, V. Down the staircase: A socio-educational novella. Soviet Education, 1977, 20 (2), 10-102.

Bárta, B. Analýza chyb v současných názorech na výchovně psychologické poradenství v ČSSR. Sborník prací Filisofické fakulty Brněnské university, 1962, B-9, 191-202.

Blažek, J. Rozmístění patnáctiletého dorostu v roce 1975 v ČSR. Výchovný poradce, 1976, 13 (2), 1-12.

Brančić, B. Vocational guidance in Yugoslavia. Belgrade: Yugoslav Federation of Vocational Guidance Associations, 1970.

Chistiakova, S. The school Komsomol and the guidance of graduates into workers' occupations. Soviet Education, 1975, 17 (5), 71-79.

Eichberg, E. Berufsbildungsberatung in der Sowietunion. In Heller, K. (Ed.) Handbuch der Bildungsberatung, Vol. 1. Stuttgart: Klett Verlag, 1975, pp. 225-238.

Gericke, B. Weiterbildung der Berufsberater im Jahre 1974-75. Forschung der sozialistischen Berufsbildung, 1975, 9 (3), 49-52.

Great Soviet Encyclopedia. (Translation of the 3rd Edition.) New York: Macmillan, 1974.

Hodovský, I. Vědecký světový názor a problem hodnot. Filosofický časopis, 1973, 21, 24-40.

Ivanov, Iu. Attainment and tasks of the Soviet school. Soviet Education, 1976, 19 (1), 29-42.

Kochemasov, V. I. The 25th Congress of the Communist Party of the Soviet Union and the labor education and vocational guidance of youth. Soviet Education, 19 (11), 72-88.

Koščo, J. Psychologické poradenstvo v školskom a profesionálnom vývine. Bratislava: Slovenské pedag. nakl., 1971.

Koščo, J. Postavenie psychólogie a problémy práce psychologov v poradenstve. Psychológie v ekonomické praxi, 1975, 10, 195-205.

Koščo, J. Školské a profesijné poradenstvo v podmienkach rozvinutej socialistickej spoločnosti. Bratislava: Slovenské pedag. nakl., 1976.

Koščo, J., Rapoš, I . & Rybárová, E. Súčasná vývinová psychológia a psychológia "životnej cesty." Psychológia a patopsychológia dieťaťa, 1974, 9, 201-216.

Kotásková, J. Sociální chování chlapců a děvčat v souvislosti se sociálním posilováním a osobnosti rodičů u dvou populací. Československá psychologie, 1972, 16, 404-419.

Kotliar, A. Certain aspects of keeping working youth in production. Soviet Review, 1974, 15 (2), 29-42.

Krevnevich, V. The manpower needs of the national economy and vocational guidance of youth. Soviet Review, 1973, 14 (3), 14-29.

Krupskaya, N. K. On education. Moscow: Foreign Language Publishing House, 1957.

Linhart, J. K jednotě ideologické a odborné práce v psychologii. Československá psychologie, 1973, 17, 105-106.

Litviniak, F. Problémy zabezpečovania a potrieb vedeckých, technických a pedagogických kádrov a ich príprava. In Koščo 1976, pp. 32-39.

Ministry of Education of the Czech Socialist Republic--Ministerstvo školství České socialistické republiky. Instrukce o soustavě výchovného poradenství v oboru působnosti Ministerstva školství České socialistické republiky. Výchovný poradce, 1976, 13 (2), 75-80.

Novák, T. Některé možnosti změny postojů u dificilních chlapců. Psychológia a patopsychológia dieťaťa, 1974, 9, 125-141.

Ottenberg, N. Changes in the occupational structure of the work force and training requirements. Soviet Education, 1978, 20 (8), 59-69.

Rókusfalvy, P. Chápanie rozličných biopsychických determinačných činiteľov regulujúcich aktivitu vo voľbe povolania a v príprave na voľbu povolania. In Koščo 1976, pp. 148-152.

Smirnov, V. F. Always prepared! Soviet Education, 1972, 15 (2), 6-71.

Svoboda, J. Rozvoj poradenské soustavy v západočeském kraji. Výchovný poradce, 1976, 13, 28-36.

Tarbuk, D. (Ed.) Education, training, and vocational guidance in Socialist Federal Republic of Yugoslavia. Belgrade: Yugoslav Federation of Vocational Guidance Associations, 1976.

Ticktin, T. Introduction to "Down the staircase." Soviet Education, 1977, 20 (2), 5-9.

Zalecki, W. Školské a profesijné poradenstvo v Poľsku. In Koščo 1976, pp. 107-115.

Suggested readings

Blunden, G. Eastern Europe: Czechoslovakia, Hungary, Poland.
New York: Time, 1965.

Bronfenbrenner, U. Two worlds of childhood: US and USSR. New York:
Russell Sage Foundation, 1970.

Fischer-Galati, S. (Ed.) Man, state, and society in East European
history. New York: Praeger, 1970.

Great Soviet Encyclopedia. (Translation of the 3rd Edition.) New
York: Macmillan, 1974.

Katz, Z. et al. (Eds.) Handbook of major Soviet nationalities. New
York: Free Press, 1975.

King, E. J. The Soviet Union--the claims of communism. In King, E.J.
Other schools and ours. Comparative studies for today. New York:
Holt, Rinehart & Winston, 1973, pp. 316-362.

Kovrig, B. The Hungarian people's republic. Baltimore: Hopkins, 1970.

Piekalkiewicz, J. Communist local government: A study of Poland.
Athens: Ohio University Press, 1975.

Rutkevich, M. N. The career plans of youth. White Plains, NY : International Arts & Science Press, 1969.

Shimoniak, W. Communist education: Its history, philosophy, and politics. Chicago: Rand McNally, 1969.

Shulman, C. (Ed.) We the Russians. New York: Praeger, 1971.

Smith, H. The Russians. New York: Quadrangle, NY Times, 1976.

Staar, R. F. The communist regimes in Eastern Europe. (2nd Ed.)
Stanford: Hoover Inst., 1971.

Svitak, I. The Czechoslovak experiment. New York: Columbia Univer.
Press, 1971.

Watson, J. W. The Soviet Union: Land of many peoples. Champaign, IL:
Garrard, 1973.

Journals:
Soviet Education, Soviet Psychology, Soviet Review, Soviet Sociology
(English translations of primary sources from the USSR.)
White Plains, NY: Sharpe Publishing.

Section Six

THE MIDDLE EAST

This Section dealing with guidance and counseling in the Middle East is a study of basic contrasts that exist in the profession. Israel has a formal system of fully established guidance services, including psychological services in the schools. The system has been professionally designed, with heavy input from foreign countries that shared their experiences with the Israelis; and the guidance personnel has been college-trained for the job. In contrast, the Arab population depends largely on informal guidance functions exercised by the Moslem culture. Young people are helped to adjust to the environment, to find work, and to enter marriage by society in general and by the close-knit and authoritarian family in particular.

The assessment of underlying social and cultural dynamics currently prevalent in the Middle East offers clues to a better understanding of that part of the world, far beyond the field of comparative guidance studies. The ongoing unrest which on the surface appears to be a power struggle of political rivals is fundamentally an intercultural confrontation of values, national traditions, and life styles.

Furthermore, the analysis of Islamic mentality sheds light on the revolutionary ferment within the Arab community, and in particular, on the upheaval in Iran. The Islamic creed proclaims the unity of religious and governmental processes which are to be guided by the same divine law. This theocratic point of view is reinforced by the belief that Islam, as the final developmental stage of religion and ethics which supersedes Judaism and Christianity,

195

is absolute and unchangeable. Chapter 17 underscores the ensuing, profound conflict situation that exists between this cultural heritage and the inevitable modernization of Arab countries entering the technological era.

John Moracco, who authored the essay on Arab guidance, served for five years at the American University in Beirut as professor of counselor education and administrator of academic programs and testing services. As an American, he worked also with various organizations of the area in a consultative role, e.g., the Beirut regional Counselors' Association and the regional office of the World Health Organization. These experiences and the personal contacts with people of the area provided him an opportunity for insight into the dynamics of Arab cultures.

The three authors of Chapter 18 which deals with guidance in Israel present a combined Israeli-American perspective. Theodore Landsman, an American counselor educator, has made four trips to Israel in recent years and served as visiting professor at universities in Tel Aviv and Haifa. He is particularly interested in promoting positive Arab-Jewish relationships. Ruth Malkinson has been associated with the school of social work at Tel Aviv University and is in the process of completing her doctorate at the University of Florida. Avner Ziv, a professor at Tel Aviv and Bar Ilan Universities, has published books in Hebrew, French, and English. Currently, he is writing a volume (in Hebrew) on the psychology of humor. His professional degree is from the Sorbonne in France.

17

ARAB COUNTRIES

John Moracco

Until recently, the Arab Middle East held minimal interest to Westerners except for its importance as a seat of three major religions. Even considering the religious significance, most Westerners feel that it was circumstantial that the Middle East was the birthplace of Christianity, Islam, and Judaism. (Carmichael 1977) Somehow, the concept of an Arab as a person means little to the average European or American. Most images of Arabs by Westerners entertain two equally incorrect representations. One image has the desert nomad (Bedouin) riding on a superb horse in a fashion not unlike the stylized American cowboy. On the other hand, cinema and television sometimes portray the Arab as an unshaven, sneaky, not to be trusted individual whose motives are beyond a Westerner's ability to comprehend.

If those representations are not true, then questions arise as to who the Arabs are. What political, cultural, and religious traditions contribute to making the Arabs what they are today? And what implication do these conditions have for counseling? This chapter will attempt to answer these questions and provide information about counseling in the Arab Middle East.

The Arab Middle East

The Middle East has been the catalyst for people and ideas since the beginning of civilization. It is an area that has been occupied by many nations, that has been changed and assimilated by a number of cultural and religious events; and yet, despite this

197

flux, a sense of continuity and timelessness permeates the land and its people. (Goldschmidt 1972)

Today, the Arab-speaking Middle East stretches from the North-African states of Morocco, Algeria, and Tunisia on its western border to the Gulf states of the United Arab Emirates on its eastern border. Twelve hundred years ago, the Arab Empire extended from Spain to India. This was an area conquered in less than eighty years and it was considerably larger than the whole of the Roman Empire which took more than eight centuries to consolidate. (Carmichael 1977) During its zenith, the Arab Empire experienced an age of enlightenment while European civilization was in the Middle Ages.

The focus in this Chapter will be on a considerably smaller area than the whole of the Arab Middle East. Included in the discussion will be the Eastern Mediterranean states: Lebanon, Syria, Jordan, and Egypt; the Arabian peninsula and the Gulf states: Saudi Arabia; the United Arab Emirates, Bahrain, Kuwait; and Iraq. Several factors make this limitation realistic. First, the area and its various cultures are extremely diverse and need to be delimited in order to make constructive generalizations. Secondly, the chosen states share at least two major attributes: language and religion. That is, these states have Arabic as their national language and the vast majority of their people are Muslims. For these reasons Iran and Turkey--Muslim countries whose natives speak Farsi and Turkish, respectively--were not included in this Chapter. However, it is probably safe to say that generalizations can be extended to these countries without too much risk.

It is possible to posit cultural generalizations that cover the Middle East and some Latin-American countries. These developing countries share many common features of a cultural phenomenon that stretches from Pakistan to Peru. The personality traits that these cultures generate seem to group around two characteristics. The first is an allegiance to kinship loyalty and trust to such an extent that affiliation with groups outside of family (village, state, etc.) is severely limited. The second characteristic is patriarchal systems that advocate female inferiority which result in relationships with women that are psychologically tense. In these societies the concept of honor is interwoven with female sexuality. (Gulick 1976)

The importance of examining the Middle-Eastern culture is to determine what aspects of the culture contribute to behaviors that are ineffective. As Gulick (1976) points out, all cultures offer a set of customs that help people cope with problems of daily life. Yet they also create problems which have to be borne for long periods of time until they get to be clearly dysfunctional. I will attempt to describe those features of Middle-Eastern culture that, in my opinion, have potential dysfunctional consequences.

The outstanding features of Middle-Eastern culture include the extended family pattern, religion, Bedouin mythology, and the Arabic language. Each of these will be described with the intention of highlighting those features which may contribute to dysfunctional behavior. However, it should be noted that when a culture is described in this fashion, it tends to distort the Gestalt of the culture. This runs the risk of presenting a culture that seems to be unidimensional. Also, a flaw in this approach is to grant finality to phenomena that sometimes border on conjecture.

Arab Middle-East family patterns

The family system in most cultures is the foremost vehicle for transmitting values and behavior. This is especially the case in the Arab Middle East as the premium placed on the family is exceedingly high. Certain aspects of the Middle-Eastern family seem to stand out and to possess potential explanations for behavior. These aspects of family patterns group around three features: (a) child-rearing practices; (b) marriage patterns; and (c) the status of women in society. Obviously, these features are interrelated and separating them may be an exercise in artificialness. Clearly, they are all of a piece and they need to be viewed as such.

Unlike in the U.S., the prevailing family pattern in the Middle East is a variation of the extended family. (Moracco 1978) The true extended family structure consisting of husband and wife, their unmarried children, married sons and their wives, and children living under one roof rarely exists today in the Arab world. This has been caused by economic considerations and by pressures emanating from industrialization. (Goode 1970) However, some of the attitudes derived from the extended family still prevail. This is true about many other parts of the world. In Latin America, for instance, the general family pattern is also a variation of the extended family and some of the guidance implications for Latin Americans are similar to the Arab Middle East. Additionally, concerns centering around work values, authoritarianism, and personal decision-making are remarkably similar in Africa (Esen 1972; Pulleybank 1974), Latin America (Espin and Renner 1974), and to a lesser extent in Europe. (Ronnestad 1974)

The social pattern of control in families in the Middle East is authoritarian in nature (Diab 1959; Melikian 1956; Prothro and Melikian 1953), as expressed through the male members of the household. This concept extends to the predominate child-rearing custom in the Arab Middle East. Children are brought up in a situation where most of the decisions are made by the father. He is seen as the main authority figure who is respected and whose council is sought in almost any situation. To do otherwise is to violate the most fundamental social pattern in the culture. This is a common feature of most developing countries. African (Esen 1972), Latin-

American (Espin and Renner 1974), and Chinese (Scaff and Ting 1972) cultures stress the central role of authority in child-rearing patterns. Thus, in these cultures children are not supposed to make independent decisions and they are not rewarded for doing so. On the other hand, in Western cultures, especially in the U.S., children are encouraged to make choices on their own. Independence is given high priority. As a result, less authority-ridden cultures may have a greater need for counseling because of the amount of flux inherent in the process. (Espin and Renner 1974)

In the Arab family, individuals are subordinate to the group and in decision-making they are influenced strongly by the values and needs of the family. If these values conflict with their own, individuals are expected to conform to family values, expressed in most cases by the father. This authoritarian structure provides psychic support and security but stifles individuality. (Khalaf 1971) However, Gulick (1976) contends that the "psychic support" which Khalaf alludes to is, in reality, a myth and that the result of the authoritarian climate in the family is a tendency toward emotional isolation and lack of trust in the personality structure. He describes this as the "atomistic" trait of the Arab personality structure which results in an individual who is distrustful of almost everyone, egocentric in thinking, and who does not have the ability to sustain group effort. This personality is unable to take risks, especially in any activity that does not bring immediate and clear personal gain.

The concept of the common good, or what the British call the "social contract," makes little sense to an Arab in the Middle East. The idea of helping others is geared to family and close friends. (Moracco 1978; Carmichael 1977) It is customary in the Middle East for the family to arrange for its own social security, that is, to look after the aged, the ill, and the unemployed. This family function is a much more generous one than in the U.S.

Such an attitude is reflected in Arab architecture. Classical design has the house situated so that it is turned inward. These stone structures, built on narrow, winding streets for protection, gather their light from inner patios. Little regard is given for life outside, on the streets. Trash and garbage are thrown into the streets as if to proclaim that, once out of the house, they become someone else's problem.

Child-rearing practices encourage what seems to be contradictory behavior patterns—egotism and conformity. (Gardner 1972) The Arab is both self-assertive and prideful on one hand, yet deeply conforming on the other hand. Boys are reared to be combative with peers and siblings, with ridicule and shame used as controlling agents. At the same time extreme loyalty is demanded, especially in matters dealing with the respect and honor of the family. This creates conditions that foster divisiveness in the Arab character

200

supported by child-rearing practices relying heavily on shaming and instigation of jealousy among siblings. Clearly, such upbringing creates ambivalent feelings in the Arab, especially toward family members, and may contribute greatly to the development of the atomistic personality. (Gulick 1977)

Vocational choice

In very primitive societies the concept of vocational choice is unknown. Vocational life styles are few in number and a person's occupation is fixed into a class structure where men tend to inherit their fathers' occupations. As traditional societies move along the industrial continuum, vocational life styles become more varied, but hereditary determination still predominates. In traditional societies, young people are shunted into careers at a very early age, in terms of vocational schools or apprenticeships. Life career decisions are made as early as ten or eleven years of age, and there is a degree of finality about them. Many countries in the Middle East and in Europe still operate according to this model. If there is counseling, it takes the form of interaction where the counselee is passive and the counselor is active, mainly giving advice. This is expected and in no way is it thought that it could be otherwise. (Stump, Jordan and Friesen 1967)

In addition to these considerations, in the Middle East it is expected that young men will carve out their careers through nepotism. The Protestant work ethic does not have a strong tradition in the culture. (Moracco 1976) Ideas that an identity can be found in work, that hard work and frugality should be valued, and that work which helps others is rewarding are not deeply ingrained in the conceptual framework of the Middle-Easterner. (Suleiman 1972) The concept of helping others outside of family and close friends is difficult for Middle-Easterners to understand. Jobs are arranged for and dispensed through "wasta"--influence and access to power. The rags-to-riches concept does not have much viability in the Middle East. It should be noted that Espin and Renner (1974) identify parallels (early vocational choice, the lack of work ethic, and the absence of identity formation through work) in Latin America.

As societies become more dynamic, life guidelines become less definite and vocational identity becomes a very complex process resulting in uncertainty. Under these conditions, early commitment to a vocation becomes more tenuous. This seems to be an integral part of mobile, highly technological societies. Apparently, it is the price to be paid for dynamism in free societies.

The Middle East is seeking dynamic modernization. Many of the countries of the region have vast financial resources. Yet all suffer from a lack of trained manpower to accomplish the elaborately drawn modernization plans. While for the immediate future, imported technology, manpower, and materials may assuage the situation, long-term planning obviates this approach. It is clear that the indigenous population must be educated and trained for modernization. Some of the Arabian Gulf oil states are realizing that in addition to the cost of importing skilled workers at all levels, there are other factors to consider; that there is a price to be paid in terms of motivation and ethics, when most of a country's human services are imported. The full ramifications of this situation are not yet known.

Women, honor, and marriage

Perhaps in no other area are the cultural effects of Middle-Eastern society as pronounced as that of the role of women. In comparison to modern societies, women are second-class citizens in Arab countries. One obvious indication of the worth of females is that in some Gulf states they were not registered officially. However, the apparent superior status of males is not without consequences for both females and males, especially in the area of sexuality. Since femininity is viewed as sexually irresponsible, uncontrollable, and irrational (whereas masculinity is seen as life-giving, good, and rational), ambivalent attitudes are generated in the Arab male. He is on psychologically unstable grounds, as these attitudes foster exploitive feelings on one hand, and protective feelings on the other. This conflict contributes to the generally insecure and atomistic character of the Arab. (Gulick 1977)

The result of this phenomenon on women's perceptions of their sex role has found conflicting interpretations. Gulick (1977) presents research findings that Arab women are satisfied with their lot in life, as well as other research data that demonstrate frustration and deep dissatisfaction of women with their roles. However, most Westerners have distorted views regarding women in the Middle East. The harem is rarely practiced and the veil is all but gone, except for conservative Arabian Gulf states. In most countries, especially the more revolutionary ones, girls have equal rights in many areas. This is especially true in access to education. This is not to gloss over the fact that, while there is a degree of equality at the legal level, everyday practices would indicate quite a different situation which is rooted in a long tradition of suppression of women.

Men, by virtue of their position in society, are responsible for women in almost every endeavor. Parenthetically, it should be noted that the adherence to "machismo" in Latin America is very similar to what is found in the Middle East. While some writers have described the Arab woman as little more than "a bearer of water and a hewer of wood," the attitude expressed in the phrase is more important than the degree of accuracy. There is definitely "women's" work and "men's" work. More importantly, men are the protectors of women's honor. Great emotional attention is awarded to female sex-

ual purity. It falls upon the father's and brothers' shoulders to
guard the chastity of their female blood relative. She is their
"'ird" or their honor. Transgressions are punishable even "till
death." Though a woman may marry, her father and her brothers, not
her husband, are responsible for her virtue. (Goode 1970)

That these customs are changing, is very much in evidence on
the streets of Beirut, Bagdad, Damascus, or Cairo. Women can be
seen fashionably dressed for the evening. Massive efforts by governments in the last decade devoted to female education will make an
even greater impact in the years to come. Governments are beginning
to realize that if they are to attain their political and economic
goals, they must alter the present position of the women. This, of
course, will result in a new role for women. Whenever roles are in
flux or rapidly changing, the potential for counseling is great. Men
and women will be mixing increasingly in social and work situations
and relationships between the sexes will have to take on new dimensions.

In addition to education, the likely area in which change will
take place most rapidly is the occupational realm. In the past, the
general feeling was that it was not quite respectable for women to
engage in gainful employment; that women who work, may be exposed
to situations leading to promiscuity, since they are not supervised.
Additionally, women working for wages were seen as reducing the status of their husbands or fathers.

As Arab societies develop economically, they will become mass
producers and consumers, which will undoubtedly result in greater
vocational opportunities for all. Since the modern Arab woman is
better educated than her sisters in the past, she will have access
to a wider variety of jobs. It is reasoned that as women become
integrated fully into the economic fabric of the country, as assured-
ly they must, values and behaviors of females will become more like
those of their male counterparts, as their occupational roles will
overlap. (Stump, Jordan and Friesen 1967) These new roles for women
may be at odds with what the male-dominated society used to allow.
It is conceivable that sex will not differentiate occupational roles
at all, if the West is an example of what can be expected to happen.
This will not be an easy transition in that it implies a different
male-female relationship that sharply digresses from the present
norm.

At present, marriage, its value, purpose, and the process
of choosing one's partner are being valued differently from
Western traditions and customs. Arranged marriages are still the
custom in many Middle-Eastern families. Traditionally, the Arab
groom had very little to say about his potential wife, while the
bride had almost no say at all. As young males had no access to
wealth, elders in the extended family made all the arrangements including settlement of the bride-price. This arrangement insured

that the power of the family was enhanced through a wise marriage choice and that alliances were made through it to provide mutual protection for the family tribe in time of need. This situation is further enhanced by the custom, and in some cases a considered right, of a young man marrying the daughter of his father's brother. While this custom is rapidly declining today, the concept of marrying within the family (second or third cousins) is still in evidence today. (Goode 1970)

As a result, courtship was an unheard of phenomenon in the past. However, as urbanization and industrialization take place, personal choices of courtship patterns and marriage mates are rapidly emerging in the Arab Middle East. This situation, which has arisen most rapidly in the last decade, places young people in choice-making positions for which they may not have been properly prepared. Furthermore, parents, especially fathers, will have to accept a lessening of authority and of the assumed right to make marriage decisions for their children. Increasingly, young people are rejecting limitations placed upon them by the extended family pattern. They are witness to the worldwide youth revolution of the sixties and early seventies by virtue of television, magazines, books and the cinema.

Religion

In almost every culture religion plays an important role in influencing behavior of individuals. In the Arab Middle East it is an all-persuasive factor that leaves no aspect of human behavior untouched. Islam, the religion of more than 90% of the people of the Arab Middle East, must be understood to appreciate fully the influence it has on its faithful. It was undoubtedly Islam that provided the unifying element for the Arab Empire thirteen centuries ago, as it welded the tribes of the Arabian Peninsula into a people, and created a new civilization. (Carmichael 1977)

Islam and Arabic culture are so fundamentally intertwined that they are of a piece. Morality, art, politics, medicine, sexual behavior, and personal conduct are all delimited by Islam through its book of scriptures called the "Quran". The religion has set the standard for living that is absolute and permanent. Muslim people need only to refer to the tenets of their religion to evaluate the worth of any act. This has an aspect of security, while at the same time it constricts potential for change.

Islam is the last of the great religions developed in the Middle East. Similar to its predecessor religions, Judaism and Christianity, Islam is monotheistic and borrows heavily from both religions. Muslims, the followers of Islam, believe that their religion is the final stage following Judaism and Christianity, and as such is absolute and without fault. The ramification of this is that there can be no change in Islamic beliefs.

Islam was the work of one man, Mohammed. It is believed that at an age of around forty years he began to receive messages from God through the angel Gabriel. Mohammed received a series of these messages which he dictated in Arabic. Thus Arabic became the official religious language of God. Mohammed is thought of as the last prophet form Abraham to Jesus (in Islam Jesus is considered a prophet).

Fundamental to Islamic theology and Arabic psychology is the belief that fate is in the hands of God and that the laws of nature exist only because it suits the Almighty. (Carmichael 1977) This complete submission to God has ramifications for the Arab character. There is a fatalistic component in the thinking of the Arab. Politically, Islamic theology militates against change, since God has ordered everything as exemplified through the sayings of Mohammed. The only change allowed is to return to the erstwhile purity and reject the corruption of the present. (Carmichael 1977) The upheaval in Iran, a Muslim country, has been rooted to this concept of political change.

Although a fairly simple religion, Islam exacts heavy demands on its followers. Basically, these have come to be known as the "five pillars of Islam." They include: (a) the belief in one God and Mohammed as his prophet; (b) the journey ("hajj") to Mecca during one's lifetime; (c) prayer five times a day; (d) the giving of alms to the needy; and (e) fasting during the holy month of "Ramadan." In addition to the Quran, there is the "Hadith", a body of tradition that provides the foundation for nearly all aspects of life, and the "Shari'a", a compendium of rules that ritualizes Islam. With these three sources, Quran, Hadith and Shari'a, the proper conduct of nearly all human behavior is codified. The Muslim believer can judge his or her behavior against what is known to be good. If this assessment is somehow less that adequate, the individual conforms to established religious norms. There are few possibilities, at the present time, that the interpretation of religious norms will change from the prescibed ones.

Language

In the Arab world there is an interesting interplay between language and religion. Mohammed's insistence that the Quran be written in Arabic, when written Arabic prose was largely unknown, had a tremendous effect. This act provided a written standard for the language and it gave the Arabic language a religious and sometimes mystical quality. (Carmichael 1977) One consequence of this is that, apart from classical Arabic, dialects developed among the regions of the Arab world. In some cases the dialects are so disparate that a speaker of colloquial Arabic in one country may not be able to understand the dialect spoken in another Arab country. However, in all Middle-Eastern countries, classical Arabic must be learned as a second language. Because it is a language fixed into a time period of thirteen and a half centuries past, it cannot cope with many present-day subjects and situations.

Regardless of the dialect used, Arabs have a special love and, indeed, reverence for the oral use of language. Individuals are praised and highly regarded because of their adherence to the oral tradition of Arabic. Arabs are often powerful and eloquent speakers capable of generating much emotion and persuasion. (Gardner 1972) Listeners are expected to be moved by a speaker's words. Consequently, speakers do not always say exactly what they mean, preferring to have words make an emotional rather than a factual impact on listeners. When engaging in overstatement and exaggeration, they do not intend to be deceitful; rather they attempt to use language for more that information sharing.

Aggression is often exhibited through language rather that physical action. A Westerner viewing the results of a minor traffic accident in Beirut may think that the participants are at each other's throats and are in mortal danger. Shouting, gesturing, and passer-by participation give the Westerner an impression that may not be accurate. In this situation, and many others, there are predetermined roles to be played out consistent with what the culture and its oral tradition demand. Not to play these roles, in this example not to proclaim, in no uncertain terms, "before God and upon your mother's eyes", your innocence in the accident may be looked upon as deviant behavior.

Bedouin tradition

Though the Bedouin--people engaged in a nomadic way of life-- constitute a small part of the total Arab population, their tradition and culture have made an impact disproportionate to their numbers. Many Arabs, far removed from the Bedouin life-style, strongly identify with Bedouin values. Similar to the frontier heritage of early American West, values and mores of Bedouin life are felt to be an important part of the Arab character. Bedouin people, perhaps because of their close link with the desert environment, value independence and consider themselves to be equal to anyone. This may come from the unique timelessness of the desert. The oneness and tranquility of desert life, where survival is a testament to courage, breed a deep faith in oneself. The endless desert environment may make the act of deferential attitudes toward others seem inconsequential. (Carmichael 1977)

While few monuments were ever constructed by them and while they left little in the way of the arts, the Bedouin developed a poetic legacy and a love of language and its use that remain to this day. Their poetry has perpetuated and glorified their code of values. These values center around courage in war, patience in misfortune,

persistence in exacting revenge, defense of the weak, boldness in
dealing with the strong, tribal loyalty, hospitality, generosity,
and trustworthiness. (Goldschmidt 1972)

The great Bedouin tradition which bred a sense of independence to
even the lowliest tribesman, has given the Arab a reassuring sense of
time and place. However, Bedouin tradition and values are rooted in
a way of life whose very existence seems endangered today. This phenomenon may create flux in the Arab value system.

The status of counseling in the Arab Middle East

Counseling in the professional sense is practically nonexistent
in the Arab Middle East. In view of the way the family system operates, it is unrealistic to think that an individual should go to a
counselor for help. This is a family function and such an act would
result in the family losing face. The family is supposed to take
care of all its members' concerns. There are a few practicing psychologists, psychiatrists, and counselors in the Middle East, but
these are exceptions. Given this situation, what is the future for
counseling services in the Arab Middle East?

The tentative answer to this question rests on two assumptions.
The first is that counseling (or psychological services) is needed
least in traditional societies. As societies become more fluid, role
instability increases and creates conditions for ambiguity. This, in
turn, makes people more apt to question major life concerns of self-
concept, vocational choice, and role definitions. Obviously, the
need for counseling increases as traditional societies change and
values became less certain.

The second assumption is that the Arab Middle East is changing.
This assumption is based on the great economic wealth generated by
oil which, in turn, forces the Arab world out of its traditional culture. The geopolitical ramifications of being an oil producing area
cannot be disregarded. Since oil makes a global impact, the Arab
Middle East will experience the results of this impact as profoundly
as any other area of the world. Apparently this is the ubiquitous
nature of oil politics. As comforting as it may seem, the oil producing Arab Middle East cannot remain a traditional society on one hand
and a major producer of oil on the other.

Future prospects

Counseling can play an important role within countries which are
in the process of change. The form that it takes depends on a number
of factors related to the cultural milieu of the individual country.
Industrial countries usually have counseling models which have developed over the last seventy-five years. It is a great temptation for
developing countries to adopt counseling models that have been devel-

oped and highly advanced abroad, e.g., in the United States. However, most countries, including those of the Middle East, resist that temptation. They realize that counseling practices should be in concert with the philosophies of the societies in which these practices are exercised. Esen's (1972) remark is worth repeating:

> All developing nations that see guidance as worth importing into their social or educational system will do well to heed this warning,...more problems might be created than solved, if guidance practices were based on indiscriminately imported alien philosophies. (p. 792)

In all probability counseling programs in the Arab Middle East will approximate what we consider vocational guidance. It appears that most countries begin their counseling programs at this stage. (Wrenn 1976) Vocational concerns may not center on vocational choices as much as they will on manpower development. That is, the primary question considered will be: What kind of trained individuals do we need to fulfill our development schemes? Interestingly, this could lead to the inclusion of women in national vocational development plans. For example, Jordan, faced with a labor shortage, has instituted a woman's labor department with the Ministry of Labor to help tap a large reservoir of educated women. (Dajani 1978)

However, considerations regarding manpower development may be different from considerations stemming from individual vocational choice processes. It is important that individual concerns in a variety of spheres (personal, social, academic, etc.) are not overlooked in a country's effort to modernize.

Counseling for vocational choice must take these considerations in stride, if it is to make an impact in the Middle East. The counselor must take the family constellation into consideration when interacting with students and young adults. It would seem that the counselor would have an enormous educational job to do with parents. Especially fathers will have to be made to realize that counselors should be seen as collaborators, not as competitors. Students must be introduced to the world of work at an early age and information on changing occupational patterns should be made available to them. More importantly, work values and attitudes must be developed at the elementary school level, if the Middle East is to fulfill its modernization plans.

Counselors must also be aware that as traditional cultures change, people become unsure of their vocational identity. As a result, vocational choices are apt to be less realistic. This often leads to apathy in vocational choice or a distortion in terms of vocational reality and vocational choice. (Stump, Jordan and Friesen 1967) In the U.S. some effects of this can be seen in subgroups that have been uprooted, e.g., American Indians and Blacks.

It's an exciting time in the Middle East. And it is one in which counseling has an unlimited potential to develop as a profession and aid in the area's struggle toward modernity, provided that an indigenous counseling philosophy is developed. This counseling philosophy needs to wrestle with the problems of modernization on the one hand and traditional value systems on the other. It also must face the reality that deeply rooted value systems may be at odds with attitudes that are required for the modernization process.

Countries interested in building modern national structures must provide supportive services so that the transition from traditional to modern society is accomplished with as little psychological disruption and accompanying alienation as possible. Ministries of education, by providing proper guidance and counseling services to their students, can help ease the shock of modernization. Counseling can play a significant role in the Middle East, as individuals struggle to reach a new identity that will reconcile the past with the future.

References

Carmichael, J.E. The Arabs today. Garden City, NJ: Doubleday, 1977.

Dajani, A. The manpower boomerang hits Jordan. ILO Information, 1978, 6, 4.

Diab, L. N. Authoritarianism and prejudice in Near-Eastern students attending American universities. Journal of Social Psychology, 1959, 50, 175-187.

Esen, A. A view of guidance from Africa. Personnel and Guidance Journal, 1972, 50, 792-798.

Espin, O.M. and Renner, R.R. Counseling: A new priority in Latin America. Personnel and Guidance Journal, 1974, 52, 297-301.

Gardner, G.H. Socio-cultural determinates. In Al-Marayati, A. (Ed.) The Middle East: Its governments and politics. Belmont,CA: Duxbury, 1972.

Goldschmidt, A. E. Jr. Historical perspectives. In Al-Marayati, A. (Ed.) The Middle East: Its governments and politics. Belmont, CA: Duxbury, 1972.

Goode, W. J. World revolution and changing family patterns. New York: Free Press, 1970.

Gulick, J. The Middle East: An anthropological perspective. Pacific Palisades, CA: Goodyear, 1977.

Gulick, J. The ethos of insecurity in Middle Eastern culture. In DeVos, G. (Ed.) Responses to changed society, culture, and personality. New York: Van Nostrand, 1976.

Khalaf, S. Family associations in Lebanon. Journal of Comparative Family Studies, 1971, 11, 235-250.

Milikian, L.H. Some correlates of authoritarianism in two cultural groups. Journal of Psychology, 1956, 42, 237-248.

Moracco, J. Vocational maturity of Arab and American high school students. Journal of Vocational Behavior, 1976, 8, 367-373.

Moracco, J. Implementing self-concept in vocational choice in the Arab Middle East. Journal of Vocational Behavior, 1978, 13, 204-209.

Prothro, E.T. and Milikian, L.H. The California Opinion Scale in an authoritarian culture. Public Opinion Quarterly, 1953, 17, 353-363.

Pulleybank, E.F. Crossing cultural barriers: A view from Lagos. Personnel and Guidance Journal, 1974, 53, 217-221.

Ronnestad, M.H. From Norway... Personnel and Guidance Journal, 1974, 53, 52-53.

Scaff, M.K. and Ting, M.G. Fu tao: Guidance in Taiwan seeks a value orientation. Personnel and Guidance Journal, 1972, 50, 645-653.

Stump, W.L., Jordan, J.E. and Friesen, E.W. Cross-cultural considerations in understanding vocational development. Journal of Counseling Psychology, 1967, 14, 325-331.

Suleiman, M.W. Crisis and revolution in Lebanon. The Middle East Journal, 1972, 26, 11-24.

Wrenn, C.G. Values and counseling in different countries and cultures. The School Counselor, 1976, 26, 5-14.

18

ISRAEL

Theodore Landsman, Ruth Malkinson, and Avner Ziv

So dappled and diverse is the color and the substance of the contemporary state of Israel that it is a special kind of pleasure to simplify the description and call it simply a "Jewish State." It does contain almost three million Jews but also almost half a million Israeli Arabs. And as is true in any contemporary society, its problems and its characteristics are mirrored in its schools.

Israel's cultural diversity is both a crown upon its head and a pain in its neck. It prides itself in its attempt to absorb a vast collection of persecuted, hounded, and courageous people. In the midst of constant wars, economic disasters, and high taxes the tiny nation manages somehow to provide a superior education and a dedicated group of guidance and psychological counselors.

Can the sophisticated observer who long ago melted his ethnic differences in the legendary pot of the late 19th and early 20th century comprehend the estimated 127 differing cultural subgroups which make up the society in which Israel's counselors serve? These include Ashkenazim--those coming from the European countries bringing with them a high level of culture and education, and the Sephardim--a majority but who come from the Asian and Arabian peninsula areas and whose cultural and economic level was often at the poverty line and who averaged perhaps seven or eight children to each family. (Garcia 1974; Landsman 1970)

This cultural disparity has resulted in one of Israel's most important social problems and in one of its greatest educa-

211

tional innovations, "the Reforma." A whole new generation of counseling and guidance personnel emerged as well.

Early studies showed a greater number of the Ashkenazi children in the public schools and universities of the state despite the fact that the Sephardim represented the majority. In addition, positions of leadership were largely dominated by the Ashkenazim.

To further complicate the matter, other subgroups within the Jewish group include:

Chassidim of various degrees of ultra orthodoxy, a group which largely maintains the style of dress of 17th century Europe, a strong family structure, and a total devotion to traditional religion;

Russians from Georgia with a high cultural level;

Circassians; Yemenites; Indian Jews from Cochin and Bombay; Samaritans; South Africans; South Americans; British; Falashim (Black Jews from Ethiopia); the Black Hebrews (from Chicago who claim to be the rightful owners of Israel); the Sabras (native born Israelis); the remnant of those rescued from the German holocaust; vegetarians; and of course, American Jews.

The diversity continues with the Israeli Arabs among whom might be found: Moslem Arabs; Druze (a sect which maintains largely Moslem cultural appearances but which has its own religious identity); Christians; and Bedouins.

Even among the substantial Christian minority may be found Greek Orthodox, Armenians, Dominicans, various Protestant groups and a small evangelical group here and there attempting conversion of the Jews to the displeasure of the Israeli government.

Somehow or other out of this maze of ethnicity an organized educational system and counseling services emerge. The Jewish schools are organized under the Ministry of Education into separate religious and secular school systems. The Arabs and Druze are also usually found in a separate school system but also under management of the Ministry of Education. Private Greek Orthodox institutions and others are also available, including an American school which attracts children of English speaking diplomats, business people, etc.

Organization and training

Counselors in Israel work in primary schools and in junior high schools (grades 7 to 9). They are often lumped together

and referred to as elementary schools to the confusion of the
American visitors. There are some 476,000 children in this
school population according to the latest available government
statistical survey. (State of Israel 1975) Starting in the
year 1979, counselors will also work in high schools.

Some 916 counselors have been identified in Israel, a ratio
of 1 to 500. For a country with the economic problems of Israel
this seems to be a respectable ratio but one which most educators
would prefer to be 1 to 250.

Counseling is a respected and well used discipline in the
state whose traditions strongly favor educational advancement,
study and professional development. Jews have traditionally
been known as "am hasefer" or "people of the book" and despite
the ravages of war, a determiniation to maintain and improve
public education is readily apparent at all levels of government.
Interest in all professions is at a high level with fierce
competition for entrance into the schools of medicine, law,
dentistry, and engineering. At Tel Aviv University which has the
largest training program for guidance counselors, some 360
candidates applied for admission to that program in 1978. Some
40 were admitted through the use of a complicated and extensive
program of testing and interviewing.

Counselors are required to have only the B.A. degree which
is available at all universities in Israel. However, the requirement of teaching experience, more or less eliminated some years
ago from most modern programs, is retained in Israel. Some
students will be accepted for training who do not have a teaching
certificate; however, these must pursue a simultaneous program
which will lead to a teacher's diploma. Despite recommendations
to the contrary from American consultants, the counselor usually
also handles a teaching load in the schools.

Supervisors generally have the master's degree in a program
which often roughly parallels the undergraduate program. Thus a
typical training program for the master's degree and one which is
indicative of the training standards would include:

Introduction to Educational Thought	Group Testing Guidance in
Psychology and Education	Vocational Counseling
Research Methods	The Exceptional Child
Statistics	Behavior Modification
Introduction to the Sociology of Education	Case Analysis in Counseling Consulting work in Schools
Group Dynamics	Supervised Practicum
Theories of Counseling	Other courses in
Interviewing	Special Education
Evaluation of Students	Thesis

The contemporary school counselor will notice immediately
that the master's degree in Israel is much more extensive than
is the degree in most countries. In addition to the thesis, the
degree usually involves some three years of post graduate work
in comparison with the one year elsewhere. The masters degree
is in fact the mark of high level competence and is roughly
equivalent to what is euphemistically referred to as the ABD--
All But the (Doctoral) Dissertation.

Administration of guidance and psychological services

Central administration of the guidance services is a
function of the Ministry of Education and has been largely
organized under Dr. Kalman Benjamini who also heads a major
psychological clinic in Jerusalem and teaches at the Hebrew
University in Jerusalem. Like Dr. Benjamini whose degree is
from a midwestern American university, many of the counselors ,
particularly the senior counselors,have been heavily influenced
by American guidance approaches although more recently a genuine
Israeli approach to guidance problems seems to be emerging out
of the native training programs.

The country is divided into three main geographic areas,
each headed by a senior counselor with a staff of four or five
senior counselors who act as consultant-supervisors to the
school counselors in the assigned districts. Most senior school
counselors hold their master's degrees in either psychology or
counselor education. Those from psychology are likely to perhaps
emphasize a more clinical approach, diagnostic and psychotherapeutic.

School counseling services developed particularly during
the 1960s to provide elementary schools and junior high schools
with professional knowledge to deal with the specific problems
of underachievers who characteristically were children whose
parents came from Arabic countries. Cultural differences and a
high percentage of illiteracy amongst parents of those students
caused a large number of them to enter school with deficiencies
diagnosed as an environmental retardation. Thus there was need
for special additional programs within the school to help those
students bridge the cultural gap.

The "Reforma"

The minister of education at that time formed a committee
to advise him on the subject of underachievers. One of the
recommendations was to change the then existing school system in
order to bring about a better integration between the various
ethnic groups. This led to the major "Reforma" in the school

214

system in the late sixties and the early seventies. Some of the
schools organized during this period of time are known as "Reforma
Schools" which is confusing to those familiar with the term
reform schools--institutions for the delinquent. On the contrary,
the reforma schools in Israel are the modernized schools which
were extended from first to 8th grade to first to 9th grade.
Education is compulsory now after the "reforma" through the 9th
grade. Plans have been made to extend this through the 10th
grade.

Schools equivalent to our high schools are dotted around
Israel and include a magnificent selection of vocational schools
mechanics, aviation trades, agriculture, etc. but require tuition
which is a heavy strain on the Israeli parent. However, scholar-
ships are generously available and many educators boast that
any student who is capable and wishes to finish high school may
do so.

The changes of the reform were aimed at improved educational
opportunities through the introduction of comprehensive methods
including school counseling services where the role of the school
counselor was clearly defined for the first time. Each middle
or junior high school was to have school counselors for each
grade level who would become actively involved in the responsibility for enhancing students' potential, for the underachievers
in particular, through relationship with students, parents and
teachers in both vocational and therapeutic counseling.

Hitherto, school counselors were involved mostly in vocational counseling and served as supervisors to teachers involved
in special programs for underachievers, programs which were at
that time optional and depended not only on financial resources
but also on the degree of acceptability of the counselor by the
principal. Thus, they were not included in all elementary
schools. With the introduction of the reform, for the first
time the school counselor became an integral part of the school
staff. The role of the counselor in the high schools and in
the elementary schools is not as clearly established. Studies
recently completed by Prof. Michal Chen show reforma schools
with guidance counselors to have fewer dropouts than those schools
which lack counselors.

Functions of the counselor

School counselors are involved in diagnosis and therapy
within the school setting, take an active part in the process
of selecting students for the various levels in each grade, and
selecting teaching methods. They undertake individual and group
counseling for students and for parents and carry on traditional
vocational guidance as well. They are often liaison between the

215

school and other agencies in the community such as those providing
social and psychological services.

A typical problem with which school counselors deal involves
an early adolescent boy at a vocational school with overnight
accomodations whose parents are divorced. His mother is remarried
but he finds he does not get along with his stepfather and he
feels his natural father does not want him. He finds himself
alone on the sabbath weekend when all others go back to their
parental homes. In the elementary school, a ten year old girl
comes to the counselor to talk of feelings of being rejected by
her playmates. She talks openly and freely with an attitude of
trust and faith in the counselor which is perhaps rare in other
cultures. In another school a counselor maintains a mailbox outside her door for students' letters whose contents might include
requests for appointments to discuss personal problems or a plea
to be changed from one achievement level to another within a class
with homogeneous groupings.

In another setting, 20 counselors are being trained to teach
psychology in the public schools with the preventive objective in
mind as well as the developmental improvement of the school
environment.

In an Arab school, the client-centered sensitivities of the
senior author were rudely shaken by confrontation with cultural
demands when the counselors sketched their handling of a problem
involving a girl who wanted to "date" an Arab boy in the school.
Such relationships are not just frowned upon in the traditional
Arab culture--but are considered grossly immoral. The counselors
felt that they had to tell the couple that they must not see each
other. Otherwise, they insisted, the girl would be taken out of
school the very next day.

In another Arab school, an intelligent and ambitious boy who
wants to get into medical school, ponders the possibility of
learning Roumanian, a whole new language, and going to that country
or any of those in the Communist bloc which offer generous scholar-
ships to Arabs who have difficulty in getting admission to the
Israeli professional schools because of poor preparation or lack
of proficiency with Hebrew.

Postgraduate training

School counselors are paid by the Ministry of Education. The
educational or school psychologists however are usually paid by
the cities or municipalities and often serve other community
psychological needs. In the Ministry of Education there is a
service called SHEFI (Sherut Psychologi Yeutzi--Educational
Psychology and Counseling Service) whose main task is to provide

for postgraduate training for school counselors and educational
psychologists. The service also prepares and distributes tests
and encourages research in the field. It publishes a professional
journal Chavat Daat (Opinion); it is subtitled Journal of
Counseling and Educational Psychology. In 1976 SHEFI sponsored a
series of 12 courses on a yearly basis involving university
lectures all paid by SHEFI. Special summer programs are available.
During vacation times, "Hishtalmut" or inservice training is
always available.

All of these are popular with Israeli counselors who as well
as being people of the book enjoy talking about their work and do
even a generous amount of listening. The tradition of the
lecture is still strong in the Israeli school system , perhaps
following upon their Russian and German origins. In the collective settlements or Kibbutzim the lecture is still perhaps the
major source of entertainment. And many of the university faculty
members made a point of visiting the more remote settlements to
offer intellectual stimulation on a wide variety of abstract subjects. It has been said that if an Israeli doesn't hear something
in a lecture which he cannot understand he doesn't feel his time
was well spent.

School psychological services

Other related services available in the schools include
those of the school psychologist, school social worker and school
nurse. Consultative services are available in medicine and
psychiatry. The school psychological services are a well
established part of the personnel service matrix and are readily
available through psychological "stations" or clinics found even
in some of the smaller communities.

How seriously Israeli school principals take their psychological services may be seen in an international news service
story which appeared in the worldwide press telling of a strike
by Beersheva principals who were demanding more psychological
services. At the nearby city of Dimona in the Negev desert area,
another group of principals also on strike listed their grievances
one of which was that the municipality had failed to provide
adequate housing for the community school psychologist resulting
in his moving to another community. Translations of standardized
tests such as the Wechslers and the TDMH self concept scale are
available in Hebrew; in addition, data on standardized norms for
Israeli samples are becoming available. The ratio of school
psychologists to students is 1 to 1000, one of the highest in the
world according to Catteral (1977).

217

Special problems and routine crises

As indicated earlier,all of Israel's social, economic and
political problems have some impact upon the school system and
upon the guidance counselor. Perhaps the most important is one
which has not yet reached its fullest maturity but which hangs
over the heads of the school systems by deteriorating threads--
specifically the problem of integration of the Arab school
population. *

Past experiences in the United States and in South Africa
have with great certainty identified the greatest victims of
ethnic neglect as the school children. The most certain target
of such change on the part of the extremist is the school building
and the minds and emotions of the school-age child. In recent
years, frustrated Israeli Arab school children have been involved
in some of the violence in the community, burning tires, stoning
police, etc. There are no integrated Arab-Jewish schools in
the entire country. On occasion, some Arab children have
quiently been made a part of an otherwise all Jewish class.
In one experimental situation, an Arab class and a separate
Jewish class existed side by side in a Haifa school. Arab
schools have suffered the neglect which is inevitable in a
segregated situation, according to Mar'i (1978). His studies
show financial support which actually reaches Arab classrooms
to be considerably less than what is allocated for all
schools. Guidance counselors will, no doubt, be called upon <u>when</u>
the crisis worsens (not, <u>if</u> the crisis worsens, for such is a
certainty). An experimental program is long overdue and an
effort should be made to develop carefully an integrated Arab-
Jewish school with preparation of parents and students and the
community, with evaluation and with high level educational
opportunities. Lest the critical American be too certain of such
success, it must be noted that the problems in such integration
far exceed those of similar ethnic crises in the United States or
in South Africa. Particularly language barriers are greater in
Israel and the security problems of Israel with her Arab neighbors
make such an undertaking exceedingly risky but necessary.

In late 1978 an experimental program of psychological services
to the Bedouin, the traditional desert wanderer, was initiated
by Moshe Landsman operating out of the Negev town of Yerucham.

Constant war and terrorism have taken their tolls. In
particular after the 1973 Yom Kippur war, many counselors were
called upon to provide help to the grief stricken. Hardly a
family in Israel escaped without some serious casualty. Two

---

*Opinions expressed in this paragraph are the responsibility
of the senior author.

groups of American psychologists and psychiatrists volunteered to provide mental health and counseling services and did so with distinction. In the ministry of welfare a special program was initiated for group counseling of war widows. It was a deeply moving experience for the therapists and one which illustrates a society which has known too much death and which prizes life passionately and which is deeply compassionate to the children and the wives of war's victims. One of the most tragic of the terrorist acts was the machine gunning of a school bus near the northern border. Children who survived the slaughter and their school mates refused to go to school for a time and developed a form of school trauma, fortunately unknown in most other nations. Professionals were flown in to facilitate a readjustment both on the part of the children and their parents.

Immigration

Each new wave of immigration brings with it its own special kinds of problems--not the least of which is illustrated in the Ashkenazi-Sephardi issues. As indicated earlier, the reformed school system was partially aimed at coping with this problem and among other things new schools were created which intentionally integrated a wide variety of such ethnic groups with the expectation that the children of these diverse cultures would build a common culture around the school experience. However, each new group had its difficulties: the Indian Jews, the Russian-Georgian Jews, the Black Jews, and not the least of the problems, the American Jews who were accustomed to a higher standard of living and for whom adjustment to the economic hardships was too much to bear. Thus, the American immigrants were amongst those showing a high percentage (32%) of failures and return to their previous country and home. Throughout however, and despite the constant criticism which the absorption agency receives in the Israeli press, the idealism and the survival necessity have forged a determination to take in the homeless and pursued and help them to build a meaningful life for themselves. The agencies involved have pioneered in the development of adaptation procedures to new vocations for older immigrants, matching talents to jobs, providing re-training opportunities for those whose specialities are not in current demand, and in some circumstances even creating new jobs. The traditional vocational counseling approaches have found full use in the complex problems of immigrant absorbtion.

The Kibbutz

The collective settlement has perhaps attracted more atten-tion than any other facet of Israeli society. Actually no more than 3% of the population live in the kibbutz although another

219

2% or more live in other forms of collectivization. The Israeli
kibbutz is perhaps one of the few utopian societies which have
survived more than one generation. However, kibbutz children
do have problems. Personal, social, and vocational counselors
are available in the kibbutz schools and are trained at Israeli
universities. On occasion, the collective spirit overlaps into
the guidance function and a guidance committee is in operation
rather than a single guidance counselor. The kibbutzim use all
psychological services including group counseling, group dynamics
and organizational development despite the fact that they are so
steeped in the group approach that one might think they would
seek relief from "grouped" treatment. They are avid consumers of
all available approaches and have available, for example, special
clinical facilities for special education problems. On occasion
the cultural pressure for college education seems to conflict
with the work ethic in the kibbutz and compromises have to be
effected to permit a kibbutznik to go to college even though the
special training may not be in demand in the kibbutz.

Guidance for women

Israel is a land of strange contrasts in its attitudes
toward women. Placards on the buses encourage women to work.
Past prime minister was the late Golda Meier. Women serve in the
army alongside men although rather rarely in combat. Yet there
is little doubt but that the home is a female responsibility with
male domination of the family as the general rule. Furthermore,
religious dictates separate women from men in the synagogues.
Within the Arab and Moslem culture, the separation is even more
distinct with educational opportunities beyond the elementary
school being severely limited. However, the winds of change are
being sensed in both the Jewish and Moslem communities and
promise greater freedom, educational opportunity and shared home
responsibility. The generation gap seems much minimized in
Israel, particularly with respect to mothers and adult daughters
who can be seen walking hand in hand or arm in arm in any street
in Tel Aviv. The kibbutz which literally pioneered in the
freedom of women has in recent years found some sentiment in
favor of greater involvement of mothers with their own children.
In some of the strictest communal structures, children were to
be considered as belonging to the entire group. However, this
has been much modified and even in a few kibbutzim, children
are permitted to live with their parents. Finding women still
being pressed into the traditional female occupations such as
working in the kitchen or the nursery, some kibbutzim have with
great dedication created special work situations suitable to
women. For example, a group in the south of Israel abandoned
its cattle business as too difficult for women to handle and
created a rose growing business which was light enough physically
to utilize the female kibbutzniks.

The Israeli Defense Force functions additionally to provide major training opportunity for many young people. All serve right after the high school graduation, men and women. It is a great mixer, marriage maker, job teacher and of course defender. Through its annual requirements of 4 to 6 weeks of reserve duty, it is also a great interrupter of the college year. This the Israelis consider to be perhaps the smallest of their problems.

The relationship of kibbutzniks to Israel in general and the relationship in turn of Israeli children to other national groups is by no means clear. Many value differences have been found in studies. However, in a study by Magen (1971) it was apparent that urban Israeli children and urban American children seem to report the same kinds of positive experiences. Highest in frequency for both groups were experiences dealing with human relationships. However, the kibbutz children surprisingly report fewer of these than do either the Americans or other Israeli children and show a tie of 27.6 percent each for frequency of positive experiences dealing with excitement and with human relationships. In generalizing techniques or solutions from the Israeli situation to the American or vice versa, considerable caution is necessary in the light of the cultural diversity of both countries.

Thus crisis by crisis, and balancing compassion with toughness to survive in a hostile world, and utilizing all that the sciences of human behavior can provide for them, the Israelis have been creating a modern society upon the most ancient of lands. Guidance counselors have a favorable image if only because they have functioned at a high professional level. By borrowing from the Americans, the French, the Russians, and countless others, and mostly by their own wits and determination, the Israelis are determined to provide their children with the best of possible educational opportunities and the most of an always precarious life.

References

Catteral, Calvin (Ed.) Psychology in the schools in international perspective. Columbus: International School Psychology Steering Committee, Vol. I, 1976; Vol. II, 1977.

Garcia, Sandra, J.A. A comparison of assimilation and acculturation of Moroccan Jews in Israel and Blacks in America. Report to the Ford Foundation, 1974.

Landsman, Moshe. Welfare problems of families with large numbers of children. Report to the Ministry of Welfare, 1970. State of Israel, 1970. (available only in Hebrew)

Magen, Zippora. Positive experiences: their relationship to
  some personality traits and their influence on the characteristics of adolescent aspirations. Masters thesis,
  Tel-Aviv University, 1971. (available in Hebrew only)

Mar'i, Sami K. Arab education in Israel. Syracuse: Syracuse
  University Press, 1978.

State of Israel. Statistical abstracts of Israel, 1975.
  Jerusalem: Central Bureau of Statistics, 1975.

Suggested readings

Amir, Yehuda; Bizman, Aharon & Rivner, Miriam. Effects of inter-
  ethnic contact on friendship choices in the military.
  Journal of Cross-Cultural Psychology, 1972, 4, 361-373.

Bentwich, Joseph S. Education in Israel. Philadelphia: Jewish
  Publication Society, 1965.

Curtis, Michael & Chertoff, Mordecai, S. (Eds.), Israel: Social
  structure and change. New Brunswick, N.J.: Transition
  Books, 1973.

Elon, Amos. The Israelis. New York: Holt, Rinehart and Winston,
  1971.

Goitein, S.D. Jews and Arabs. New York: Schocken, 1964.

Harkabi, Y. Arab attitudes to Israel. Jerusalem: Keter
  Publishing House, 1972.

Hermon, Simon K. Israelis and Jews. Philadelphia: Jewish
  Publication Society, 1970.

Hofman, Jochanon. Identity and intergroup perception in Israel:
  Jews and Arabs. Occasional Papers on the Middle East No. 7.
  Haifa: Institute of Middle Eastern Studies, University of
  Haifa, 1976.

Kugelmass, Sol.; Lieblich, Amia & Bossik, Dorit. Patterns of
  intellectual ability in Jewish and Arab children in Israel.
  Jounral of Cross-Cultural Psychology, 1974, 5, 184-198.

Lieblich, Amia; Ninio, Amat & Kugelmass, Sol. Effects of ethnic origin and parental SES on WPPSI performance of pre-school children in Israel. *Journal of Cross-Cultural Psychology*, 1972, 3, 159-168.

Litvinoff, Barnet. *To the house of their fathers*. New York: Praeger, 1965.

Rabin, Albert I. *Kibbutz studies*. East Lansing, Mich.: Michigan State University Press, 1971.

Sachar, Abram C. *A history of the Jews*, 5th edition. New York: Knopf, 1965.

Segre, V.D. *Israel, a society in transition*. London: Oxford University Press, 1971.

Wiesel, Elie. *One generation after*. New York: Random House, 1965.

Zim, Jacob. *My shalom, my peace*. Tel Aviv: Sabra Books, 1975.

Ziv, Avner; Shani, Abraham & Nebenhouse, Soshana. Adolescents' education in Israel and in the Soviet Union: Differences in moral judgement. *Journal of Cross-Cultural Psychology*, 1975, 6, 108-121.

Ziv, Avner and Iraeli, R. The influence of bombardment on children living in the kibbutzim. *Journal of Counseling Psychology*, 1973, 40, 287-291.

Section Seven

THE FAR EAST

The ancient civilizations of the Far East are like the tribu-
taries of a mighty river that moved slowly through its long history
of rich cultural epochs. It has forged a set of value orientations
and life styles all of its own. Its peoples' national traditions
are the outcome of strong religious tenets, tribal and family customs,
and above all, of the centuries-long isolation from the rest of the
world.

While this aloofness helped generate relative homogeneity of
cultural patterns, philosophical perspectives, and life-styles, it
kept the rulers and the masses of Far-Eastern nations out of the
mainstream of world affairs. With the exception of a few travelers
who moved sporadically between East and West and brought information--
often inaccurate tales--back home, there was little contact or dialogue with the outside world. Modernization of life and technological
progress were slow in coming.

At present, the Far East is full of contrasts and conflicts,
many of them resulting from the stagnant past confronting the age of
technology. The contrast of high levels in cultural awareness and
of low levels in living standards creates tensions in some countries.
Rapid technological developments in a relatively short time creates
another set of tensions in striving societies, characterized by confrontations between traditional values and modern exigencies of daily
life.

The three countries discussed in this Section--Japan, South Ko-

225

rea, and Malaysia--have instituted, to varying degrees, guidance
services in their educational systems, particularly with an emphasis on vocational planning. The countries differ from each other
in many ways. Japan was for long the conqueror of Korea which opposed the cultural and political hegemony and managed to maintain
its ethnic uniqueness under great hardship. Malaysia existed under
colonial rule for generations and reflects the European influences
of that era even now. There are also major differences in the levels
of modernization of the three countries. By now, Japan has become
a technological giant, with all the blessings and curses that accom-
pany the status. On the other hand, South Korea and Malaysia have
attained lower levels of modernization and industrial development.

The author of Chapters 19 and 20, Walter L. Powers, is an American professor with long experience in the Far East. Since 1945,
he has been there more than twenty times as visiting professor, consultant for UNESCO, and adviser to the Korean Ministry of Education.
The author of Chapter 21, A. G. Watts, writes from the British perspective. A guidance researcher of the National Institute for Careers Education and Counselling in Cambridge, he went to Malaysia
to become acquainted with the present state of guidance services in
that country.

Stuff It

Containers, Gifts & Silk Flowers

Portia Leah Brewster

Portia Leah Smith

Margo Lynne James

Mrs. Portia B. Smith

Mrs. Margo B. James

Mrs. Cassandra B. Austin

2829 New Boston Road • 838-8710

19

JAPAN

Walter L. Powers

Recorded history does not provide the exact date when the ancestors of the Japanese people settled in the Japanese island and developed their own culture. Since there was no mass migration or military conquest, it is assumed that the Japanese nation developed gradually over a long period of time. Since the early history of most countries is derived through legend, Japan is no exception. It has only been since World War II that interest in the beginnings of Japan shifted from legend to research of material data. For example, extensive research is being carried out with the aid of ancient Japanese documents, Chinese and Korean historical material and archeological artifacts.

Contemporary scholars tend to classify history of Japan in three periods: ancient and medieval Japan to C 1550; the early modern history (1550-1850) and Japan since 1950. Since counseling and guidance is a modern phenomenon, the historical development of Japan as it relates to the counseling and guidance movement will be restricted to Japan since 1950.

The Educational System

Prior to the modern restoration of Japan schools in 1792, education of their children was based primarily upon the social class. Children of the ruling class were given special instruction in the military arts whereas children of the merchant class were taught reading, writing and mathematics in inferior facilities. These

inferior facilities were called temple schools. The Meiji restoration in 1868 was the beginning of a new Japan and a new educational system. A system of elementary schools, middle schools and
colleges and universities was established with no social distinction. Compulsory education in the beginning was only three years.
At the same time, normal schools were established and the imperial
university was recognized. The pattern of development seemed to
be highly influenced by the German system of education with a
great deal of western European influence. For example, in 1887
E. Hausknecht from Germany gave a series of lectures on the
science of education at Tokyo University. After this series of
lectures, German educational approaches experienced remarkable
progress, and many German books were translated.

Following the Russo-Japanese war in which Japan was victori-
ous, compulsory education was increased to four years by 1900 and
to six years by 1908. The education system became free at that
point in time and attendance began to increase significantly due
to the change in financing. In fact, it grew to 95% attendance
within a very short period of time. For forty years the education facilities increased significantly along with the improve-
ments of the capitalistic economy and the development of Japan.
During the war period of 1940-45, a "national school system" was
introduced primarily because of the war efforts. The number of
years spent in the middle school and high school were reduced
greatly in order to meet the war effort with which Japan was
faced.

Sweeping changes were made when the American occupational
force arrived. The system which had not changed greatly since its
introduction in 1872 was streamlined and democratized. A 6-3-3-4
plan was established. Not only was the structure changed but also
the purpose of education changed significantly. The educational
program which had led to imperialism and World War II had to be
changed in the establishment of a new purpose which laid the
ground work for peace. The fundamental educational law provided
a framework for education leading toward respect for the worth and
dignity of the individual. In the development of the democratic
culture, it was envisioned that education was the key. Through
such a system the nation would ultimately contribute to the welfare of mankind and the realization of world peace. By 1947 many
sweeping changes had been made. Compulsory education was
increased to nine years. Co-education was introduced at all
levels, affecting government universities most significantly since
they had only been previously opened to male students. De-
centralization of education, allowing greater freedom at the provincial and local levels, was established. Textbooks and curriculum regulations could no longer be dictated by the central
government. Elementary and lower secondary schools were maintained by the cities, towns and villages, while special schools and

228

upper secondary schools were financed by the provincial government.

Entry into elementary schools begins at six years of age and is continuous for six years. Pre-school education is not generally attained. For example, in 1956 only 21.8 percent of the first grade pupils had attended a kindergarten. Following six years in elementary school, entry into lower secondary schools is automatic in the government-controlled schools because the lower secondary school is also compulsory. Entrance to upper secondary schools, after completing the six-three plan, is by way of entrance examinations. More than half of the students pass the examination for entrance into the upper secondary school. The number of school leavers following lower secondary school is diminishing.

Soviet books on education have recently come into Japan and are having an effect on the educational system through extensive leftist student movements. However, it will not be easy to replace the long tradition of German influence as well as recent American interventions.

The Guidance Movement

Guidance in Japanese schools can be traced to almost fifty years ago. Professor G. Kohachi Fujimoto of the Rekkyo University in Japan places the history in two main periods: pre- and post-World War II. Each must be considered separately because of differing influences during these periods.

Before World War II, the primary purpose of guidance in all compulsory education was to prepare skilled workers for the society. The guidance services were primarily directed toward assessment through testing and placement. The principles of guidance were introduced to Japan primarily from influences of the industrial development in the United States. In 1920, the city of Osaka, second largest in Japan, opened a Vocational Guidance Bureau for Youth patterned after Frank Parsons' Vocational Bureau in Boston. This Bureau was the first public facility in Japan for Vocational Guidance. The following years, the Employment Exchange law was promulgated in Tokyo which instituted public employment exchange offices for testing and counseling youth. The introduction and standardization of translated American intelligence tests and other psychological tests were carried out in the Employment Exchange and Counseling Center for youth. The Minister of Education in 1927 issued directives throughout Japan to utilize individual personality assessments in guiding elementary school children going into middle school by matching children's abilities and school vocational goals. Also, during this year, the Japanese Vocational Guidance Association was formed for the purpose of publishing a journal, holding training institutes for vocational

229

counselors, conducting research, and publishing children's career oriented textbooks.

Beginning in 1938, with growing Japanese imperialism, the pressures to mobilize the nation toward war industries somewhat changed the original vocational guidance goals of "adjustment between the development of individuality and the social need." Vocational guidance was used as a means to mobilize the necessary labor force for the sake of the war. In 1942 the elementary schools were ordered to be called Kokumin Gakko (Japanese people's schools) and the central ideas of vocational guidance were lost.

Guidance activities following World War II influenced in part by the U. S. military occupational government plowed a new direction. Two new laws were promulgated which gave direction and purpose to vocational guidance. Under the new school Education Law, the 6-3-3-4 system of education was established with 6-3 grades made compulsory. The role of vocational guidance in the secondary school was directed "to develop individual student's ability for self choice in career planning." The Employment Security Law was established to undertake vocational placement for persons seeking employment and to act in cooperation with vocational guidance in schools. During this period, in-service training for vocational guidance workers was established as a cooperative venture between the Japanese Vocational Guidance Association, the Ministry of Education, and various universities, including Tokyo University, Kyoto University, Nihon University and Rikkyo University. Later, the in-service programs were limited to teacher-counselor training only and were conducted through the Ministry of Education.

In 1949, with the establishment of the Educational Personnel Certificates for teachers and administrators, vocational guidance specialists were offered certificates for junior and senior high schools. At the same time, the Employment Security Law required graduating seniors of the junior and senior high schools and universities the opportunity for placement services through cooperation between the public employment security office and the school. This free service was located in the schools.

Placement service as a single purpose of guidance did not last very long. Under sponsorship of the Japan Vocational Guidance Association, Don Super of Columbia University provided a two-week lecture tour which laid the theoretical foundation for developmental guidance. Later, Henry Borow of the University of Minnesota lectured extensively. The teacher-counselor approach began to improve with the publication of manuals for home-room teachers in junior high schools and high school. With the publication of the Teacher's Manual for Pupil Guidance in 1965, the social and personal adjustment aspects of counseling began to take shape. In-service training programs for teacher-counselors from two to eight weeks duration was provided by the Ministry of Education.

Present Condition of Guidance

Counseling and guidance as conceived by the Ministry of Education is directed to accomplish the following at the junior high school:

(a) Guidance should be given not only to those going directly into the labor market immediately upon graduation, but also to those going on to high school and those leaving school for family business.

(b) Guidance in the school should take place throughout the three grade levels in a systematic and continuous process.

(c) Home room and group guidance activities should be provided:
1. To help the pupils to understand their own individuality and family environment.
2. To help the pupils to develop an awareness of self through various tests and the relationship between test results and their plans for vocations and careers.
3. To help pupils to understand the nature of the world of work in terms of job specifications, qualifications, requirements, supply and demand.
4. To help the pupils gain an understanding of the high school curriculum and programs leading to vocational careers.
5. To help the pupils to understand the adjustments needed in the transition from school to work.

(d) Individual educational and vocation counseling should take place for each student.

In the secondary high schools, educational and vocational guidance is directed in a similar manner and purpose as in the junior high school. That is, it emphasizes the vocational aspects of all areas of the curriculum with the teacher-counselor concept. Counseling is conducted in the framework of the "home-room" activities. However, they differ because of the diversity of high schools in Japan where the conduct of vocational guidance is left to the discretion of each school on the basis of its own unique nature, i.e., Agricultural High Schools, Commercial High Schools, etc.

According to Osao Mizutoni of the Ministry of Education, the present condition leaves much to be desired although the system has

231

been rather well spelled out. For instance, he believes that many
of the home-room teachers do not have a full understanding of vocational guidance and lack the ability to guide pupils. Many of
the teacher-counselors do not have enough professional knowledge,
counseling techniques, counseling room facilities, and individual
data on each pupil. However, strenuous efforts are being made to
correct deficiencies through cooperation of the National Ministry
of Education and the local school authorities by providing courses,
handbooks, reference materials, and research information.

Vocational Testing

The adoption and modification of foreign-born tests in
Japan has required considerable effort. The major problem was
social-cultural differences. Direct translations cannot be made
because of semantic differences. All tests developed abroad are
not culturally free; consequently, the validity needs considerable effort in developing and refinement of the instrument for
the Japanese. The early testing movement in Japan was limited to
tools and apparatus used in experimental psychology; for example,
reaction time, basal discrimination, sensation and mental sort-
ing were used as a means for predicting occupational aptitude.
Testing has lagged behind American and European efforts, although
since 1970 significant movement has occurred in the utilization of
tests and their use in vocational counseling. It was not until
1925 that Suzuki developed a Binet-Simon test into Japanese. In
1947, Tanaka developed the revised Stanford-Binet test of 1916.
The WISC and WAIS have been translated and validated by Token for
use in Japan.

Vocational interest tests have been in use in Japan now since
1961 when Kadana developed the Kadana-Strong Vocational Interest
Inventory, thirty-four years after Strong first developed the test
in the United States of America. The Kuder Preference Record was
developed for use in Japan during World War II by Token. In 1948
the Japanese Vocational Guidance Association published a vocational
interest test which is presently in wide use. Special aptitude
tests such as the Seashore Measure of Musical Talent and the
Minnesota Clerical Test were translated for the Japanese in the
1950's. It only took two years after the GATB was introduced in
the U.S. for the Japanese Vocational Guidance Association to develop the equivalent form in Japan.

Sources suggested for additional reading

Dore, R. P. Education in Tokugawa, Japan. Berkeley: University of California Press, 1965.

Foreign Affairs Association of Japan. Japan year book. Tokyo: Author, 1944.

Hirano Ken'ichiro. Japanese educational policy. Asian Research, 1968, 15, October.

Japanese National Commission for UNESCO. Development of modern system of education in Japan. Tokyo: Author, 1960.

Japanese National Commission for UNESCO. Japan, its land, people, and culture. Tokyo: Author, 1964.

Keenleyside, H. I. and Thomas, A. F. History of Japanese education and present educational system. Tokyo, 1937.

Passin, H. Japanese education. New York: Teachers College Press, 1970.

Proceedings of the First Asian Regional Seminar on Educational and Vocational Guidance and the Second General Assembly of the Asian Regional Association on Vocational and Educational Guidance. Tokyo: Japan Vocational Guidance Association, 1974.

Silberman, B. S. and Harootunian, H. D. (Eds.) Japan in crisis: Essays on democracy. Princeton: Princeton University Press, 1974.

20

REPUBLIC OF KOREA

Walter L. Powers

National Traditions

The racial origin of the Korean people is obscure but the primary stock is believed to be Tanguisic which is related to the Mongols with some Chinese mixture. The earliest written record of the Korean peninsula occurs in a Chinese history of about 109 B.C. During the Chow Dynasty, a Chinese prince was set up as Lord of "Chosun," a name applied to Chinese colonies along the northwest coast of the peninsula. During most of its recorded history, beginning with the Chow Dynasty and proceeding through the Yi Dynasty which ended in 1910, Koreans have been subject to presence and influence of either China or Japan.

From 1910-1945, Korea was once again under the rule of Japan and the long awaited liberation of 1945 was to be shortlived. At the time of Korea's liberation from Japan, and in accordance with the Potsdam agreement, U.S.S.R. combat forces entered North Korea and the military troops from the United States entered South Korea with the 38th parallel acting as boundary between the now divided country. On June 25, 1950, troops from North Korea attacked the South Korean forces to begin a war which ended in 1953. Many Americans and United Nations troops were killed but the Korean people bore the brunt of warfare with over 1,300,000 civilian and military casualties and 100,000 children orphaned with millions rendered homeless.

The Republic of Korea began, then, in 1953 beset with a myriad of problems: economic deprivations, a ravaged land and homeless and demoralized people. The Koreans, however, are an intelligent, industrious people who have fought back against these obstacles to create a republic advancing toward economic self-sufficiency with an awareness of the advantages of comprehensive education.

The Educational System

Education, in any formal sense, seems to have come to Korea from China during the earlier Buddhist period when scholarship was confined to the priesthood. Priests served as teachers for the children of the kings after the formal adoption of Buddhism as the state religion in 371 A.D. There were no attempts to set up schools for the people.

With the introduction of Confucianism in Korea, the impetus for education took place. Confucianism brought the belief that real problems in society could be solved by learning the rules of social conduct and the wisdom of the past. The teacher, as the transmitter of this wisdom and its interpreter, had a high place in society. Position of power in the government went to those who scored high on civil service examinations. The content of these examinations was based on the Classics as taught in schools. A school system was established with the best teachers brought to the capital city to instruct advanced students, supervise the examinations, and advise the court.

The schools were staffed by teachers who were qualified by examination of the content of the Classics, the same as government officials had been examined. The method of instruction was primarily memorization of the Classics written in Chinese characters. The students proceeded at their own pace in an ungraded situation. Some Koreans of today, when hearing of some tendency toward upgraded schools in the United States, say it is the return to the old village Confucian school. Some elements still exist today. I visited rural village schools in which memorization took place by pupils going over and over the material aloud chanting their passages in a loud singsong.

Toward the middle of the nineteenth century, Korea was locked against the outside world and became a hermit nation for several generations. This isolation had developed over the years due to repeated invasions from Japan and China. Western missionaries sometimes were killed, and armed expeditions were met with force. However, toward the end of the nineteenth century, both internal and external pressures proposed treaties to be extended with Japan, Britain, Russia, France, and the United States.

The educational destiny of Korean schools was extremely influenced by three wars--one between the Chinese and Japanese in
1894-95, one between Japan and Russia in 1904, and World War II.
The Japanese won the first two of these wars by sending their
armies into Korea, developing ports, building railroads, and
fighting battles on Korean territory. Under the Japanese, the
elementary schools became the training grounds to educate the
citizens of the expanded Japanese empire. The curriculum emphasized the study of the Japanese language, history, and culture.

The defeat of the Japanese Empire in 1945 brought about almost as great an upheaval in Korea as it did in Japan. The modern
government, industry, and schools developed by the Japanese had
also been managed by Japanese to serve their purposes. As all of
the Japanese leaders and technicians returned to their homeland,
Koreans, with the assistance of the American Military Government,
attempted to take over and operate. Since the Korean schools had
been developed to produce citizens or workers of Japan, the textbooks were now in the wrong language and had the wrong content for
teaching Korean children how to live in a full and hopefully democratic country. Almost all of the administrators left the school
system, and so did many of the teachers. Also, those Koreans who
had received training under the Japanese were indoctrinated thoroughly with the authoritarian approach to educational problems.
There was very little understanding of democracy as an ideology,
or as a means of operation.

The five-five pattern of organization of the Korean school
system was abandoned in favor of the six-year elementary school,
three-year middle school or junior high school, and a three-year
high school. This added two years at both the elementary and
secondary schools. With the development of the junior high
schools, it became possible to put some secondary school education
in reach of many country children who were not able to go to urban
centers. Korean parents realizing a privilege that had long been
denied them sent their children to school. For example, the number of children enrolled in primary school in the three years
immediately after the liberation of Korea from Japanese rule rose
from 1,370,000 to 2,490,000.

Administration and Control of the Educational System

All schools in the Republic of Korea are under the direct
control and supervision of the national government through the
Ministry of Education. Organized under the Minister of Education
are various bureau chiefs who have control over specific domains
of the educational system, i.e., Common Education; Higher Education; Technical Education; Cultural Affairs and Textbooks. There
are eleven city, country, and provincial boards who report to the

bureau chief. All curriculum changes must be channeled through and approved by the Ministry of Education which also is responsible for textbook selection and ordering.

In 1968, seventeen percent of the National Budget was allocated for national and public education. Seventy-one percent of the funds are allocated for national and public education, while twenty percent go to secondary education and nine percent to higher education. Free compulsory education is available through the sixth grade not including kindergarten and more than 95% of all elementary aged children attended school.

Secondary education covers the six years beyond elementary school. The secondary schools are divided into two three-year units; middle school (grades 7-9) and high school (grades 10-12). Secondary education is not compulsory, although recent moves had been made by the Ministry of Education to provide compulsory comprehensive high schools. Until recently, students have been admitted to middle school and high school only upon the completion of an exacting competitive examination. Although the examinations are still utilized, students compete for placement in neighborhood high schools rather than take open exams for all high schools. Students are expected to pay entrance fees and tuition.

The Korean spoken and written language is quite distinct from both Japanese and Chinese. Its alphabet which was devised during the reign of King Syong from A.D. 1418-1450 is considered one of the most ingenious writing systems ever devised. In its modern form, Hangul consists of 24 phonetic symbols. During the Japanese occupation of Korea, the children were forced to use the Japanese language, consequently affecting the literacy of the language. Since the 1945 liberation, Hangul with its one-to-one correspondence between symbol and sound, has been again in use and has contributed to a high literacy rate in South Korea estimated to be 90 percent.

Programs for adult education are divided into two broad categories: (1) education for illiterates, and (2) training careers in trades and vocations. Many of these adult programs have been accomplished through governmental sponsorship conducted by professional and volunteer teachers. The government has also published and distributed thousands of free copies of Basic Korean. There are twenty-six schools for adult education open to anyone. Of the total number of courses offered, one-half are vocational and the other half are cultural in nature. In addition to these schools, there are 527 privately operated institutes for adult vocational education. Adult education in the Republic of Korea has so far shown gratifying results in elementary illiteracy and has made marked achievement in raising the standard of literacy in less-developed agricultural and fishing communities.

The basic criteria for the curriculum of all elementary schools are set by the Ministry of Education. The Korean language, arithmetic, social studies, natural science, moral education, and physical education are taught in grades one through six. Simple vocational training such as homemaking, gardening, and working with tools is provided in grades four through six.

In middle schools, the basic curriculum includes the Korean language, mathematics, social studies, art, music, and physical education plus electives selected from a list including several languages and vocational training. Although a foreign language is an elective subject, practically all middle school students begin the study of English in the seventh grade.

The academic high school offers the classical curriculum plus electives and extra-curricular activities. Required courses include the Korean language, social studies, Korean history, mathematics, science, music, art, physical education, and vocational training. English is offered as an elective but it is taken by most students. Many high school students are employed full-time so the schools run shifts with a regular high school curriculum offered evenings.

Colleges and universities have expanded rapidly during the post-liberation years. This expansion has, however, often been accomplished with a distinct lack of planning at the expense of quality. Since no adequate survey of human resources and job opportunities has been made, the school curriculum is not adequate to fit the real needs of the country.

The Ministry of Education program is now placing more emphasis on natural and applied science. The Ministry of Education also is dedicated to: (1) improving the facilities of national universities and extending financial subsidies for private institutions to improve their facilities; (2) establishing "guidance centers" at all national universities; (3) creating ties between national universities and industrial corporations for coordination in research; and (4) increasing the number of professors in graduate schools of all national universities.

Concept of Guidance

The moral and ethical values of the South Koreans which have historically been built upon Confucian attitudes have exerted a strong influence on the concept of guidance.

These attitudes can generally be classified as time orientation, man-nature orientation, and power-status orientation.

All people must examine problems rooted in the present or past and yet must try to anticipate the future; however, the differences toward the view of time are related to the degree of precedence given. Korean culture, which historically has been oriented in the past, views the good life, defined in terms of past living, where history has largely been viewed as cyclical and the future regarded as mere repetition of some position of the past. Koreans historically have not viewed their institutions as developmental. Education in this setting has not been dynamic or experimental, and until the Japanese introduced colonial-flavored modern education in the twentieth century, the Korean school system was designed only to perpetuate the best of the past in unaltered form. From the tender age when the child memorized the first Chinese character until many years later, if exceptionally able, he studied to pass the royal examination and become a government official. The curriculum of the scholar was the literature of the past. The student studied to imitate rather than exceed, to conform rather than create. Education was divorced entirely from the social, economic, and scientific problems of the present.

The second cultural attitude lies in the relation of man to nature. In the East-Asian culture, man has not been as concerned with gaining mastery over his environment as he has been in living in harmony with it. Mountains, even though they might obstruct travel, and rivers, even though they might be impassable during certain seasons, have not been viewed as frustrating inconveniences. Rather, these are facts to which man must discipline himself. The challenge lies not in constructing new weapons for mastery but in developing a new degree of resignedness. Like the time orientation, the traditional view held by Koreans with respect to nature has not contributed to a dynamic educational system. If man does not seek mastery over nature, there is little need for schools to be concerned with the skills for manipulating the physical universe. Rather, schools with this attitude would be concerned with developing the person of meditation who seeks to avoid the common, tedious, daily environment by finding and developing problems in a more abstract and aesthetic realm. The educated man is the man of contemplation who carries about him an air of peace and tranquility. His view toward the natural environment is shown in many and diverse ways, but perhaps best expressed in his works of art.

The third attitude results in a cultural condition called power and status orientation. A power structure has existed in Korea that equated position with authority, while social custom has further equated authority with validity. This hierarchial structure and manner of decision making are also reflected in the classroom, counseling office, and in the family. The teacher, counselor, and father each occupy positions of ultimate respect, trust, and power. Their word is law. The obvious difficulty in using modern educational or counseling methods within this frame-

240

work is readily seen. The schools, in both fostering cooperation
and stressing at the same time reliance on the individual's
ability to solve his own problems, runs into conflict with family
and societal traditions, and the self-concept of the student.
Moreover, the school finds it difficult to break down its historical authoritarian structure for fear that the teacher or
counselor may lose the traditional respect felt for him.

Development and Training of Guidance Personnel

The general theory of guidance was introduced about 1949 by
Korean professors who had studied in the United States following
the liberation of 1945. In 1954 the Central Education Institute
provided in-service training courses for teachers in which
"Guidance and Mental Hygiene" were introduced. It wasn't until
1957 that training of guidance teachers was introduced and the
Ministry of Education designated "Teacher-Counselor" posts within
certain schools.

Seoul National University and Kyungbuk National University
developed in-service training for teachers to fill these newly
developed "Teacher-Counselor" positions in the schools. More
than 240 hours of training courses were held at these two universities. Courses covered in the training program were: (1) Psychology of Human Behavior; (2) Principles of Guidance and Counseling; (3) Human Mental and Physical Development; (4) Psychological
Tests; and (5) Mental Health. Consultants in these in-service
training programs and subsequent seminars including this author
were: Professors Bum Mo Chung, Sung Ik Kang, Young Duk Lee from
Seoul National University, Sang Loh Lee of Kyungbuk, Hee Kyung
Chung of Ewha Women's University, and Won Shik Chung of the
Central Educational Research Institute. The institute type programs conducted at Seoul National University and Kyungbuk National University consisted of 40 and 30 participants each.

The major thrust of the counselor role in the early years of
school counseling in Korea focused on testing and vocational education. The first psychological test battery in Korea was prepared by Bum Mo Chung as early as 1955. In April 1960 the Central
Education Research Institute began standardizing Individual Intelligence tests for adolescents and adults. A research team
composed of Professors Bum Mo Chung, Youg Shen Jun, Ki Suk Kim,
and Won Shik Chung, translated and constructed alternate items for
the WAIS to compensate for cultural differences. The test was
standardized on a group of about 4,000 subjects. The Korean Institute for Research in Behavioral Sciences founded by Dr. Bum Mo
Chung now provides services similar to Educational Testing
Services in the United States. The testing movement has grown and
counselors now have available in Korean language the following
type tests:

Intelligence tests	14 kinds
Achievement tests	20 kinds
Aptitude tests	9 kinds
Interest tests	3 kinds
Personality tests	12 kinds
Attitude tests	7 kinds
Other tests	9 kinds

The second major thrust of guidance activities in Korean schools was aimed toward vocational counseling and vocational education. This emphasis was brought about when the people of Korea were faced with the enormous task of building their own economy following the Korean conflict. There arose a huge demand for engineers, artisans, businessmen, experts in fisheries and agriculture, and technicians in all fields; this still exists today. Aware of this need, the Ministry of Education, with advice from the United Nations and the United States, instigated a long-range program of vocational guidance and vocational education. Beginning with simple prevocational projects in the elementary schools and continuing prevocational education as a required subject in the middle schools, this program is most strongly implemented at the secondary level in the vocational high school, and continues upward through technical and professional courses in colleges and universities. Counselors with vocational guidance orientation are being prepared with increasing numbers to meet the challenge required in the development of their nation.

At the elementary level, girls in the fifth and sixth grades are taught homemaking and boys simple work with tools--usually for two to three hours per week. In all middle schools, both boys and girls spend five hours per week at required vocational courses in which the counselor is expected to play an important role. At the high school level, three types of institutions offer vocational training: the vocational high school, the comprehensive high school, and junior technical colleges. Unfortunately, most counselor positions are located primarily in the comprehensive high school.

Since the traditional concept of education in Korea has always been classical scholarship, the idea of practical vocational training and vocational guidance as a vital part of education is new to parents and students. A special effort has, therefore, been made to attract vocational students by providing buildings and facilities in every way equal to those of the best academic high schools. School counselors have attempted to emphasize the dignity of vocational competence as well as the need for vocational skills in building for a future. In spite of this, counselors have encountered the problem that neither the parent nor students have yet generally accepted the idea that a vocational education carries as much prestige as an academic school. Students still

242

throng to the academic institution for programs, while some vocational programs have enrollments far below their training capacity. Full blame for this condition cannot be placed upon the parents and students--because counselor training itself follows classical academic models of abstract, ideological, and scholastic theory.

Student Personnel Services

This author assisted Seoul National University and Kyungbuk University in Taegu to establish a student guidance center in 1962. The objectives were to assist in the personal and social adjustment of the students and provide a meaningful university life. Psychology Professor Lee Sang Lo of Kyungbuk was appointed the first director of the center. Under his direction and with assistance from Dr. Jesse Tarwater of The Asia Foundation, the center services were expanded through the establishment of three departments and several sections to provide counseling, guidance, research and training.

The objectives of the student guidance center as described in its first brochure were: 1) to promote mental health with emotional stability; 2) to assist efficient adjustment by developing the ability to solve problems; 3) to make efforts for the fullest individual development by helping in the choice of careers or the bases of correct and reasonable understanding and reliable materials; 4) to encourage the spirit of cooperation through student activities; and 5) to endeavor to promote consistent and scientific research. The organization was structured as follows:

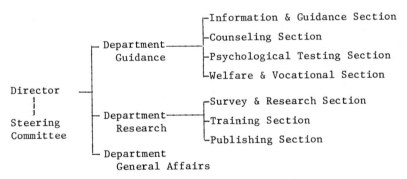

The steering committee consists of professional members of the related fields which plan services, activities, oversee the budget, and elect the Director of the Center.

The Department of Guidance has the following functions: gather and make available vocational and job information; provide scholastic information regarding Korean and foreign colleges and universities; give information regarding study and study methods; provide orientation for freshmen and transfer students; conduct conferences; arrange interviews between professors and students; provide counseling services on emotional and personal problems, family and family relations, sex and courtship, career problems, study methods, etc.

A section of Psychological Testing provides individual and group testing of intelligence, aptitudes, interests, personality, etc. The Welfare and Vocational section provides the following: scholarship and financial aid; job and vocational aptitude analyses; job placement on a part-time or full-time basis.

The Department of Research conducts research, investigations, publishing, and training services. It is within this department that in-service and pre-service training takes place for persons specializing in Counseling and Guidance. The Center provides counseling practice, case conferencing, and counselor qualification examinations. The Research Department also publishes journals, guidebooks for student life and work, etc.

Guidance and counseling in an advancing nation is always in a state of evolution. This is true regardless of the level of development in the country. The Republic of Korea has made remarkable progress with its counseling and guidance program in the last two decades. Korean citizens are unusually dedicated to seeking an education for their children and youth. It has been a privilege for this author to have shared in the advancement of the goals of counseling and guidance in the schools of Korea.

Sources suggested for additional reading

Asian Regional Conference on Educational and Vocational Guidance
   (Proceedings). Tokyo: Japan Vocational Guidance Association,
   1967.

Bartz, P. M. South Korea. Oxford: Clarendon Press, 1972.

Beauchamp, G. A. Comparative analysis of curriculum systems. Wil-
   mette: Kagg Press, 1972.

Bereday, G. Z. Corporative method in education. New York: Holt,
   Rinehart and Winston, 1964.

Chung, Tae-Shi. Yesterday of Korean education. Korea Journal, 1963,
   3, (4).

Eckstein, M. A. Scientific investigations in comparative education.
   New York: Macmillan, 1969.

Fifty facts on Korea. Washington D.C.: Korean Pacific Press, 1950.

Fisher, J. E. Democracy and mission education in Korea. New York:
   Teachers College, 1928.

Goslin, W. E. Teacher education in Korea. Nashville: Peabody College
   for Teachers, 1965.

Handbook. Student Guidance Center, Kyungbuk University. Taegu,
   Korea, 1963.

Holmes, B. Problems in education, a comparative approach. New York:
   Humanities Press, 1965.

Korean Report. (Korean Information Office). 1966, 6, (3), July-
   September.

Korean Report. (Korean Information Office). 1967, 7, (1), January-
   March.

Korean Report. (Korean Information Office). 1969, 9, January-March.

Olt, Chae Kyung. Handbook of Korea. New York: Pageant Press, 1958.

Reeve, W. D. The Republic of Korea. Oxford: Oxford University Press,
   1963.

Wood, C. W. Secondary education in South Korea. The Educational
   Forum, 1959, 24, 99-106.

21

MALAYSIA

A. G. Watts

Formal career guidance services are a product of economic and social development. In relatively primitive societies, allocation to adult roles is determined largely by the family, caste or class into which one is born. As the society becomes more complex, these systems start to break bown, and career guidance services are needed to lubricate—and, perhaps, catalyse (Daws 1977)—increasing levels of social and occupational mobility. How then is the role of career guidance evolving in those Third World countries that are trying to accelerate the pace of economic and social development that they will be able to catch up with the living standards attained by the Western world? How far are they being influenced by the approaches to career guidance that have evolved in such industrialised countries as the USA and Britain? How applicable are these approaches to cultures that in many ways are very different?

An opportunity to examine these questions in the context of one developing country, Malaysia, was afforded by a three-week study tour which I carried out in February-March, 1977. This report outlines my impressions of the career guidance system that seems to be emerging there. Attention will be focused mainly on career guidance, because

This Chapter is a revised version of a paper published in the May 1978 issue of the International Journal for the Advancement of Counselling and is published here with the permission of that Journal's Editors.

this was the primary focus of my visit, but some mention will also be made of other aspects of guidance and counseling services.

The country and its educational system

Malaysia consists of the former Federation of Malaya, Sarawak, and Sabah (North Borneo). It is one of the richest of the developing countries, its wealth being principally based on tin, rubber, oil palm, and timber. There are though great disparities of wealth, many people living little above subsistence level. The population is multi-lingual and multi-racial: nearly half are Malays, about a third are Chinese, and the rest include Indians as well as Dayaks and other indigenous groups. The integration of Sabah and Sarawak with the Malay states is not yet complete, but gradually their educational systems, for example, are being brought into line with that in Peninsular Malaysia. The comments here will relate mainly to the latter, though most will be applicable to Sabah and Sarawak too.

The educational system is very centralised, with uniform curricula prescribed by the Ministry of Education. It has been greatly influenced by the British system, and is predominately academic in character and heavily examination-oriented. Bahasa Malaysia has gradually been replacing English as the main medium of instruction, though this process is not yet complete. The basic structure of the system consists of six years in primary school, followed by three years in lower secondary school, two in upper secondary school, and two in the sixth-form school. Automatic promotion operates from primary Standard 1 (1st grade) to Form 3 (approximately 9th grade) of secondary school. Nonetheless, a study of children born in 1956 in Peninsular Malaysia found that 13% had dropped out by the end of primary school, and 55% by the fourth year of post-primary education; for children born in 1960, the former figure had been reduced to 10%. (Murad Committee 1975) Drop-out rates are particularly high in the rural schools which serve the socio-economically most disadvantaged sector of the population.

Guidance provisions and problems

The origins of career guidance in Malaya (as it then was) date from 1939 (Ministry of Education 1966), and in 1959 a Youth Employment Service was established by the Ministry of Labour, though--as we shall see later--it has not been developed. The Ministry of Education's first circular on career guidance was published in 1960, and this initial display of interest was accentuated when, five years later, the abolition of the entrance examination for admission to secondary schools meant that the schools became comprehensive. The intention initially was that the curriculum would allow scope for student choice (in practice, the system has tended to become very rigid). A small group of people was accordingly sent overseas-- notably to the University of Reading in England--for training, and in 1967 a circular was published which proposed that every primary and secondary school should appoint a guidance teacher. Such

248

teachers should do about 25 periods of classroom teaching (as against the usual 30 or so) and should be exempted from extra-curricular duties: Their role was defined mainly in terms of career guidance, though they were also expected to interview pupils on personal and behavioral problems, to visit pupils' homes if and when necessary, to be responsible for the environmental health conditions of the school, and to organise (where possible) Parent-Teacher Associations.

A systematic training program of one-week courses was started in 1969, and in the following five years 1,772 teachers attended such courses. (Iyer 1975) In 1970 the post of regional guidance officer was created in a number of states to act as a link between the Ministry of Education and school guidance services, to organise and act as a tutor on guidance training courses, to collect and disseminate occupational information, and to serve as a referral person for difficult cases. A revised guidance manual was published in 1971. (EPRD 1971)

The formal system as it stands at present makes guidance primarily the responsibility of the Ministry of Education, with a network of skilled regional guidance officers co-ordinating the work of guidance teachers who have been trained for a minimum of one week and have some teaching periods set aside for guidance work. However, due to lack of resources, it has not yet been possible to implement this system in full. Thus for example, all the states in Peninsular Malaysia have a regional guidance officer, as does Sarawak, but in 1977 only four of the ten had attended a one-year training course overseas, and most were expected to perform other administrative chores in addition to their guidance responsibilities.

So far as training is concerned, an unpublished survey of guidance teachers in Peninsular Malaysia, conducted in 1974, found that 66% had received training in the Ministry's one-week courses. Evidence from the workshops conducted by myself in 1977 suggested that this figure had fallen to under 40%. Clearly staff turnover meant that the effects of the initial training effort were being eroded. A few shorter seminars on particular problems and techniques have been held, but many guidance teachers are expected to operate without any training at all. Moreover, there are very few who have had more substantial training, though one or two have taken a one-year course overseas, and a guidance and counseling option has now been introduced in the one-year postgraduate diploma course at the University of Malaya (comprising between a quarter and a third of the course).

The other obvious major problem is that of time. Despite the statement in the Ministry's 1967 circular that guidance teachers should have a teaching workload of only about 25 periods a week, the 1974 survey and the evidence from my workshops suggest that only about one-third of secondary schools have implemented this recommendation. Moreover, only about one-fifth have released their guidance teachers from their extra-curricular duties. Many schools, therefore, seem to expect guidance teachers to carry out their guidance work in their own time, without additional pay. This causes much resentment and disillusionment: indeed, the first article in the inaugural issue of the Jernal Panduan Mavoga was partly entitled "Career Guidance in Schools: Is It a Sham?". (Yunus Noor 1975) This is largely explained by the low level of staffing in Malaysian schools: about half the population is 16 or under, and classes tend to average 45-50 in size. Nonetheless, it seems clear that a decision should be made as to whether guidance is part of the guidance teacher's responsibility, in which case time and/or additional pay must be provided for it, or whether it is a voluntary activity. In the latter case it should be left open to volunteers rather than, as is often the case at present, assigned by school administrators to sometimes unwilling teachers. The possibility that no-one will volunteer has to be accepted.

The problems posed by lack of time are exacerbated by the sheer profusion of tasks which the guidance teacher is expected to perform. Initially the role was seen as being mainly concerned with educational and career guidance, but the 1967 circular extended it into such areas as personal counseling and relations with parents. Since then, a major responsibility for drug education and social and moral education has also been added: the guidance teacher is expected to "help pupils acquire desirable attitudes and behavior in their day-to-day living both at present and for the future." (Iyer 1975) Such attempts to fit more and more quarts into the same pint pot seem to lead to confusion and discouragement, particularly as little help seems to be given to helping guidance teachers to set objectives which are realistic and which therefore give them a reasonable chance of being--and feeling--effective. Moreover, there is a strong danger that guidance teachers will be tempted to neglect the long-term aims of career guidance and spend all their time responding to immediate and pressing behavioral problems. This tendency is an important counterweight to the arguments--so persuasive in logical terms--about the essential interrelationship of personal, educational and career problems and the consequent need for broadly based guidance services. In the USA, too, counselors have come under severe attack for neglecting the career guidance part of their role. (Ginzberg 1971)

One response to the problem of lack of staff time, adopted by a few schools, has been to try to build on the role of home-room teachers, recognising that they often know their students best. The role of these teachers is at present mainly administrative and disciplinary, and they are not given any guidance periods in which to talk with students individually or in groups about guidance problems. Moreover, the size of classes again poses a major difficulty in attempting to extend the guidance role.

Nonetheless, attempts are now being made to give some attention to guidance in initial teacher training. A short course in guidance

has been held for lecturers in teacher training colleges that provided information for them to incorporate in their own courses.
This suggests that Malaysia is not moving towards the kind of professional separation between counseling and teaching that has occurred in the USA and now seems to be developing, for example, in
Ireland. (Chamberlain and Delaney 1977) Instead, it is moving
towards the more integrated kind of approach that has emerged in
Scotland and seems to be emerging also in England and Wales, accepting the problems of role conflict that may result. Further evidence
to support this judgement is provided by the fact that in the schools
where investment in guidance has been heaviest--the federal residential schools provided for rural students who would have too far to
travel to day schools from their homes--it has officially (though
not always actually) been entrusted to two half-time rather than one
full-time guidance teacher. A few of these schools have also introduced a tutor system for pastoral-care purposes (cf., p.143).

In addition to the problems of training and time, a further
major deficiency at present is the paucity of occupational information. This was mentioned as one of the main problem areas in a survey of guidance teachers conducted in 1973. (Loser and Nichols 1975)
My own visits to schools suggested that in many cases the occupational information resources amounted to a few books and booklets
(usually from overseas and often ten or even fifteen years old), a
few mimeographed sheets, and a few hand-made posters. The extent of
the problem can be judged from a statement in the official guidance
manual that, "as the collection of occupational/educational information in Malaysia is still meagre, it is recommended that the information be filed alphabetically." (EPRD 1971) Yet without good occupational information, more sophisticated forms of career guidance
activities are likely to be of limited value. It would seem that in
this case the importing of relatively advanced ideas from Britain
and the USA has meant that insufficient attention has been paid to basic
priorities. The system has attempted to run before it was ready to
walk.

The lack of occupational information would seem to be related to
a more basic structural weakness in the Malaysian system as it exists
at present. Career guidance is concerned with the interface between
education and employment, yet the current services are based almost
entirely within education. Despite the visit of a British expert in
1969 recommending an extension of the Ministry of Labour's career
guidance services (White 1969), this Ministry seems to have with-
drawn from its involvement in guidance work and to have concentrated
on providing job placement services. The reasons for this are complex, and may well be related to pressures arising from the lack of
training facilities and the national policy of positive discrimination (parallels the USA concept of affirmative action--Ed.) in favor
of the indigenous "bumiputras," notably the Malays, who form just
over half the population in Peninsular Malaysia and considerably less
in Sarawak and Sabah. This policy represents an attempt to even out

some of the past economic imbalances between the various ethnic groups and to reorientate the predominantly agricultural and rural culture of the "bumiputras" to the needs of modern science and technology.

Whatever the reasons, the split between guidance and placement services impoverishes both, making it difficult for guidance to stay in touch with the realities of the labor market, and for placement work to pay attention to the long-term needs of the individual. It also means that virtually no career guidance services are available to adults, though institutionally based services are now provided by the Malaysian universities for their students.

Employers, too, seem so far to have done little to support the development of guidance work. By and large--apart from certain areas of specialization--they have been able to recruit their labor force through informal and direct methods, and have not been very cooperative even in supplying information when asked to do so. A work experience program for 139 students was organised in 1974, but though successful (Selangor Vocational Guidance Association 1975), was an isolated experiment. The main involvement of employers has been through the Vocational Guidance Associations, the first of which-- in Selangor--was initiated by Rotary Club members in 1966. Associations have now been set up in a number of states, usually again with strong Rotary Club support, and in 1973 a Malaysian Vocational Guidance Association (MAVOGA) was set up to coordinate their work and give it a national focus. MAVOGA is a voluntary service organisation, containing representatives of business and industrial firms, guidance teachers, and civic leaders, as well as public administrators. It provides some services, including publications (notably a journal and three "guidance notebooks"). It also acts as a pressure group to improve the public guidance services.

Cultural factors and implications

The reasons that such services have not been developed further are not difficult to find. The very size and rigidity of the educational system, the ill-effects of which guidance is expected to mitigate, make it difficult to implement guidance services effectively. The system tends to be formal, monolithic, and unable to pay much attention to individual differences, or to the curricular facilitation of vocational development. (Watts 1979) Moreover, the labor market is by no means an open one. Unemployment is a constant problem and the allocation of available opportunities is heavily dominated by nepotism, private contacts, and by the "bumiputra" positive discrimination policy.

There may be other cultural factors which make guidance, and particularly the counseling-oriented approaches to guidance which seem to be dominant in official thinking, difficult to implement. Esen (1972) pointed out that in Nigeria the central concept of coun-

252

seling--that of the self-determining individual--appeared inappropriate, since individual identity was considered subordinate to
group (and especially tribal) identity. Guidance principles and
methods, accordingly, needed to be adapted to encompass the importance of that group structure, so as to "reflect true African thinking." This observation serves as an important reminder that the
assumptions which underlie guidance are culturally relative.

Since Malaysia is a multi-ethnic and a rapidly changing society, it is not easy to define precisely the cultural factors which
need to be taken into account in devising the nature of guidance
services. However, Asians as a whole tend to be more authoritarian
in their social attitudes and tend to regard self-disclosure as a
sign of weakness rather than strength. Arkoff et al. (1966) found
that in contrast with American students, Asian students tended to
be acquiescent, to believe that mental health could be enhanced
through will power and through avoidance of unpleasant thoughts, and
to view counseling as a directive and paternalistic process. Furthermore,
although the Ministry of Education (1970) has clearly asserted
"the democratic principle that it is the duty and the right of every
individual to choose his own way of life in so far as his choice
does not interfere with rights of others," this principle is still
not widely accepted in practice. The family is still very influential. The pay and status of the job entered by the student is regarded as affecting the status of the family as a whole. Since the
public pension plan covers only government employees, the parents'
own future depends in a very practical sense on the student's choice,
and it is considered rightful for them to influence or even determine that choice.

In such a culture, the predominantly client-centered
approach to guidance which seems to have been officially adopted
may be in danger of consigning guidance permanently to a marginal
and ineffectual role. Major structural changes are certainly needed
both in education and in the operation of the labor market, before
such guidance is likely to be truly effective. In the meantime,
guidance can point the way to the changes that need to be made,
although its voice is still a weak one.

References

Arkoff, A. et al. Mental health and counseling ideas of Asian and
   American students. _Journal of Counseling Psychology_, 1966, _13_.

Chamberlain, J. and Delaney, O. Guidance and counselling in Irish
   schools. _British Journal of Guidance and Counselling_, 1977, _5_.

Daws, P. P. Are careers education programmes in secondary schools
   a waste of time? A reply to Roberts. _British Journal of Guidance
   and Counselling_, 1977, _5_.

EPRD (Educational Planning and Research Division). _Guidance in
   schools_. Kuala Lumpur: Ministry of Education, Malaysia, 1971.

Esen, A. A view of guidance from Africa. _Personnel and Guidance
   Journal_, 1972, _50_.

Ginzberg, E. _Career guidance: Who needs it, who provides it, who
   can improve it_. New York: McGraw-Hill, 1971.

Iyer, G. K. Guidance services: Its current status in schools. _Jernal
   Panduan Mavoga_, 1975, _1_.

Loser, J. and Nichols, T. P. Perceptions of guidance teachers: A
   study. _Jernal Panduan Mavoga_, 1975, _1_.

Ministry of Education. _School guidance services_. Kuala Lumpur:
   Author, 1966.

Ministry of Education. _Education in Malaysia_. Kuala Lumpur: Author,
   1970.

Murad Committee. _Kajian keciciran_ (Dropout study). Kuala Lumpur:
   Ministry of Education, Malaysia, 1975.

Selangor Vocational Guidance Association. Evaluation report of the
   job experience programme organised jointly by the Selangor
   Vocational Guidance Association and the Selangor Education Department. Kuala Lumpur: SVGA, 1975 (Mimeo).

Watts, A. G. The interaction between careers guidance and the
   school curriculum in Malaysia. In Watts, A. G. and Ferreira
   Marques, J. H. _Guidance and the curriculum_. Paris: UNESCO,
   1979 (In press).

White, G. C. The development of vocational guidance in Malaysia.
   London: Central Youth Employment Executive, 1969 (Mimeo).

Yunus Noor, M. Career guidance in schools: Is it a sham? Where has
   it led the students? _Jernal Panduan Mavoga_, 1975, _1_.

Section Eight

AUSTRALASIA

As a geographical region, Australasia covers a vast area of the Pacific that includes Australia, New Zealand, and a myriad of widely scattered islands of Polynesia, Melanesia, and Micronesia. The present section of this book limits itself to exploring the guidance scene in Australia and New Zealand, two countries so closely related that they once considered forming a political union. Traditionally, both countries had strong ties with Great Britain-- a major influence in the development of their educational systems, social mores, and cultural preferences. But especially since World War II, the cultural and social configurations have been changing.

Undoubtedly, the world at large has numerous inaccurate opinions about life in the South Pacific region as exemplified by a number of exotic stereotypes which die hard in the minds of people. One of them is the image of an Australian as a tall, rugged individual with a heavy sunburn, wearing a wide-brimmed hat. By now, this image has become largely a myth. Both in Australia and in New Zealand, the population is predominantly urban and so is the life-style.

Both chapters of this section indicate the lively liaison that exists between Australasia and the rest of the world. Counseling and guidance professionals of the two countries are well informed about parallel work done by their colleagues abroad, especially in English speaking countries whose literature is readily available. Parenthetically, it should be recalled that Frank Parsons, the founder of the guidance movement in America, had close contacts with like-minded people in New Zealand while planning his helping efforts in the Boston area. Thus, the American guidance community may feel a special affinity to this part of the world.

Chapter 22 was authored by an Australian psychologist, John Urbano, whose primary emphasis is vocational guidance. In Chapter 23, John Small, a counselor educator at a New Zealand university, focuses primarily on guidance in educational settings. These two emphases help form a comprehensive perspective on the professional scene in the area.

22

AUSTRALIA

John M. Urbano

As a nation Australia is undoubtedly very young. Although several nations landed, or claimed to have landed, on the shores of Australia on various occasions during the sixteenth and seventeenth centuries it was not until August 22, 1770, that the history of Australia was brought into definite political connection with Western civilization. It was on that date that Captain Cook took possession "of the whole eastern coast" on behalf of His Majesty King George III. At that time Australia's population comprised 300,000 aborigines. (Australian Bureau of Statistics 1978)

More recently, on June 30, 1976, Australia's population was assessed at 14,074,000 of which 116,000 were aborigines. Approximately two-thirds of this population is situated in eleven major towns throughout Australia. Australia itself is a large land mass approximately the size of the United States of America. Immigration has contributed substantially to Australia's post-war population growth. In the post-war years to 1976 some 3.5 million migrants have arrived of which an estimated 80 per cent settled. (Australian Bureau of Statistics 1978)

Australia is made up of seven separate States: Victoria, New South Wales, Queensland, South Australia, Western Australia, Tasmania and the Northern Territory. Australia has a three-tier system of government, consisting of a federal government, seven state governments and local municipal councils and shires.

Society

Despite its distance from Europe and America, Australia sees itself as a Western society and shares many of the values and attitudes of the Western world. At the centre of these is the belief that the individual has a right to personal growth and development and the economic belief in continued expansion and progress with the underlying acceptance of the work ethic.

Australia until the last few years has enjoyed many years of almost full employment and concurrently a very high standard of living. It enjoys one of the highest levels of home ownership in the world. In recent years the rate of technological and social change has been rapidly increasing. This has put into question many of our established values about the intrinsic worth of work and the role of the educational system and has put heavy demands on the individual in society to come to an early decision regarding alternative values and life-styles.

At the national and the individual level one is aware in Australia of a transitional unrest where a nation is moving from an economically secure and socially structured society to an uncertain and constantly changing community. Despite its stresses on the individual, one encouraging trend overall seems to be an ever-increasing awareness and concern for individuals and their rights, which is reflected in recent legislative programmes.

Aspects of the educational system

The six State Governments administer their own systems of primary, secondary and technical education through Government departments responsible to State Ministers. Education at all Government primary and secondary schools in Australia is free with attendance being compulsory for children between the ages of 6 and 15 years. Australian schools generally operate between approximately 9:00 a.m. and 3:30 p.m. for three terms between early February and mid-December.

The schools in Australia have a considerable degree of autonomy. In fact, in recent years most States have established regional or area administrators responsible for planning schools and deploying staff within a group of schools. Also, there has been encouragement given for the establishment of school boards, with community representation, to take part in policy and decision making.

The six years of primary school are followed by six years of secondary school. In the primary school children have the same teacher throughout the day, whereas in the secondary school children generally have different teachers for different subjects.

When students have attained the minimum school leaving age, they have various options. They may leave school and seek employment. They may enroll in a vocationally oriented course of a "technical and further education" (TAFE) institution or a private business college. For many TAFE courses, completion of Year 10 of secondary school is minimum entry requirement. For those continuing to the end of secondary school (Year 12), opportunities for further studies are available in TAFE institutions, universities, colleges of advanced education and several other post-school institutions. Entry into the universities or the colleges of advanced education is restricted by quotas in the various faculties (academic divisions--Ed.) and students must have completed a full secondary education or demonstrate capacity to successfully complete a course.

At present there are two main criticisms of the Australian educational system. For the last few years journalists, teachers, parents and employers have bemoaned the decline in the literacy and computational skills of present-day students. However, very little empirical evidence has been produced as to the nature and incidence of illiteracy in schools. Studies that have been done (Keeves and Bourke et al. 1976) indicate that on reading tests administered to ten and fourteen year old students there were no marked differences of their performance levels in comparison with students in Britain and the United States.

The second criticism is not solely a criticism of the educational system. Certainly at the moment Australian society is concerned about secondary and post-secondary education and its relationship to the reality demands of the labour market. This seems to have influenced the present Government's decision in 1976 to set up a Committee of Inquiry into Education and Training aimed at looking at the desirable pattern of post-secondary education over the next twenty years or so, and especially considering the ideal relationship between the labour market and the education system.

This hiatus between the aims of the educational system and the demands of the labour market has meant that school leavers often have transition problems when taking employment for the first time. These problems are aggravated by the high levels of unemployment being experienced amongst young people in recent years.

The national Department of Employment and Youth Affairs and the Department of Education have introduced schemes to improve the chances of school leavers for obtaining employment. One such scheme is the Educational Programme for Unemployed Youth. Under this programme money is made available to the States for the development and conduct of pilot remedial schemes in such subjects as English, mathematics and communication for young people under twenty-one years of age whose educational qualifications are low or inadequate for today's labour market conditions.

Concept of guidance

Vocational development is seen as a process of exploration and learning during which persons come to some understanding of their values, interests and aspirations, and relate these to the demands of the world of work. Vocational development is used here as a generic term which encompasses a process of decision-making and planning which begins early in childhood and continues into maturity. The initial vocational choice is regarded as only a small part of the individual's total vocational development. Generally, too, the vocational development of an individual is seen in the context of the total human development of that person.

Often in Australia the term "vocational guidance" is used to encompass the many services which might be offered to the person during the process of vocational development. These services or activities ideally form part of a total program for enhancing vocational development which might include work experience, career education, and job-exploration courses as well as counselling.

It may be helpful to state in some detail the objectives of a typical vocational guidance programme. Vocational guidance programmes in Australia are often aimed at:

(1) Assisting individuals toward self-understanding in vocationally relevant terms. As an objective, this means encouraging individuals to become actively involved in deciding the kinds of work satisfactions and values which are personally important to them; the social and personal competencies necessary to obtain and keep employment; the abilities, aptitudes, skills, interests and preferences which will have vocational application for them; the occupational limitation that any disability might impose on the client.

(2) Assisting individuals towards an understanding of the world of work. This means encouraging individuals to come to an understanding of the demands that working life will make upon them; the range of occupations which are available; the tasks and activities involved in various occupations; the entry requirements for various occupations, in terms of education and training; and those extrinsic features of the job which have to do with salary, promotional prospects, working conditions; the actual restrictions imposed by their disability.

(3) Assisting individuals to gain those life-skills which will enable them to cope with vocational change and adjustment throughout their working lives. This means encouraging individuals to gain the skills and attitudes which are important for independent vocational decision-making throughout that person's entire working life. This acquires particular significance when career itself is thought of as a longitudinal, developmental concept. A career may embrace more than a single occupation and certainly more than a single job. Similar jobs may be held with different employers or somewhat different

260

jobs with the same employer, perhaps in different departments. Career denotes a succession of jobs within a sequence of occupations,
a sequence which may proceed much more rapidly in a world of work
subject to constant change on the scale increasingly experienced
today.

The need for vocational guidance may commence prior to entry to
the work force but is likely to occur also at later stages. For
example, assistance may be needed by adults re-entering the work
force after an absence from it for any reason, and others who, while
still working, are experiencing work adjustment problems. The need
for guidance services for these special, mainly older, groups has
been increasingly recognized and is coupled with the growing needs
of those adults experiencing unemployment.

Organization of guidance and counselling

The scene in relation to the organization of guidance and counselling services in Australia is complex and somewhat uncoordinated.
There are three levels of service.

First, there is the within-the school guidance service. Although the detailed picture varies from State to State it would be
accurate to say that all States have their own school guidance
officers who are called "careers advisers", "careers teachers", or
"career education co-ordinators". These are in the main people who
are drawn from the teaching stream and who still maintain a small
teaching load. This team of careers advisers in schools is a very
recent phenomenon in Australia, gathering momentum in the last four
or five years.

It is obviously due to a number of factors but with the high
rate of youth unemployment in Australia and the heavy publicity of
the transition problems from school to work there has been some
recognition of the demands of the labour market by the school system. The career education movement is concerned with ensuring that
the student becomes more vocationally self-aware, develops better
decision-making skills and acquires a knowledge of occupations and
what they require. Unlike some overseas approaches, career education
in Australia is seen as a distinct subject and as yet is not infused
or incorporated in the content of curriculum subjects.

Second, there is the guidance service within the educational
system provided on a visiting basis from a regional or area head-
quarters rather than being permanently attached to a school. This
is a guidance service which is staffed by trained counsellors or
psychologists whose charter is to deal with behavioural or personal
problems, educational problems or vocational problems. Often their
workload is so heavily concerned with other educational problems
that vocational guidance would not receive a high priority.

261

Third, there are guidance services provided <u>outside the school</u> <u>system</u>. These include services provided by the national Commonwealth Employment Services (CES) and the Division of Vocational Guidance Services in New South Wales. Most universities in Australia also provide guidance services on their campuses for potential and present students. Even within some large industrial organizations there are indications that counselling services are being provided for employees. (Green 1974)

The Commonwealth Employment Service supports guidance activities in schools by preparing and distributing occupational information and by offering other supportive services to teachers and parents. For example, occupational films are made available to schools and visits are arranged to various firms and training institutions where young people can observe work being performed and training being provided. Special counselling services are provided for unemployed youth, handicapped and other clients needing special attention.

As a further support, a staff of one hundred psychologists functions as a back-up service to the Commonwealth Employment Service and their activities fall into three broad groups: (1) counselling and assessment services for clients; (2) training activities directed at CES staff; and (3) consultation services directed at career teachers and others involved in career orientation in schools. These services are described more fully in later paragraphs.

The Division of Vocational Guidance Services in New South Wales has a staff of approximately one hundred psychologists whose work is very similar to the national Vocational Psychology Sections of the CES. However, their work is limited to one State.

Prevalent methodology

The current practices employed in the vocational guidance field in Australia may be best described in terms of the three levels of service mentioned previously.

Within the <u>school setting</u>, "careers advisors" who are mostly practicing teachers, would not see offering individual interviews to every school leaver as their most critical responsibility. Rather, if one can generalize, their main responsibility is to stimulate interest in career planning and to enhance the students' vocational development. This is done, for example, by setting up career reference rooms in schools; conducting individual or small group discussions on careers; influencing the development of curricula to include career issues in subject areas; and designing career orientation or exploration material for students.

Within the <u>educational system</u>, the "school psychologist" or "guidance officer" deals with academic, emotional and behavioural problems of students , and administers group and individual intell-

262

igence and achievement tests, particularly at the primary level. His or her work may include some vocational counselling, insofar as career problems are often associated with personal, educational and social problems of students. But the case load of these counsellors is such that unless they have a strong personal interest, vocational counselling will be only an incidental component.

While ten or twenty years ago the school psychologist was testing and "streaming" students into educational groups of comparable competence, these functions are steadily diminishing. Yet, the vocational counselling aspect of the school psychologist's role will probably not increase in importance. (Hall 1977) A trend is apparent for school psychologists to work as consultants to teachers in matters of classroom performance, setting learning objectives, etc.

Counsellors outside the school system do much of their counselling work on an individual basis. The Vocational Psychology Sections of the CES conducted 17,167 counselling interviews during 1977-78, approximately 90% of them on an individual basis.

To meet the primary obligation to its own clients, the Commonwealth Employment Service defined the range of activities for its vocational psychologists. Their case-work involves clients who are registered with the CES or who are referred by the Commonwealth Rehabilitation service. In particular, vocational psychologists counsel and assist people who are already in the labour market and who are experiencing serious personal difficulties in finding work or adjusting to it. They see a wide range of people of all ages with a variety of problems, including those who are physically, mentally, or socially handicapped; those who have a history of changing jobs; older people faced with sudden change in employment; the young unemployed; and young clients who have found their initial choice of occupation unsatisfactory.

As regards young people who are still in school, CES psychologists limit their work to those who will likely encounter serious difficulties in choosing, finding, or maintaining suitable employment. The majority of contacts receive preliminary counselling over the telephone or are asked to contact an Office of the Commonwealth Employment Service first. In this way many young clients whose primary need is for occupational information rather than counselling are redirected to the Career Reference Centres (job information centres) run by the CES.

For youth who are still in school, the CES psychologists provide assistance of a different kind, in the hope that serious employment problems can be prevented before they leave the school environment. To this end, the Vocational Psychology Section is offering consultation and advice for the establishment of career education programmes at both the in- and out-of-school levels, while keeping counselling to a minimum. One product of this effort has been

263

the "Career Planning Pack" which may be used in school curricula or in group counselling programmes to help students develop skills in vocational decision-making. These efforts, which are of a preventative nature, are complementary to the efforts of the CES to establish career development resources centres (Career Reference Centres). A more effective vocational preparation during the school years will reduce the number of people needing individual help at the point of entry into the work force and release psychological resources for counselling people of all ages who really need it.

In relation to testing practices it is interesting to note that in 1968 approximately 80% of clients seen by CES psychologists were routinely group-tested before an assessment of the problem was undertaken. (Urbano and Lovell 1976) By 1977-78 the philosophy of the service became more client-oriented and testing had dropped to 27%. With the increase of unemployment, especially youth unemployment, clients are now seen, on the average, two or three times compared with the "once-only" contact typical of 1968.

The Division of Vocational Guidance Services in New South Wales interviewed around 49,000 clients in 1977-78, of which approximately 50% were administered tests of intelligence. In addition another 19,061 clients received group guidance. Although the Division has been involved in recent years in automatic testing and large scale interviewing, there are indications that changes have occurred. The automatic testing of all Year 9 students has stopped and the Division will most likely adopt a more individual approach to student's problems. There are indications that their work will closely parallel the work of CES psychologists in other States in the offering of consultation and training services to schools.

It is very difficult to obtain accurate information about the work of commercial agencies offering vocational guidance. Many of these agencies are part of larger management consultation firms. However, it is not unusual to read in local newspapers advertisements to the effect that "a vocational guidance test battery plus counselling and a detailed report costs $100." Most of the private agencies conducting vocational guidance would use psychological testing regularly as part of their guidance routine. In fact, although the use of psychological testing appears to have fallen in public agencies, some private agencies report an increase in their use of such tests. Braun (1977) reports an increase of the use of psychological tests in one major private agency in excess of 30% between the years 1972-1976.

However, the overall tendency in Australia is marked by a decline in the reliance on testing. In the future, any tests administered to clients are more likely to be the result of a perceived need on the part of both the client and the psychologist rather than being automatically administered as a prerequisite for guidance.

Turning to the question of counselling orientations, Australian practices have clearly moved through several phases. From the post-war period to around the early sixties, Australian guidance practice was very prescriptive or directive in orientation. This was the period of the industrial and the applied psychology movement. In the sixties and early seventies, Australian guidance and counselling went through an almost religiously non-directive phase stimulated by the work of Rogers (1951) and later by the research of Truax and Carkhuff (1967). At present guidance is still non-directive but with a reality emphasis. Guidance and counselling are geared to the total life-style of the individual. Counselling has a healthy blend of reality basis, of accountability, and of valuing the personal growth of every client.

Guidance personnel

While attempts are made to select suitable teachers as careers advisors, the training provided for them at the moment is minimal. Blakers (1978) indicates that most States provide only a week's training each year for careers advisors. One State, Victoria, does provide ten days per term. These courses invariably focus on training in decision-making, the setting up of a careers library, the development of a careers curriculum, and the establishment of facilitative relationships with students.

In at least two States, tertiary institutions are providing graduate and post-graduate courses in career counselling. For example, the Royal Melbourne Institute of Technology in Victoria offers a two year part-time course in career education for graduates of universities or teacher training institutions. In Blakers' (1978) description the course focuses on educational and vocational information. Emphasis is placed on the collection, analysis, classification and communication of this information, and on its use in developing career and self-awareness, in promoting decision-making skills, and in career education. It also examines work and industry, their relationships with society, the changing nature of work, issues raised by work, such as job design, labour turnover, and the rationale of work. Other units deal with vocational development theory and vocational choice and with problems of particular client groups such as migrants, aborigines, women, and the chronically unemployed.

In relation to the training of school psychologists or guidance officers, all State Departments of Education offer their own in-service programmes which vary from a six month part-time course in one State to a three year part-time course in another State. These courses provide training in the principles and practice of guidance in educational settings. Post-graduate study in educational psychology is provided by several universities and colleges throughout Australia.

265

Vocational psychologists employed by the CES and the Division of Vocational Guidance Services in New South Wales are trained by their own organisations in intensive one-year training programs aimed at increasing self-awareness of the trainee and imparting counselling and diagnostic skills.

One feature of Australian counselor education which is worth commenting on is the almost total neglect by universities--until a few years ago--of providing any training in counselling or interviewing in the undergraduate psychology curriculum. Consequently, many organizations employing large numbers of psychologists have their own counselling training programmes. Some of these were so well regarded that several years ago they were deemed equivalent to a fourth year of university study for accreditation with the Australian Psychological Society.

An assessment of the number of personnel involved in vocational guidance in Australia is difficult because of the rapidly changing scene and the paucity of data in some areas. However, from data collected from various sources (Blakers 1978; Department of Education 1976) it appears that at the end of 1978 there were no less than 1,000 career advisors in schools. Of course, some of these are involved in the career adviser's capacity only part-time. At least 1,400 vocational guidance officers and psychologists were active in the country. This figure includes psychologists and guidance officers involved in schools, universities, colleges of advanced education, the Division of Vocational Guidance Services, the CES and in private consultancy agencies. An earlier survey by Kidd (1971) indicated that in June 1970, there were only 834 psychologists involved in the guidance field. One obvious reason for the difference in these figures is the steady growth of the ranks of psychologists in Australia. Secondly, the figures for 1978 include both psychologists and guidance officers from any discipline.

If the number of careers advisers and guidance officers-psychologists is compared with the number of school students, one can estimate the counsellor-student ratio. The most recent census figures (for 1976) indicate 2,960,250 school enrollments. (Australian Bureau of Statistics 1978) In other words, there is one career guidance officer (career adviser, guidance officer, or vocational psychologist) for about 1,200 students.

It would be fair to say that these counsellors and psychologists do not enjoy a high status in Australian society. To begin with, the general public is poorly informed about counsellors and psychologists. The latter are still surrounded by a professional-medical "mystique" which implies illness and weakness in clients who are referred to them. In one of the few studies available on this topic (Small and Gault 1975) it was found that relatively few members of the general public selected a psychologist as their consultant for various hypothetical services. In this same study most respondents selected a school teacher as the most suitable person to consult for career guidance. Furthermore, the same number of respondents would contact a social worker for career guidance as would contact a psychologist for such advice. This study underlines the ignorance of many people about the work of psychologists in the community and their preference for professionals they have some acquaintance with.

Professional associations

The main professional body for those counsellors who are trained as psychologists is the Australian Psychological Society which at present contains 3,600 members. To obtain full membership in the Society, an individual must have completed four years of graduate studies in psychology followed by two years of supervised professional experience. The Society functions as a professional association, very similar to the APGA or APA in the USA, which sets guidelines in such areas as ethical standards, professional practices, fees to be charged, and other related matters. It also serves as a scientific body which endeavors to ensure that the latest professional knowledge and skill is disseminated to its members. The Society does not serve as a registration (licensure--Ed.) board, although membership of the Society facilitates registration with the various State Psychological Registration Boards.

A very recent development is the growth in the number of Career Education Associations. Presently almost every State in Australia has such an association, and in the last few months a National Career Education Association has been formed to represent the state bodies at the national level. These associations, whose main focus is the development of career education in Australia, do not exclude from their membership teachers or psychologists. Membership, which currently numbers several hundred, is open to all people interested in career education.

Informal guidance systems

Professional associations, unions, and employer groups in Australia offer some limited vocational assistance by supplying career information and recruitment literature, and providing speakers for careers nights and seminars. In addition, several private publishing firms produce career guides for distribution to secondary school students at a nominal price.

Currently the media are very active in focussing on vocational guidance issues through newspaper supplements on careers or through radio and TV programmes. However, apart from these limited activities, the informal guidance network plays a minor part on the Australian scene.

Summary

Work is a very important concern in Australian society. Hence vocational guidance has been historically linked with employment goals and its practice often geared to the short-term aim of securing suitable, satisfying work for the individual. Vocational guidance is now beginning to be more concerned with long-term aims: e.g., vocational maturity of the individual; insights that the individual needs to have for survival in a rapidly changing technology and in a society with higher levels of unemployment. Vocational guidance programmes are beginning to prepare the individual for work more comprehensively. They focus on the individual learning about jobs, on his or her attitudes and values, and on incorporating these insights in a strategy for career choices in a changing environment.

Vocational guidance is currently receiving more emphasis in the educational system than had been the case in the past. Also, more welfare and counselling services are being housed within the school and the educational system. To a large extent this is the result of a few enthusiastic and highly motivated individuals.

Nationally, one has the impression of a lack of coordination among the various vocational guidance programmes and services available in Australia. One key indicator is the growing proliferation of committees of enquiry which have been looking at this problem in the last few years. Several changes will need to occur to assure the optimal use the vocational guidance resources at the national level.

First, the problems of relationships between the school, the labour market, and the rest of the community will need to be overcome. It is not unusual to hear vocal criticisms of the schools' failure to produce adequate candidates for the labour market. The various key agents in vocational guidance (schools, employers, the CES, parents, unions, etc.) need to be coordinated in a cooperative national machinery which will facilitate more unified and concerted work.

Second, career education will need to be taken more seriously to become a pervasive component of the Australian educational picture. The OECD Educational Committee (1976) examiners clearly indicated that every average-size Australian secondary school needs at least one full-time, adequately trained professional who would be responsible for career education. They also suggested that career education should become a compulsory subject, at least in grades nine and ten.

Furthermore, the training system and promotion prospects of career advisers should be improved. Finally, education programmes of the future should focus on life-skills training. They need to

look at decision-making, interpersonal relations, instilling flexibility to cope with the "future shock" in the labour market, and
provide the resources needed to enable individuals to make several
job changes in their lifetime. Vocational counsellors will have to
be resource persons rather than counsellors for individuals. They
should train other "career helpers" as well as coordinate the total
career program in a particular school.

References

Australian Bureau of Statistics. Year Book, Australia 1977-78.
    Canberra: Australian Government Publishing Service, 1978.

Blakers, C. School and work. Canberra: Australian National Univer-
    sity Press, 1978.

Braun, N. Whither psychological testing? Personnel Management
    (Australia), 1977, 15 (1), 24-35.

Department of Education. Transition from school to work or further
    study. (A background paper for an OECD review of Australian
    education policy.) Canberra: Department of Education, 1976.

Green, M. Counselling for employees. Personnel Practice Bulletin,
    1974, 30, 234-243.

Hall, J. A. Educational psychology in public service. In Nixon, M.
    and Taft, R. (Eds.) Psychology in Australia. Sydney: Pergamon
    Press, 1977.

Keeves, J. P. and Bourke, S. F. et al. Australian studies in
    school performance: Literacy and numeracy in Australian schools.
    Canberra: Australian Government Publishing Service, 1976.

Kidd, G. A. The employment of psychologists in Australia. Sydney:
    University Appointments Board, 1971.

OECD Education Committee. Review of educational policy in Australia.
    Paris, 1976.

Rogers, C. R. Client-centered therapy. Boston: Houghton Mifflin,
    1951.

Small, J. and Gault, U. Perceptions of psychologists by the general
    public and three professional groups. Australian Psychologist,
    1975, 10, 21-31

Truax, C. B. and Carkhuff, R. R. Toward effective counseling and psychotherapy: Training and practice. Chicago: Aldine, 1967.

Urbano, J. M. and Lovell, A. B. Vocational guidance and counselling --the contemporary scene. Educational Magazine, 1976, 33 (2), 40-41.

23

NEW ZEALAND

John J. Small

Introduction

A number of qualifications need to be made about the organization of this report. First, except where otherwise stated or clearly implied, data cited here have been extracted from two government sources published by the Department of Statistics (1977, 1978). Secondly, there has been a deliberate emphasis on guidance and counseling services to education, with only brief references to those in the wider community. Thirdly, except for some background information from earlier years, current developments are described as they emerged since 1970. Finally, the only references cited are those originating from within New Zealand. Although not an exhaustive list, it is a representative selection of recent publications relevant to guidance and counseling.

New Zealand society

New Zealand is a nation of three million people living on two main islands in the South Pacific, 1,600 kilometres south-east of Australia. The topography is rugged and varied and is increasingly attracting tourists. The people are mainly of British origin, but Maoris--the indigenous race--and other Polynesians constitute about ten per cent of the population, and this proportion is increasing. There are no racial barriers to citizenship. Politically, the country is a representative democracy in the Westminster tradition, linked with Great Britain and its Commonwealth. Every three years,

all citizens over the age of eighteen are eligible to vote in an
election for a unicameral parliament. New Zealand's economic, cultural, and political dependence upon Great Britain, once marked, is
weakening as a result of its closer trading associations with other
countries.

By conventional criteria such as longevity, infant mortality,
literacy, public provisions for education, health, and welfare, car
ownership, and amenities in homes, New Zealanders have long enjoyed
a high standard of living. However, because of economic difficulties,
sombre predictions are being made about the future. The agricultural basis of the economy is seen to be increasingly precarious.
With few natural resources for heavy industry and commerce, the
nation has frequent unfavorable trade balances, thus paying a heavy
price for its way of life.

As in other Western nations, the country is undergoing rapid
changes in its employment structure. In the ten years preceding
1976, the proportion of the labour force employed in service jobs
rose by six per cent to 55% at the expense of primary production
jobs (now 10%) and employment in secondary industry (now 34%). Until
the late 1970's, the annual inflation levels were low, the net immigration figures were high, and unemployment was but a memory of
the 1930's. Now unemployment and inflation are high, and there are
net external migration figures with heavy losses of trained people.
There are other marked social changes. The urban drift is increasing, over 80% of the population now being classified as urban dwell-
ers. The rate of urbanisation is especially high among the Maoris
who, as a group, have two other characteristics that together give
rise to social problems. Maoris tend to be younger (about 60% are
under twenty years of age, compared with 40% for Europeans) and they
are less qualified, as only 5% of them complete secondary education
with a university entrance qualification, compared with 25% of the
Europeans. The institution of marriage is also changing rapidly.
Birth rates are falling, divorce rates are increasing, the numbers
of one-parent families are rising (22% increase from 1966 to 1971).
Especially among the young, marriage rates are declining and extramarital fertility rates are rising.

Even during their earlier dependence upon Great Britain, New
Zealanders had a strong sense of identity as a nation. The people
still like to describe themselves as having the pioneering virtues
and values of equality, independence, fairness, thrift, and impro-
visation. The sense of nationhood has undoubtedly been fostered
by the memory of heavy casualties in two world wars and by a keen
interest in the achievements of its sports heroes. Nevertheless,
just as in its political and social ideas and institutions there
was a heavy borrowing from England, so in education, literature, and
the arts the culture has, until recently, been a derivative one.
With a few notable exceptions, scant respect was accorded those
achievements which distinctly reflected consciousness arising from

272

life in New Zealand. State support for the arts began about thirty years ago with meagre grants, and only within the last fifteen years has New Zealand's culture been seriously studied in its universities. There have been deliberate moves to preserve Maori culture by formal courses in schools and tertiary institutions and by various grants and sponsorships.

The educational system

For the vast majority of children and adolescents, education means compulsory attendance from six to fifteen years of age in schools which are secular and free of tuition fees, although other costs are involved. Most children enter primary school at five years and secondary school at age thirteen or fourteen. The latter are usually coeducational and comprehensive, offering a wide variety of courses and serving the immediate neighbourhood. Over 80% of 15-16 year olds remain at school, but there are progressively smaller proportions of older students. At the end of the third year of secondary school most students attempt the School Certificate examination. In the fourth year the most successful seek a Sixth Form Certificate and a University Entrance qualification; of these, a small proportion return for a fifth year in order to prepare more thoroughly for tertiary education. At the technical institutes most students (over 95%) take courses through correspondence or part-time study. Teachers' colleges enroll the smallest numbers of tertiary students, but all of them are full-time for periods of between one and three years, depending upon their prior qualifications. More than one-third of university students study part-time or through extra-mural arrangements. A full range of general courses in arts, science, and commerce for undergraduate and graduate students is offered by the six universities, but each has also developed specialised schools. Some restrictions are placed upon entry to these schools, but every person holding an entrance qualification is entitled to claim a place in a general course at a university. Most full-time students at tertiary institutions are subsidised by the state through various financial arrangements. An increasing number of cooperative relationships are developing locally and nationally in tertiary education.

A summary of the provisions for education is given in Figure 8.1. Just over 30% of the population are receiving education in one of the institutions listed in the table. In 1974, 5.6% of the gross national product was spent on education, compared with a mean of 5.7% for eleven other advanced nations. On international tests of reading comprehension and responses to literature, the overall achievements of a sample of fourteen and eighteen year olds in New Zealand schools surpassed those of nine other countries, including England and USA. (Thorndike 1973; Purves, Foshay and Hanson 1973) These indices of usuage, financing, and literacy point to an education system of high quality.

273

Figure 8.1. Institutions and students in the New Zealand education
system in 1977

Type of institution	No. of institutions		No. of students, in thousands	
Pre-School (subsidized, non-compulsory)		1,143		57
Primary				
private	324		49	
state	2,222	2,546	474	523
Secondary				
private	107		32	
state	292	399	200	232
Tertiary				
technical institutes	16		123	
teachers colleges	13		7	
universities	7	36	48	178
Totals in the education system		4,124		990

However, there are also signs of stress in the system and some
public concern is voiced about it, especially at the secondary level. This disquiet was reflected in two recent official reports
(Department of Education 1976, 1977--the McCombs Report and the
Johnson Report) where among the topics discussed were moral and social education, schools as communities, and ethnic identity. The
Johnson Report documented increases in venereal diseases, alcohol-
ism, heart disease, and extramarital fertility. Among the measures
needed to improve education, health, and social well-being, there
were specific recommendations in both Reports for adequate guidance
and counseling services.

The concept of guidance and counseling

Guidance and counseling services are provided in both educational and other settings. It is difficult to distinguish them from
social and community work and psychotherapy, and from other helping
efforts such as teaching, remedial work, advising, supervising,
nursing, etc. These recent statements help clarify the concept of
counseling and guidance in New Zealand:

> When we speak of guidance we shall have in mind all the
> influences in a school that bear on the choices and de-
> cisions that pupils make in respect of their own personal,
> educational and vocational concerns... We see guidance
> as a network of influences--some of them formal, others

informal and incidental--which, taken together, reflect
a school's awareness of its responsibilities to its
pupils as persons. (Department of Education 1971, pp. 4-5)

Counseling is both a process and a relationship. It is
a process by which persons evaluate themselves, make
choices, and decide on courses of action that are consistent with those choices. This process brings counselors and their clients into relationships requiring
trust and understanding. (Department of Education 1971,
p. 5)

Counseling is a dialogue in which one person helps another who has some difficulty that is important to him
or her. It may be psychotherapeutic or guiding or problem solving and may be practised under a counseling
agency or in the context of other professional work or
by trained volunteers. (Nuthall 1978, p. 3)

Each method counts as counseling when certain other
conditions of the relationship are met. These conditions are of an ethical nature and include the following:
a higher degree of confidentiality than is normally expected of, say, teachers; an insistence on the voluntary
nature of the relationship; and an emphasis on the personal responsibility of the client for her own behavior.
(Munro, Manthei and Small 1979, p. 1)

Counseling is generally seen as an activity virtually equivalent to psychotherapy, and within the helping professions it involves more and more job titles and descriptions. It is this
attractiveness of the title that makes it difficult to determine
who should be called counselors and how to take a census of them.
In reviewing all the counseling services and training programs for
Christchurch, a city of 250,000, Nuthall's (1978) solution was to
assess the extent to which each statutory and voluntary helper was
engaged in counseling as a primary function. A clear-cut case at
the first level would be a marriage counselor; an example at the
second level would be a liaison officer at the university whose
primary function is educational guidance but who quite often provides counseling; on a third level would be a nurse whose major
work is medical care but who occasionally does counseling. With
those distinctions as a guide, a summary was prepared of the work
done by those fully employed at the first level, and engaged in
guidance and counseling work with children and young people, rather
than with families or with adults.

Psychological services

The ultimate objective of these services is to assist children

275

and adolescents to overcome difficulties associated with their development and learning. Originally this included the provision of vocational guidance, but very few cases are now dealt with in which the need for such assistance is predominant.

In general, psychologists work as consultants, examining children on request, reporting on their educational and personal-social needs, and discussing with parents, teachers, and others the most appropriate courses of action. Referrals to the service may be made by anyone concerned with the welfare of children and adolescents. Primary schools make many more referrals than do secondary schools--up to ten times more in some areas. However, psychologists regularly visit those secondary schools which have fully developed guidance networks, as well as other secondary schools on request. Indeed, close cooperation is maintained with all branches of the education services, especially in the field of special education, and with child health clinics provided by hospital boards. The preventive aspect of the psychologists' work is carried out by their involvement in pre-school services, community agencies for mental health, and inservice training courses offered by the Department of Education. Psychologists also do research work both as individuals and in teams.

The principal change in recent years has been the shift from casework to consultation. Instead of doing most of their work in offices and clinics, psychologists now tend to deal with cases in the settings in which the complaints originated. For example, in the Christchurch center over half of all the children seen in 1978 by psychologists were dealt with in schools and only 17% in the center's facilities. Glynn, Thomas, and Wotherspoon (1978) have described an innovative project of consultant psychological service in one area of Auckland and evaluated it in comparision with a more conventional approach.

All psychologists are graduates in either psychology or in education with strong components of psychology, and most are trained teachers. The usual method of entering the service is via a special university course at a post-master's level, but alternative methods of entry have also been devised.

Vocational guidance

The objective of this service is to assist individuals to recognise their own potentialities and limitations and help them relate interests, abilities, temperament, and other characteristics to the planning and development of an appropriate educational program and eventually to the choice of a suitable career.

Vocational counselors seek to achieve these objectives by providing three main types of service--individual casework, group guidance, and careers information. Casework may include assessment of physical handicap, counseling, standardised testing, information giving, and consultation with and referral to other agencies. Some clients refer themselves, but a large proportion are referred from schools and from employment offices. A good deal of group work is done, especially through visits to secondary schools in the district (two visits a year as far as possible), consultative activities with guidance counselors and careers advisers in schools, seminars and careers visits, and week-long training courses for newly appointed careers advisers. Careers advisers are secondary teachers who are given a special time allowance for this purpose.

Information is disseminated through two types of publications --bulletins and careers leaflets. The former originate in each center and include notices about center activities and the service generally, brief notes updating careers information, and articles of professional interest, e.g., "Youth employment in crisis--the OECD outlook" and "Breaking occupational carriers--Girls in traditionally male occupations".

There are research and training officers at the head office of the service. In recruiting new staff, the selection panels look for people with good academic qualifications in such subjects as education, economics, psychology, and sociology, and also relevant work experience. Induction and inservice training is provided, but there is a growing practice of sending new counselors to the university training programs.

Departmental control of the service was transferred from Education to Labour in 1978. Coincidentally, if not causally, there seems to have been a rejuvenation and an upturn in morale in the service, perhaps because of the change of job title to counselor, and because of a closer association with the Labour Department employment officers and the public generally. Another factor may have been an ambitious five-year (1978–1982) development plan, which provides for adding nine new centers to the previous seven and recruiting counselors for fifty new positions.

Visiting teacher service

This service investigates cases in which home circumstances or other factors outside the school may be adversely affecting a child's education and general well-being. This obviously overlaps with activities of other helping professions. However, good working relationships with other professionals are the rule rather than the exception, largely as a result of effective coordination. A visiting teacher may be based in a primary or intermediate school and serve all state schools (primary and secondary) in the area. Such a teacher attends regular meetings with other specialists, such as the guidance counselors, social workers from the Social Welfare

277

Department, educational psychologists, and public health nurses.

Visiting teachers are in effect educational social workers whose special task is the strengthening of links between schools and homes and other agencies. They do a good deal of interviewing, counseling and home visiting, and they offer supportive help and guidance. Ideally they seek to work in preventive roles before marked maladjustment has occurred. They are not truant officers, although they may be asked to investigate cases which school principals have found difficult to handle. To be successful they need to have much personal contact with their immediate clientele (children, parents and teachers), an intimate knowledge of the local area and all the helping services within it, and good working relationships with individual professionals and voluntary workers.

Their casework comes from referrals, usually from the school principals. Visiting teachers frequently serve as consultants to administrators and school personnel. Perhaps the greatest weakness of the service is that, with a few exceptions, visiting teachers are given no formal training for their duties, although there have been a number of official recommendations that this be provided. The selection criteria seem to be that they present a friendly, sympathetic and tactful manner and that they have shown an ability to establish good working relationships with parents, teachers, and children.

Counseling service

Guidance counseling began mainly as a local version of American school counseling. Most programs were conceived as remedial aids to large secondary schools which were unable to cope with students who were disruptive and disinterested. Despite variations in the aims and functions of guidance counseling, there has been a transition from a remedial emphasis in most schools to one aimed at providing direct and indirect service to all students.

The administrative manual used by principals states that guidance counselors may be required to teach up to four half-days per week, and that they are engaged partly in career work and partly in teaching. It says nothing about guidance or counseling. However, an official memorandum about the duties of guidance counselors was drafted in 1969. It states that each guidance counselor is expected to

> assist the principal and his staff to provide each pupil with the school program best suited to his needs and abilities; assist each pupil in choosing his career and planning his further education; help overcome the difficulties which may impede a pupil's educational progress and his personal and social development. (Department of Education 1971; Appendix I, ii)

278

The organisation of guidance and counseling in the schools presents a varied picture, ranging from a minimum of specialised services (one part-time careers adviser) to a complex organisation coordinated by a senior administrative teacher and served directly by one or two full-time guidance counselors supported by part-time careers advisers and guidance teachers. Panckhurst (1975) described and evaluated five of these systems of guidance. Some differences in pattern are due to differences in size of school; other differences are due to the preferences of the principal and the governing authority. Regardless of these differences, the term "guidance network" has found wide acceptance as the sum of all formal and informal guidance responsibilities accepted by teachers.

Most guidance counselors are teachers of at least five years experience before appointment. As far as possible, they are sent for additional training in a specialised curriculum at an education department of a university. About thirty to forty counselors per year graduate from these programs which consist of one year of combined academic and practical studies followed by another year of approved supervised experience in the school.

Counseling in tertiary schools

There are relatively few full-time counselors at the upper level of the educational system. This is mainly because there is no national policy on such matters in tertiary education, and thus financial support of counseling services comes out of other funds. Each institution decides whether or not it will have counseling services, and if so, what qualifications it will require of counselors.

Another important factor affecting tertiary school counseling is that the institutional ethos at that level differs from that of primary and secondary schools. Especially at universities, students are in effect simply supplied with the means of learning, remediation, and self-development. Seldom are they coerced, however gently, into accepting help which is more likely to be the case at lower levels. Thus many university students who could probably profit from the services of a counselor skilled in, say, reducing examination anxiety or teaching better social skills, choose not to avail themselves of such opportunities.

Current trends

The consultative function of guidance and counseling services is increasingly emphasised, although there is still a long way to go in building consultative skills and training programs. McBeth and Nuthall (1978) point to the rising consciousness of the need for consultation work in the helping services. However, Webster's (1970) strong plea for consultation as the preferred mode of counseling

279

has been largely ignored. The most striking research contribution on the subject has been made by Glynn and a group of professionals whose work is impressive by its amount, variety, and thoroughness. (E.g., Glynn, Thomas and Wotherspoon 1978)

The use of tests and measurements has undergone a noticeable change. Tests are now used with more discretion than formerly, particularly as the bases of educational and vocational decisions. Although in many schools group tests of scholastic aptitude are still routinely administered, the fine distinctions between different ability levels have been largely abandoned in favour of what is called "broad band streaming." Considerable test sophistication has emerged.

The status of vocational guidance has experienced a distinct improvement. The Renwick Report (Department of Education 1971) recommended that counselors accept more responsibility for vocational guidance. Some counselors who preferred to concentrate on personal social aspects resented this. However, a nationwide survey by Strang (1974) has shown that vocational guidance was the main activity of most counselors. On the average, they spent between eleven and fifteen hours per week on this work--considerably more than on either educational or personal social guidance.

Eclecticism of outlook is evident in current counseling practices and in training programs in this small country with many interdisciplinary contacts. Some trainers give a strong behaviorist orientation, some emphasize sensitivity and client-centered approaches, some feature skill training in a micro-counseling format, and some are avowedly eclectic. Apart from formal training courses, there are frequent opportunities to attend interdisciplinary lectures and workshops. The current ethos suggests that counselors be acquainted with a wide range of skills and viewpoints, e.g., behavior modification, transactional analysis, grief counseling, sensitivity training, assertiveness training, etc. (Manthei 1979) Awareness of the multi-racial character of New Zealand society has stimulated action on improving communication between different cultural groups. Various organizations became involved, but the contributions most relevant to counseling were made by Hermansson (1974) and by Metge and Kinloch (1978).

The work of a counselor

Both in New Zealand and elsewhere there are few published data about the minutiae of guidance and counseling activities. Three valuable sets of data were used in a review of guidance in schools (Small 1976): one was Wadsworth's (1970) summary of a year's work as a counselor; another was the survey by Strang (1974); however, the most detailed data came from a third source, the unpublished work records done by Munro. These data constitute probably the most accurate and comprehensive description of a guidance counselor's activities published anywhere. They appear in Figure 8. 2. which

280

is presented with an expression of thanks to Miss Munro for permitting its reproduction in abridged form.

Figure 8. 2. One counselor's activities at a New Zealand high school (analysis of four school year programs)

	1972	1974	1976	1978
Total enrollment in school	1110	1158	1280	1341
Guidance personnel: Couns.	1	1	1	2
Career adv.	1	1	1	Adm. staff
Other	8	8	9	6
Total No. of cases	271	212	262	209
Boys of total	10%	9%	15%	17%
Girls of total	90%	91%	85%	83%
Counseling cases (educ., pers.)	132	82	102	105
No. of interviews per case:				
one	61%	59%	24%	54%
two--four	29%	32%	28%	30%
five or more	10%	9%	48%	16%
Parent interview & home visits	34	29	38	29
Consultation: with agencies	103	64	92	42
analysis of needs		16 meet.	27 meet.	61 meet.
implementing plans				
& staff consult.	112 hrs.	293 hrs.	182 hrs.*	167 hrs.*
with parents	33 hrs.	31 hrs.	45 hrs.	27 hrs.**
Teaching assignments (periods)	147	170	106	192

* Additional time spent in inservice training experiences.
** Additional time spent in family consulting-counseling.

Counseling in other social services

A review of guidance and counseling in New Zealand would be misleading, if it omitted reference to statutory and voluntary organisations where the largest number of guidance workers are found. There is a great variety of human services available in statutory agencies other than educational institutions. In large cities these include emergency services by the Social Welfare Department; outpatient clinics; alcohol rehabilitation programs; crisis intervention teams; etc.

Although staff members of these agencies receive induction and inservice training, a substantial proportion of them is not well trained. Bygate (1977) reported that 184 of 633 social workers had "no qualifications." On the other hand, there are fully trained profes-

sionals involved in the ranks of human services personnel such as
psychiatrists, psychologists, licensed social workers, nurses, etc.

A large proportion of guidance and counseling services are provided for the community by voluntary organizations. Some of them
receive grants from public funds--and deservedly so--for in some
cases their selection, training, and supervision of personnel are
more rigorous than those provided by the state. The most active and
professionalised of these is the Marriage Guidance Council which is
supported by the Department of Justice and which provides some 200
counselors in 24 centers. Other voluntary organisations are the
telephone services such as Lifeline and Youthline (Donnelly 1974;
Hattie 1975) and some of the social services of the largest churches
in the main centers.

While census-taking of these agencies is difficult, an exhaustive
study by Nuthall (1978) identified 68 agencies providing counseling
in Christchurch alone. The success of voluntary organisations in
the guidance field may be responsible for the trend toward decentralisation of statutory services. The hospital authority in Christchurch, for instance, established a community health center staffed
by a psychologist and by social workers in a suburban shopping center. Harray (1975) and Lowe and Rainey (1974) report on earlier
developments involving comprehensive health care.

Training provisions for personnel in non-educational helping
services are so varied that they cannot be detailed here. Some are
organised by government departments, as universities have programs,
e.g., in clinical psychology, that are highly selective and lengthy.
Increasingly, technical institutes and teachers' colleges are providing courses directly relevant to counseling and social work. Many
such courses, e.g., assertiveness training, are very attractive to
the interested public. (Manthei 1979)

Professional associations

In New Zealand, persons employed in the helping services often
meet under the official auspices of their employers. Outside such
"in house" meetings, there are four main groupings of people in the
field of guidance and counseling:

New Zealand Psychological Society.--At first a branch of the
British Psychological Society, it has become a fully independent
body in 1969 and is affiliated with the International Union of Psychological Sciences. The Society publishes a bulletin several times
each year and The New Zealand Psychologist twice a year. Total membership is about 500.

New Zealand Counseling and Guidance Association.--Formed in
1974, it serves mainly the interests of school guidance counselors.

A large number of vocational counselors is about to join. The Association organises annual conferences, publishes a newsletter and the New Zealand Counseling and Guidance Association Journal. It has about 200 members.

New Zealand Association of Psychological Therapists.--Formed in 1946 and reorganised in 1974, it is a multidisciplinary group that includes pastoral counselors, nurses, psychiatrists, and art and music therapists. Its membership is about 100.

New Zealand Association of Social Workers.--This organisation, begun in 1964, serves professionals in social work by holding annual meetings and by publishing monthly newsletters and a quarterly, New Zealand Social Work. There are nearly 700 members.

Conclusion

Guidance and counseling are developing fields in New Zealand--in terms of practical provisions, training programs, and theoretical and empirical research. A need for decentralisation of the services into smaller units is felt both in education and in social services, along with the need to further develop the training of professionals, paraprofessionals, and lay helpers. Compared with counseling, consultation as a mode for providing helping services may be still less developed than many would think desirable, but its acceptance is growing.

Despite their geographical isolation, professionals in guidance and counseling in New Zealand are well acquainted with developments in their field in similar societies elsewhere. What is needed now--it seems to me--is a determination to continue developing New Zealand responses to New Zealand needs. This calls for ingenuity in providing better services and training, and in cultivating a critical attitude to the whole field of guidance and counseling. There have been few examples of the latter, apart from Webster's (1970) criticism of the casework model of counseling and my own critique (Small 1978) of the ways in which behaviorists account for changes resulting from counseling.

References

Bygate, P. S. Social work within the state services. New Zealand Social Work, 1977, 1, 17-22.

Department of Education. Growing, sharing, and learning. (Johnson Report) Wellington: Department of Education, 1977.

Department of Education. Guidance in secondary schools. (Renwick Report) Wellington: Department of Education, 1971.

Department of Education. Toward partnership. (McCombs Report) Wellington: Department of Education, 1976.

Department of Statistics. New Zealand official yearbook. Wellington: Department of Statistics, 1978.

Department of Statistics. Social trends in New Zealand. Wellington: Department of Statistics, 1977.

Donnelly, F. C. Youth aids youth. New Zealand Medical Journal, 1974, 80, 5-10.

Glynn, E.L., Thomas, J.D. and Wotherspoon, A.T. Applied psychology in the Mangere Guidance Unit: Implementing behavioral programs in the school. The Exceptional Child, 1978, 25, 115-126.

Harray, A. S. The role of the counselor in a medical center. New Zealand Medical Journal, 1975, 82, 383-385.

Hattie, J. A. Youthline Dunedin: An evaluation of a telephone counseling service. New Zealand Medical Journal, 1975, 82, 80-81.

Hermansson, G. L. Counseling Polynesian youth. In Bray, D.H. and Hill, C.G.N. (Eds.) Polynesian and Pakeha in New Zealand education. (Vol. 2) Auckland: Heinemann Educational Books, 1974.

Lowe, J. N. and Rainey, H. B. Social work in a New Zealand group medical practice. New Zealand Medical Journal, 1974, 79, 739-742.

McBeth, L. and Nuthall, J.J. Community health services--an approach to planning. New Zealand Social Work, 1978, 2, 15-17.

Manthei, M. Positively me: An assertive training guide. Wellington: Methuen, 1979.

Metge, J. and Kinloch, P. Talking past each other: Problems of cross-cultural communication. Wellington: Victoria Univers., 1978.

Munro, E.A., Manthei, R.J. and Small, J.J. Counseling: A skills approach. Wellington: Methuen, 1979.

Nuthall, J.J. A review of community counseling services and training programs. Christchurch: North Canterbury Hospital Board, 1978.

Panckhurst, J.D. Guidance in five secondary schools: An evaluation of the pilot program. Wellington: Victoria University, 1975.

Purves, A.C., Foshay, A.W. and Hanson, G. Literature education in ten countries. New York: Wiley, 1973.

Small, J. J. Guidance in action. New Zealand Counseling and Guidance Association Journal, 1976, 1, 1-7.

Small, J. J. Explaining changes attributed to behavioral counseling. New Zealand Journal of Educational Studies, 1978, 13, 144-153.

Strang, J. M. Guidance counseling in New Zealand. Unpublished Master's thesis. University of Otago, 1974.

Thorndike, R. L. Reading comprehension education in fifteen countries. New York: Wiley, 1973.

Wadsworth, E. J. The role of school counselor. The New Zealand Social Worker, 1970, 6, 13-21.

Webster, A. C. Guidance and counseling. In Bates, R.J. (Ed.) Prospects in New Zealand education. Auckland: Heinemann Educational Books, 1970.

Suggested readings

Elley, W. B. and Livingstone, I. D. External examinations and internal assessments: Alternative plans for reform. New Zealand Council for Educational Research, 1972.

Fry, J. (Ed.) Help: A directory of community activities in Christchurch (1978 Edition). Christchurch: City Council, 1977.

Piesse, D. and Lardner, J. (Eds.) Social services in New Zealand. Auckland: Auckland Regional Authority, 1974.

Progressive achievement tests. (Listening comprehension; mathematics; study skills; etc.) New Zealand Council for Educational Research, variable publication dates.

Winterbourn, R. Guidance services in New Zealand education. Wellington: New Zealand Council for Educational Research, 1974.

Section Nine

AFRICA

The rapid growth and self-discovery of youth are at once exciting and painful experiences. The days that lie ahead seem both
promising and threatening. We know this to be true in the lives of
individual persons. It is equally true in the formative stages of
newly emerging nations that have assumed the responsibility of statehood.

Those people of Africa who had achieved independence after
World War II, while cherishing their freedom, face developmental
problems of overwhelming dimensions. Spreading technology and urbanization threaten established social patterns and values. There
is a lack of professional resources and adequately trained personnel
to help overcome illiteracy, lacking health care, and indifference
among the masses. Modernization, while inevitable, presents dangers
to the identity of the people in a tribal unit before a broader
identity can be fully established.

To forge this new identity among African peoples is a challenging process in which guidance can play an important role. To do so
effectively, African guidance has to be anchored in its indigenous
traditions. When five hundred years ago, explorers sailing from
Europe discovered a new continent to be called America, they claimed
it for others. Today, the African continent--once ruled by others--
needs to be discovered and claimed by its own peoples.

The co-authors of Chapter 24, while analyzing here specifically the Nigerian scene, offer insights that are applicable to

many African countries. Both of them combine their African heritage
with professional training and experiences gained abroad. Violet
Arene, who has received her professional training in the United
States, now heads the Guidance and Counseling Unit in the Federal
Ministry of Education of her country. M. O. A. Durojaiye earned
his Doctorate in Great Britain and is now Dean of the Education Faculty at the University of Lagos.

24

NIGERIA

V. N. Arene and M. O. A. Durojaiye

    Nigeria, an independent country since 1960, is estimated to
have a population of 70 to 80 million people who live in a land
washed in the south by the Atlantic Ocean and bordered in the north
by the sub-Sahara scrubland. A wide range of geographical and cli-
matic conditions--from tropical rain forest to semidesert areas--
can be found there. It is a country of diverse cultures, languages,
and religious practices. Nearly 250 distinct languages are spoken
in the country. They fall into three major groups that closely coincide with the three principal ethnic population segments.

The social milieu

    At present, life patterns of the Nigerian society are changing.
The traditional community life which exists in rural areas is being
replaced by a new life style in cities and towns. Urbanization,
bureaucratization, secularization, technological advancement, and
monetary economy are producing fragmentation of the native culture.
Traditional values are merging with Western values in urban settings
and this "marriage" has triggered a crisis of moral standards. The
extended family system in which the adults are regarded as teachers
of good behavior for the child is fast dwindling. Schools appear
unable to step in and fill the gap at present. Thus it is becoming
increasingly apparent that guidance and counselling are needed to
help youth develop personal and social adjustment and to create a
disciplined, well adjusted citizenry.

    However, the problem is to break through the hard crust of con-

servatism or traditionalism of many Nigerians who do not appreciate
the need for personal counselling for adjustment by professional
persons. This resistant attitude is unfortunately buttressed by
traditional practices. A common feature, for instance, of many Nigerian traditional families is the phenomenon of a close-knit family and clan relationship known as the extended family institution.
In this context, everyone is related to everyone else by ancestral
ties and everyone is a brother or sister. Foreigners have been be-
wildered by the motley of sisters and brothers in a Nigerian's life.
The truth is that such subtle discriminatory terms of distant relationships as nephews, nieces, cousins, etc., are incomprehensible
to the average Nigerian, and the terms of brother and sister cover
most traceable blood relationships, no matter how tenuous. This
socio-cultural phenomenon finds expression in mutual solicitousness
about the welfare of one another and in a quasi-communal approach to
supervision and correction of the young and to social insurance. It
is in the spirit of this culture that some traditionalists deny the
need for professional counsellors, especially when the case is made
for personal adjustment counselling.

A common view of traditionalists is that religious figures,
priests, parents, teachers, friends, elders, etc. could do all the
personal counselling a child needs and that there is no need for
professional counsellors. School administrators of the old authoritarian order also think that teachers who opt for guidance and counselling are "escaping" from teaching which to them is the primary
and most important function of the school. One old school headmaster in a strong disclaimer of professional counselling said that for
seven years he was able to function as "teacher, dean of students,
dispenser, counsellor, placement officer, headmaster, house-master,
gamesmaster, choirmaster, and occasionally, duty pastor." And he
said, he survived it. Therefore, aspiring professional counsellors
appeared to him as malingerers. (Makinde 1973, 1974). The mental
health function of guidance and counselling is yet to receive the
recognition it deserves as a prerequisite for assisting individuals,
at least in the educational system, in preparation for taking on positions of responsibility.

Current educational policy

A new national policy on education was launched in 1977 with
emphasis on pre-primary and primary education, the latter to be completed by all young Nigerians. Some 75% of students who go on to
secondary schools leave at the age of fourteen plus and 25% leave
at the age of seventeen. For those interested, programmes in colleges of advanced technology or in universities are available. Life-
long education is encouraged through Adult Education Centres for
those young people who drop out at any stage of their educational
process.

A document entitled, "National Policy of Education for the

Federal Republic of Nigeria" spells out educational policies in detail. It reads in part:

> The desire that Nigeria be a free, just and democratic
> society, a land of opportunities for all its citizens,
> able to generate a great dynamic economy, and growing
> into a united, strong, and self-reliant nation cannot
> be over-emphasized. In order to realize fully the poten-
> tials of the contributions of education to the achieve-
> ment of the objectives, all other agencies will operate
> in concert with education to that end.

> Six values are essential for attaining the stated goals:
> (1) respect for the worth and dignity of the individual;
> (2) faith in man's ability to make rational decisions;
> (3) moral and spiritual values in interpersonal and human
> relations; (4) shared responsibility for the common good
> of society; (5) respect for the dignity of labour; and
> (6) the promotion of the emotional, physical, and psycho-
> logical health of all children. (Government of Nigeria
> 1977)

Development of guidance work

Although guidance services are obviously needed for the achievement of these goals, they are not as yet fully developed. The history of guidance in Nigeria is a short one. It was introduced to
the country by missionary educators. A Child Guidance Clinic was
established in 1964 under the auspices of the Federal Ministry of
Education as a grant-aided agency that was supervised by the Roman
Catholic Mission. The emphasis of the Clinic was on remedial work.
Later, a Vocational Guidance Bureau was opened and, for a time, it
ran workshops for teachers until it was phased out. However, the
idea of educational guidance lingered in the Federal Ministry of
Education and eventually led to the establishment of the present
Guidance and Counselling Unit set up in January, 1977 with proper
fiscal backing and official support.

By far the most generally acceptable role of guidance in Nigeria is in the areas of educational and vocational planning. All
agree that students should be guided in the choice of subjects for
the final secondary school education certificate and for their career planning. In other words, the "sorting-out" function of guidance and counselling appears relevant to the majority of Nigerians
for enhancing the effectiveness of education.

In a research project conducted in three Federal Government
schools in Lagos by one of the authors, V.N. Arene, it was discovered
that the most common problem of students was ignorance about the
various options in the world of work. This of course was not sur-

prising because many of the students come from homes with little knowledge of occupational options. And no well organized system of disseminating occupational information exists as yet. Students therefore, generally know only about the major common occupations such as law, medicine, and engineering.

Vocational guidance emphasis

It is in the context of these limitations that advocacy for educational and vocational counselling finds favourable response by most Nigerians who consider education as a precious commodity and a key to high social status. The implication of this trend is obvious. It means that at the crusading and pioneering stage, guidance counsellors should emphasize vocational and educational guidance as the main rationale of their efforts and make personal counselling an issue of secondary importance. The statement of the National Policy on Guidance has already taken that position:

> In view of the apparent ignorance of many young people about career prospects, and in view of personality maladjustment among school children, career officers and counsellors will be appointed in post-primary institutions. (Government of Nigeria 1977)

Thus the role of guidance and counselling in attaining Nigeria's educational objectives has been established. The Government had implicitly recognized that for education to become truly the much celebrated instrument of human and national development, it needs to incorporate guidance in its processes for appraising and grooming the nation's talents.

The Federal Government is now set on implementation. For instance, the proposed "6-3-3" educational system which will commence in 1982 will make heavy demands on the services of guidance counsellors. They will have to facilitate the selection and transition processes for at least 40% of primary school children to junior secondary schools and the eventual placement of students in further educational institutions or vocational trade schools, as their aptitudes may dictate. Guidance counsellors will also be needed to support the informal efforts at educating the nearly 80% illiterate masses through remedial schools. The function of guidance that will be most involved is psychological testing for the appraisal of vocational interests and aptitudes. These services will go on concurrently with counselling for adjustment; for instance, assistance to students in clarification of values, in value-related education, and the cultivation of self-discipline.

Organization and staffing of guidance programs

At present, a pattern of centralized initiatives at the federal

level and of decentralized developments of guidance services at the
state level are emerging. The original leadership on the part of
the central Government continues, as is evident from its mandatory
policy directives for the adoption and maintenance of guidance and
counselling services throughout the nation. These directives involve:
deployment of guidance counsellors in schools; assisting youth in the
areas of vocational planning and personal adjustment; and training of
guidance personnel from the ranks of school teachers.

The Federal Ministry of Education has adopted a dynamic strategy
for professional education of personnel. In a national workshop it
has trained a corps of guidance personnel educators. These are to
provide training at the state level for school teachers as semi-
professionals in guidance. Some of the states in the Federation have
already initiated this program. The Federal Ministry of Education
itself also offers induction and orientation courses for teachers in
federal and state schools and thus serves as a model for the State
Ministries of Education. This policy of national leadership through
example is most important.

Having adopted education as an "instrument par excellence" for
national development, the Federal Government intervened boldly in the
educational system of Nigeria and now directly owns some schools and
colleges. All fifty Federal Government schools and colleges employ
at present guidance counsellors and careers officers to render counselling and vocational guidance to students. State Ministries of
Education are to do the same for their own schools.

To establish a modest ratio of one guidance counsellor for a
thousand students, 16,000 counselors would be needed by 1982 to facilitate the innovative "6-3-3" school system. Thus, the Federal
Government intends to embark on a crash programme for personnel
training. Elements of guidance and counselling will be integrated
into teacher education curricula to acquaint teachers with the concept so that even in schools where no counsellors are available, the
benefits of guidance would still reach the students through teachers
who have been offered a smattering of counsellor education. It is
of utmost significance that the Government give a more positive
consideration to special remuneration for guidance counsellors. If
this happens, teachers will have strong incentive to opt for counselling. At the moment, teachers who become guidance counsellors
"live on hope," but do not as yet enjoy an extra remuneration.

As could be expected, there are varying levels of development
of guidance services from state to state. While some two states of
the Federation have not taken off at all, the State of Lagos where
the Capital City is located, has attained a very gratifying level
of sophistication in its services. Its Child Guidance Clinic, the
only one of its type south of the Sahara, has developed very effective tools for clinical diagnosis and has been able to offer help
to a host of "special" children. It has also organized training
workshops for teachers as potential counsellor and has supervised

293

counselling services which are becoming widely spread in the State
Schools of Lagos.

Current trends and concerns

Salient trends have already emerged in the young guidance movement of Nigeria. The peculiar Nigerian socio-cultural needs and realities are clearly influencing the role of guidance and counselling.
The dearth of classroom teachers, for instance, has made it incumbent
on the experienced teachers who usually become counsellors to teach
and to counsel. On the other hand, inducted teachers who could not
fully qualify as counsellors have been designated career masters or
mistresses.

In a small research project conducted by the senior author of
this Chapter on a group of thirty-one guidance professionals assembled for a workshop, it was found that their levels of training and
experience, and their roles varied greatly. The following designa-
tions described members of the group: (a) career master/mistress;
(b) teacher-counsellor; (c) guidance counsellor; (d) counsellor educator (usually at the Faculty of Education of a University);
(e) inspector of education.

It is also clear that guidance services in Nigeria today are
devoid of the overly sophisticated constructs, techniques, tools,
etc., described in guidance work rendered in the U.S.A., for instance,
or other advanced countries. The dilemmas and exigencies of competing
priorities within the educational system have, unfortunately, not
found guidance to be the number one priority. As one Permanent Secretary in the government put it, one has to choose between providing
classrooms and teachers to combat the near 80% illiteracy rate or the
luxury of special professionals known as guidance counsellors. Thus,
the guidance community is realistically accepting its position in the
face of so many other needs which delay its rapid progress and expansion.

Yet what is worth doing at all, is worth doing well. One of
many challenges faced by guidance counsellors in Nigeria today is
establishing credibility and securing recognition for guidance as a
vital force for the advancement of a developing country. The crisis
of values and morals ushered in by introjected Western urban culture
is another challenge for Nigerian counsellors. For instance, the
orderliness, the mutual concern and care of others which are values
of the traditional culture in the villages are not present in the
urban areas where diffusion of responsibility and amorality of behaviour appear to be the social characteristics. The role of guidance counsellors and social workers will eventually need to become
strongly consultative with governmental institutions and with parents
or members of the extended family. It is an irony that the individual who means so much to the group in the traditional culture and for
whom care is provided both by the nuclear and extended family is not

really at a high premium in the urban setting where technology and
development overshadow individual welfare. The resultant social
deprivation perpetuates a vicious cycle which retards advancement.
As Montagu (1974) has aptly put it, it is difficult for the genius
in the individual to be unleashed if he is perpetually engaged in
survival struggles. One cannot expect a well-adjusted citizenry with
self-motivated discipline from parents who do not have time to supervise their children's behaviour in the urban areas where the race
for prestige and wealth has become the foremost value of urban technological culture.

Emerging guidance philosophy

In these circumstances, Nigeria's guidance community is searching for a meaningful and effective philosophical framework. Two
attitudinal questions put to a group of guidance counsellors assembled for a three-day conference received a 100% positive response.
The two attitude-related statements were as follows:

(a) "For the most part, the Nigerian Counsellor will turn away
from Western traditional theories and therapies to Nigerian social
and cultural phenomena for explanation and appropriate remedy in
cases of maladjustment."
(b) "The Nigerian Counseloor will necessarily evolve counselling techniques suitable for the Nigerian personality."

The counselling strategy preferred by most of the counsellors
appears to be an active, interventionist, directive approach based
on the traditional respect for elders rather than the typical non-
directive model promoted in the Western world which reflects the
liberal-democratic ideology. This posture is significant. Most
Nigerian cultures are authoritarian and evince hierarchical relationships profoundly deferential to elders and superiors. Our youth
shall be definitely disappointed by the counsellors if they are not
didactic and directive. Nigerian counsellors face the dilemma of
setting limits while not stifling the development of self-responsi-
bility and independence in the youth. Nigerian counsellors have to
strike a balance between respect for their culture and respect for
the individual.

A note for non-African colleagues

A prominent issue in international counselling investigations
is the role of cultural values which determine the nature and the
objectives of counselling practice. Values in counselling philosophy and art are socio-cultural. Professionals who wish to practice
guidance beyond their shores have to avoid cultural "encapsulation"
that was labeled as counterproductive by the venerable mentor, C.
Gilbert Wrenn (1962). This consideration is necessary if guidance

and counselling are to be internationally as effective as other
professions, e.g., medicine or nursing, which a professional person
could practice anywhere. Ignorance of the cultural underpinnings
that make for success in psychotherapy has caused many a foreign
professional in Nigeria to fail and leave disenchanted.

An introduction to principal world cultures and to sociology
and anthropology may have to become part of foundational courses in
counsellor education to help students understand varying cultural
settings, social relationships, and models of adjustive behaviour.
Murray has postulated that behaviour is an outcome of the relationship between the person and the environment. (Hayes 1974) And Horney
(1964) has surmised that new psychological findings do not necessarily reveal universal trends of the human nature. Perceptions of human behaviour and models of personality adjustment vary from culture
to culture. The expert in applied psychology should have adequate
exposure to some of these insights.

Concluding remarks

The young counselling service in Nigeria, even though beset by
both pioneering and cultural problems, promises to become a dynamic
instrument of the educational process for human development. For
that purpose, Nigerian Counsellors need to analyze and synthesize
their value commitments with a view to forming a meaningful philosophical framework on which to predicate their services. They need
to have a springboard from which to develop new theories and make
contributions to the field of guidance. It has been suggested that
if one were to fully understand the problems of children in Nigerian
schools, the question of polygamy might be very relevant for inves-
tigation. Other problems of socio-cultural nature likely to be of
concern to guidance counsellors in Nigeria are: implications of
ignorance, social deprivation, superstitious beliefs, cultural hangups, and excessive dependency habits.

One can be optimistic because of the effective support supplied
by the Central Government which is determined to have the guidance
movement in Nigeria survive the present tribulations and is fully
cognizant of the relevance of guidance services. In addition to this,
there are new educational developments. There is also the acute
crisis of values linked with the policy of urbanization and the new
technological culture. All these factors augur a bright future for
guidance and counselling in Nigeria. It is only a question of time
before the mental health function of guidance will be as much in demand as its educational and vocational functions. The entire range
of guidance services is needed for the benefit of young citizens of
Nigeria.

References

Government of Nigeria. White paper on national policy of education. Lagos: Author, 1977.

Hayes, E. Environmental press and psychological need as related to the success of minority group students. Journal of Counseling Psychology, 1974, 21, 299-304.

Horney, K. The neurotic personality of our time. New York: Norton, 1964.

Makinde, O. The teacher's role in counselling. The School Master (Journal of Nigerian Union of Teachers), 1973, 1974 (11, 12, 13).

Montagu, A. Culture and human development. Englewood Cliffs, NJ: Prentice Hall, 1974.

Wrenn, C. G. The counselor in a changing world. Washington: APGA Press, 1962.

Section Ten

EPILOGUE

Victor J. Drapela

As we look back at the kaleidoscopic scene of guidance around the world, certain features stand out as though they are elements of a pattern. This Epilogue will point out some of the salient points which have repeatedly surfaced in the preceding chapters.

A large geographical territory was scanned and a wide range of guidance processes in various cultures was identified. Generically, these processes can be characterized as "assistance to people" facilitating effective behavior, adjustment to society, and contentment in life. However, these common aims of guidance are overshadowed by significant differences. Within the general framework of assisting people, some guidance models emphasize labor market needs and societal concerns; while others see the personal development of individuals as their top priority. Some are school-related, others are linked with employment agencies. Some have a unitary ideological base, others are pluralistic in philosophy and values. Some make extensive use of counseling, others provide guidance by orientation en masse.

A continuum for guidance models

To provide a platform for comparability, we need to form a continuum that would place the surveyed guidance models into perspective. Terms such as "superior" and "deficient" are not useful opposites for our purpose, since different cultures require different guidance interventions. The continuum proposed here employs other criteria.

At one end of the continuum are informal, unstructured guidance processes carried out by society itself. Individuals are helped to adjust to life through socialization within the family and tribe, with well defined roles of the head of the household or tribe, of other adult members, and of children of both sexes. Additional socialization opportunities are provided through indigenous social institutions, e.g., religious, political, or patriotic organizations. This type of guidance is found in authoritarian societies that promote and enforce explicit standards of behavior for their members. An example of this societal guidance model is given in chapter seventeen which deals with the Arab countries.

At the other end of the proposed continuum are formalized, professionally staffed, and publicly administered guidance services. These are provided for the benefit of individuals, especially children and adolescents, at considerable cost to society. Such guidance and counseling services are found in permissive societies with a high degree of industrialization and personal need satisfaction. Such societies typically suffer from a "social overdevelopment syndrome" which encompasses psycho-social problems, e.g., alienation, intrapersonal conflicts, inability to communicate effectively, boredom, and lack of purpose. Thus, guidance services in such societies have a prevalent psychological orientation. An example of this guidance approach can be found on the North-American continent (chapters three and four).

Between these two polarities there are many guidance models of different shades, with their own emphases, goals, and philosophical orientations. Most of them focus upon vocational guidance, either exclusively or predominantly. As a society develops and its job market becomes more complex, vocational guidance seems to be the logical starting point for all other guidance services. And when school curricula become flexible, educational guidance emerges; first as an assistance to students for selecting their educational goals, and eventually, as an aid in personal-social problems as well. This sequence of developmental stages is spelled out by several authors in this volume and seems to be the natural pattern of growth for guidance everywhere.

Guidance personnel

Guidance services are staffed by workers whose backgrounds and qualifications greatly differ from one country to another. However, the one single profession from which the largest numbers of counselors are recruited is the teaching profession. This has been verified or implied in all countries with an organized guidance service which have been covered in this volume. Another significant finding is the consensus among people of differing cultures about the close linkage of guidance functions with the role of an educator. In some countries, e.g., the Soviet Union, instruction and guidance are seen as inseparable, while other countries have established a formal pro-

fessional category of teacher-counselors, e.g., the German Federal
Republic. Specialized counselor training programs for teachers, such
as the one in the Netherlands, have been invariably successful.

In this context, recommendations that all teachers receive at
least a rudimentary guidance training as part of their pre-service
education, are gaining new significance. Basic guidance skills would
benefit teachers in their classroom management function and increase
their sensitivity in dealing with individual students as well. In
countries where no professionally trained counselors are available,
involving teachers in classroom guidance is perhaps the best way to
start. But even in countries with established guidance services,
there is a need for extending such services to the elementary school
level; and that involves classroom teachers' active participation,
no matter whether counselors are available or not.

Another professional group in the ranks of guidance personnel
is that of psychologists. Their training is invariably at the university level and their role and functions are clearly defined. Conversely, the least homogeneous personnel category is that of employment counselors (or advisors). Even within the same country, there
is a high degree of variability as to their education and skills.
In some cases, they are not more than clerks who provide information;
while in others, they are professionally trained specialists in behavioral sciences and labor market management. Generally speaking,
employment counselors have their procedures and activities spelled
out in considerable detail by the agency which employs them. How
much attention is given to the dynamics and unique needs of clients
looking for a job depends exclusively on the attitudes of individual
employment counselors.

Trends and prospects

As comparative studies and intercultural contacts increase on
a global basis within the guidance profession, a trend toward internationally recognized standards in counselor education may evolve.
Such standardization of Master's curricula in guidance and counseling has been attained on the North American continent, making it
possible for counselors to move from state to state in the U.S. and
from province to province in Canada, as well as between the two nations. True, certain state or provincial requirements for counselor
certification vary to a degree, but these differences are relatively
small and the regional standards can be satisfied by additional academic work or professional experience. Worldwide, well established
professions (physicians, engineers, etc.) have achieved a high degree of comparability in their professional training curricula from
nation to nation.

Individual members of the profession can influence this and
other issues by becoming actively involved in the work of their na-

301

tional counselor associations and by joining international organizations which are listed in the Appendix. Congresses and seminars of such organizations provide an excellent opportunity for sharing one's concerns with colleagues from other countries.

The spread of technology, the rapid changes in social structures, the lessening of family influences, of ethical traditions and religious commitments--these are but a few factors that are broadening the range of personal values decisions to be made by people in their daily lives. As this process continues, guidance will be increasingly in demand not only by youth but also by other population groups. The growth and development of guidance services will likely follow the earlier mentioned path--from vocational to educational and to personal-social assistance--and greater emphasis will be placed on individual and group counseling rather than on orientation and advice giving. Yet vocational guidance will always retain its significance.

Counselors around the world will have to clarify their professional commitments and loyalties. Are they to serve primarily the institution that employs them or is their first loyalty to the clients who seek assistance? Manipulating the behavior of clients or disregarding their needs in order to satisfy the institution is certainly unethical. On the other hand, promoting a philosophy of "doing your own thing" at the expense of others reinforces personality warp and is equally unethical. Genuine, caring, and sensitive counselors help their clients develop both free and responsible behavior, no matter what counseling strategy they use. While in theory these professional principles appear obvious, their implementation may at times require a high degree of integrity and courage.

As a new profession, the guidance community will have to prove itself worldwide in the decades to come. Counselors will have to succeed in strengthening the human dimension in the midst of new technologies. They will have to model and effectively promote attitudes of self-esteem, mutual concern, and creativity among the people who will seek their assistance.

APPENDIX

LIST OF PROFESSIONAL ORGANIZATIONS

INTERNATIONAL AND REGIONAL

Asian Regional Association on Vocational and Educational Guidance
(ARAVEG)
1-1 Kanda Hitotsubashi, Chyiodaku
Tokyo, Japan

Interamerican Association of Psychology
PO Box 7921
Austin, Tx 78712 USA

International Association for Applied Psychology (IAAP)
University of California
Irvine, Ca 92664 USA

International Association for Educational and Vocational Guidance
(IAEVG)
257 route d'Arlon
Strassen, Luxembourg

International Association for Educational and Vocational Information
(AIISUP)
20 rue de l'Estrapade
75005 Paris, France

International Council of Psychologists, Inc.
    2772 North Lake Avenue
    Altadena, Ca 91001 USA

International Labor Organisation (ILO)
    Human Resources Department, Vocational Training Branch
    1211 Geneva 22, Switzerland

International Round Table for the Advancement of Counseling (IRTAC)
    Livingstone House, Livingstone Road
    London E15 2LL England

International School Psychology Steering Committee
    92 S. Dawson Avenue
    Columbus, Oh 43209 USA

Scandinavian Vocational Guidance Federation
    Arbetsmarknadsstyrelsen
    10220 Stockholm 12, Sweden

NATIONAL ORGANIZATIONS

Australia:
    Australian Psychological Society
    c/o Department of Employment and Industrial Relations
    PO Box 2817-AA
    Melbourne, VIC 3001

Belgium:
    Association nationale d'orientation professionnelle (ANOP)
    28, rue Estiévenart
    7270 Dour

Canada:
    Canadian Guidance nad Counselling Association
    1895 avenue de LaSalle
    Montreal, Quebec PQ H1V 2K4

Federal Republic of Germany:
    Deutscher Verband für
    Berufsberatung (DVB)
    Platz der Deutschen Einheit 1
    6200 Wiesbaden

France:
    Association des conseillers d'orientation de France (ACOF)
    1 rue Navier
    51 Reims

    Société médicale d'orientation professionnelle
    78 avenue de Suffren
    75015 Paris

Israel:
    Association for Vocational Guidance in Israel
    4 Rabbi Benjamin Street
    Jerusalem

Italy:
    Unione italiana per l'orientamento professionale (UIOP)
    via Vancini 3
    40134 Bologna

Japan:
    Japan Vocational Guidance Association
    1-1 Kanda Hitotsubashi, Chiyodaku
    Tokyo

Mexico:
    Sociedad de estudios professionales
    Tepexpam No. 22, bulevar del Niño Jesús
    Mexico 21, D.F.

The Netherlands:
    Federatie van samenwerkende organisaties van beroepskeuzeadviseurs
    Torenstraat 36
    The Hague

New Zealand:
    New Zealand Counselling and Guidance Association
    c/o Department of Education
    University of Canterbury
    Christchurch 1

South Korea:
    Korean Association for Educational and Vocational Guidance
    PO Box 5498
    Seoul

Spain:
    Sociedad española de psicologia
    San Julio 11
    Madrid 2

Switzerland:
   Schweizerischer Verband für Berufsberatung
   Eidmattstrasse 51
   8032 Zurich

Yugoslavia:
   Yugoslav Federation of Vocational Guidance Associations
   ul. Zmaj Jovina 21
   Belgrade

United Kingdom:
   British Association for Counselling
   26 Bedford Square
   London WC1B 3HU

United States:
   American Personnel and Guidance Association (APGA)
   1607 New Hampshire Avenue NW
   Washington, D.C. 20009

INDEX OF NAMES

309

INDEX OF SUBJECTS

314

"Melting pot" phenomenon 28,
    41, 257
Methodologies in guidance and
    counseling 33, 70, 72,
    92, 185, 262-264, 280
Modernization in society 51,
    54, 67, 153, 196, 201, 207,
    209, 225, 228, 248, 251,
    287, 289, 296

Naziism 86, 87, 152

Octobrist youth organization
    176, 177
Overdevelopment syndrome
    46, 300

"Pastoral care" (in British
    education) 143, 251
Peace efforts in guidance 9
Pedology (in Soviet Union) 171
Perceptual frame of reference
    4, 9, 18
Personnel in guidance:
    Australia 265-267
    Brazil 71
    Canada 34-36
    France 106-107
    Germany (Fed. R.) 93-94, 96
    Ireland 116-117
    Israel 212-214, 216-217
    Japan 231-232
    Korea, S. 241-243
    Malaysia 248 ff
    Netherlands 124 ff
    New Zealand 275 ff
    Nigeria 292-294
    Socialist bloc 183-184
    Soviet Union 167, 178
    Sweden 132-133, 135
    United Kingdom 143-144
    United States 43-44
    Yugoslavia 189-191
Pioneer youth organization 176 ff

Rationale of guidance:
    Australia 260-261

Brazil 68
Canada 31-32
France 100
Germany (Fed. R.) 91-92
Ireland 116-117
Israel 214, 218-219
Japan 229-230, 231
Korea, S. 239-241, 243
Malaysia 248
Netherlands 122-123, 126
New Zealand 274-275
Nigeria 291-292, 295
Socialist bloc 170-172,
    184
Soviet Union 156-158,
    166-169
Sweden 131-132
United Kingdom 142
United States 42
Yugoslavia 187-188
Religious issues 54, 79, 86,
    114, 123, 130, 138, 156,
    159, 161, 171, 204-205,
    212, 236
Role playing in comparative
    studies 20

School anxiety 87
Sex education in school 132
"Socialism with a human face"
    160-161

Testing in guidance 34, 61, 70,
    92-93, 105, 117, 217, 232,
    241-242, 264, 280
Travel abroad for study 22

Vocational guidance:
    Australia 260 ff
    Brazil 69 ff
    Canada 32-33
    France 102 ff
    Germany (Fed. R.) 94 ff
    Ireland 117-118
    Israel 215 ff
    Japan 229 ff
    Korea, S. 241 ff
    Malaysia 249 ff

315

<u>Notes:</u>